WHEN THE OFFICE
WENT TO WAR

WHEN THE OFFICE WENT TO WAR

War letters from the men of the Great Western Railway

Clare Horrie and Kathryn Phelps

The National Archives

CONWAY
BLOOMSBURY
LONDON · NEW DELHI · NEW YORK · SYDNEY

Published by Conway
An imprint of Bloomsbury Publishing Plc

50 Bedford Square   1385 Broadway
London   New York
WC1B 3DP   NY 10018
UK   USA

www.bloomsbury.com

CONWAY and the 'C' logo are trademarks of Bloomsbury Publishing Plc

First published 2015

British Library Cataloguing-in-Publication Data
A catalogue record for this book is available from the British Library.

Library of Congress Cataloguing-in-Publication data has been applied for.

ISBN: HB: 978-1-8448-6280-1
ePDF: 978-1-8448-6282-5
ePub: 978-1-8448-6281-8

10 9 8 7 6 5 4 3 2 1

Designed by CE Marketing
Printed and bound in Great Britain by CPI Group (UK) Limited, Croydon, CR0 4YY

To find out more about our authors and books visit www.bloomsbury.com. Here you will find extracts,
author interviews, details of forthcoming events and the option to sign up for our newsletters.

CONTENTS

This book is dedicated to all those who worked at the Paddington Audit office for the Great Western Railway and served or lost their lives during the First World War.

INTRODUCTION

'Just a few lines to let you know that I am still in the land of the living.'
EDGAR HARRY BRACKENBURY, 16TH MARCH 1916

These words from E.H. Brackenbury are some of the few written by the many British men in the forces during the First World War. Such wartime correspondence recreates the world of combat in striking detail told by the men who were there. The letters in this book come from the members of the Audit office for the Great Western Railway based at Paddington while on active service 1915-1918. What makes this collection of soldiers' letters so different from all others is the fact that it reveals the stories of a particular group of men or 'GWR* fellows', ranging in class and education, who were writing back to their colleagues and bosses in the office over time.

The letters themselves are arranged in twelve carefully bound folders, rather like a series of scrapbooks. Starting from August 1915, each part represents what was known as the office newsletter, a collection of letters, photographs, postcards, field cards and contemporary newspaper cuttings from those who had gone to fight. Every newsletter opened with a news section listing those who had written and sent photos to the office and those who recently left to company to serve at the front. The totals at that point of all men in khaki from the Audit office were given too. Again the news section gave details of those who had died or had been injured, visited the office on leave or been promoted.

The newsletters were meant for circulation within the office departments and they were also read by men when they came home from the front on leave. People at home who had been sent their own letters or photographs lent them or typed them out to be circulated as part of the Audit office newsletter.

The whole process was clearly carefully managed. The news section listed those in the Audit office writing to the men. Letters and photographs for inclusion from the Goods, Passengers, Agreements General and Parcels, Fares and Ticket supply departments were to be handed to particular named people.

Those writing to the men clearly dealt with a large body of correspondence. Naturally, we do not have copies of any of the letters sent out, but evidently they were full of news according to the responses from the men and must have varied depending on the relationship with the sender. There was a real drive to keep in touch at all costs. Indicative of this commitment is the question posed in the August 1915 newsletter, 'are we in touch with all the fellows away, and if not, why not?'

The letters

For the 'Audit boys' who were far from home it must have been important to maintain that connection with Paddington and civilian life, a world away from the front. It provided a touchstone for what they the fighting for or allowed them to dream about life after the war. Many were keen to return to their jobs as Great Western Railway management had promised and showed concern in their letters over female workers taking their places in their absence. Some may have seen writing was a way of securing their future and wished to keep up with office politics.

Thus, through their letters this particular cast of characters mapped their personal experiences of the conflict within France, Belgium, the Dardanelles, India, Greece or Egypt. Some men who enlisted had previously been in the Territorial Army or fought in the Boer War. Others were 'mere boys' or had no previous military experience. During their time in khaki some were seriously injured and others died. All of the men in their different ways seem to be incredibly stoic and brave.

Many of those who wrote back to the Paddington Audit office showed a desire to grit their teeth and get on with it, keep a stiff upper lip and chose not to describe the hell they were going through in their letters. The fact that the letters were shared within the office and written to male colleagues must have informed their overall tone. They were open letters. As a consequence, some letters appear chipper and understated or betray a subtle sense of bravado. For example, Donald Hambly writing at the end of 1916 whilst training on the south coast with the Royal Naval Air Service said

> *'I am living in hopes of being sent out very much nearer the real thing, but for the present I must possess my soul in patience and carry on with what cheerfulness I can muster.'*

Censorship was a big issue for our writers as the correspondence makes clear. Handwriting was crayoned out in thick blue pencil by the censor in an obvious way. Writers often recorded their awareness of the censor too. Harold Watts, for example, declared that he would not give details and would save it for discussion when he next visited on leave. Some of the letters were addressed from 'somewhere in France' or else the author buried their address in main body of the letter text as advised by the censor.

Nevertheless, it is still surprising that some did describe the reality of the war as they experienced it and provided details that defied the censor, for example E. H. C. Stewart:

> *'Our casualties here amounted on the average, to about two per day killed, of course, we thought it terrible at the time at least I did.'*

Again, A.E. Rippington wrote in August 1915:

> *'Well old chap, I am glad I am wounded to get out of that hell, and if you ever meet a chap that says he wants to go back call him a liar.'*

Interestingly E.H. Brackenbury, who wrote from France and described the countryside and his various leisure activities made the following loaded comment:

'I hope you will not wonder whether I am aware that there is a War going on, for I am very well aware of it but at the same time think it quite a good scheme to talk about other things sometimes.'

The language and form of address used in the letters is a world away from today's lexicon with the use of terms like 'old chap' or 'old boy' or being in a euphemistic 'warm spot' or 'show'. Writers often seem to be pre-occupied in expressing that they were in 'good health' or 'in the pink' possibly because they were only too acutely aware this could rapidly change, indeed as W.J.E. Martin of the 3rd Battalion Grenadier Guards wrote from France in November 1915,

'To let you know I have not got shot yet and am in the best of health.'

Some letters appear more formal than others as the men addressed their superiors or bosses. 'Dear Sir' was used as an occasional form of address. Regular writer, Arthur Smith often signed off as 'yours obediently' providing a certain Victorian formality. He even apologised for his handwriting, which in fact is possibly one of the clearest hands! In other instances it is obvious that the authors were writing to close friends and used nicknames such as 'Effie' for F.E. Lewis; 'Burgie' for Mr G. Burgoyne; 'Jacko' for E.W. Jackson; 'Frosty' for R.C.S. Frost; 'Fatty' for J.W. Hyam; or 'Mug' for Morris to name a few.

Humour served as an evident refuge from their situation for some. Stanley Frost's letters often displayed a sense of humour and lightness of touch. In his first letter to the Audit office, 6th July 1915, he said,

'Fancy it being July and still we are pounding away at the Huns, or very often it is the reverse, worse luck! I suppose it is no good applying for a fortnight's leave!'

Similarly S. Smith joked in his undated letter to the office whilst training at Longmoor Camp* in 1917,

'I have had a military hair cut tonight and feel that I look like Bill Sykes. I am afraid none of your young ladies would care to be seen walking up number 1 [platform at Paddington Station] with me as I look at the moment.'

H.A. Skilling made a very dark pun, when he wrote on 5th January 1917

> *Our guns never cease down there, as soon as one section stop, another lot open out*
> *so you can tell there is <u>Somme</u> noise.*

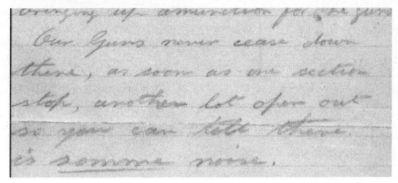

Gilbert Williams in a similar vein noted in November 1915,

> *'Oh! what a picnic it is in the trenches now. We have been in ten days up to now*
> *and except for the last two days it has been raining almost steadily. The result is*
> *mud, mud and yet more mud.'*

'Taffy' Edwards joked in one of his letters from Bordon* training camp
to the office,

> *'God what a life! What oh ye merry sapper*, no name only a blessed number like*
> *a bally convict, oh if mother could see me now? Fit, hale and hearty and as jolly as*
> *a kitten.'*

The content shared by the letters covered a range of themes from the
general to the specific. Numerous letters outline training in military
camps in the UK at Longmoor or Bordon where the sense of anticipation
appeared evident after enlistment and later conscription. We can read
details about rifle practice, physical drill, including leapfrog, the quality
and range of food and state of the beds, blankets and cutlery! Clearly, the
experience varied among men before they went abroad. Some seemed
bored waiting for their marching orders and others expressed sadness that
they were not in the same draft as other GWR men. Frank Turner, of the
18th County of London (London Irish) who sadly was to lose his right

arm in 1917, said whilst training in Winchester that a large number of men who were passed fit to join the army then were 'getting discharged on medical grounds' as most of them had heart trouble.

Once they reached their destinations abroad, letters home captured the sheer drudgery of trench conditions. Many conveyed the sense of physical deprivation from the mud, cold and shattering noise of gun and shellfire. A lot of the men documented the work carried out whilst in 'reserve' including trench digging and building parapets and dugouts. Again, the sheer sense of exhaustion is palpable, in November 1915, W.J.E. Martin wrote after the first attack on Looe and Hill 70,

> *'You should have seen us coming down the road up to our necks in white mud, rifle rusty and some of the boys walking along asleep. One of my platoon lost his rifle on the march, so that will tell you how some us were.'*

Likewise, Harold Watts stationed on the Dardanelles said in an early letter back to Audit office,

> *'I am so tired and would give anything to get away from this continual banging'*

A jaded Sidney Douce wrote in October 1916,

> *'This war is a most horrible and terrible affair... Still we keep on jogging along with the hope it will all end much sooner than some of the critics would have us believe.'*

His words were echoed in a similar way in a letter again from W.J.E. Martin,

> *'Roll on the duration of war, and England, I used to think it pretty bad out here, but I did not know it was like this, and by appearances, I shall spend my 20th Birthday and Xmas out in this awful country.'*

And F.E. Lewis whilst training in Norfolk with the 2nd Middlesex Hussars confessed,

> *'I find life very hard. You see Bertie, I am over forty and not particularly robust, in fact I am the sort of man that should have gone to the Army Pay Corps.'*

Understandably, food was a big consideration for most writers, they described what they ate in the trenches, or at the railheads* (where men and supplies were transferred from the railway network to the front) or in their billets behind the line, and what was consumed for Christmas dinner. For J.R. Higgs it was hard living on army rations and the 'fare usually is not very appetising'. We learn about their joy of having a break from the usual diet of bully beef*. Arthur Smith referring to Christmas at his railhead in December 1915 happily penned:

'For Christmas dinner we had two roasted stuffed chickens, roast potatoes, lime juice and Perrier water, Xmas pudding, nuts and last of all a bowl of champagne'

He said they had to buy these extra things and the pudding was a gift from one of the Daily papers. The quality of the local beer in France also invited comment, for Monty Pond it was 'something like onion water' and for E.W. Jackson,

'Belgium beer, it may interest you to know, is not quite as bad as the French'

The men were very keen to paint a picture of their new surroundings for those at home. And the differences between the French and English landscapes were a common discussion point in letters. Harry Beaumont stationed out in India at Rawal Pindi reported that 'the landscape is a perfect mixture of Devonshire, Scotch and Alpine scenery'. Harold Watts even sent home a piece of heather from the Dardanelles,

'Enclosed is a bit of heather which grows in great profusion all over the peninsula and the troops use it in the trenches to boil their dixies on'

Arthur Smith vividly described his crossing back to France after leave in 1915,

'The sea was calm and the night bright with moonlight and fair. All the lights were out on board and no smoking was allowed so being on the sea just in moonlight was rather nice and the scene was beautiful'

The 'GWR fellows' also regaled the office with details of recreational activities such as concert parties, bands, football matches and boxing.

Dick James, who wrote in August 1915 that he was glad that the GWR was still flourishing without him, said:

'*We are having a good time here in the way of concerts, sports, boxing tournaments etc. The latter was great especially the bout between a farrier sergeant and a cook's mate. They biffed at one another until neither could stand, it was terribly funny.*'

F.R. Morris, on the other hand, sent back a copy of a concert party programme along with details of various concerts and dramas. Monty Pond, who was a keen violinist had a violin sent out, so he managed to have some musical evenings and also enjoyed screenings of Charlie Chaplin pictures which 'were very laughable as usual.' Stanley Frost and others enjoyed camping and fishing beyond the firing line. Therefore for all these writers such experiences must have offered the chance of a more normal existence, however transitory.

References to animals loom large in the letters. Ron Dyer was delighted to have learnt to ride so easily and had a job working with canaries, as pigeon fancier in his spare time at home he certainly took to that immediately. 'Fatty' Hyam described in detail his work with horses. However, those in the Dardanelles commented on more exotic beasts. H.W. Cronin pointed out that 'the only living things are green canaries and lizards.'

Arthur Smith in November 1915 commented on the acquisition of a pet dog:

'*We have a dog in with us now. He came round once and appeared to belong to nobody…He is said to have been brought down from the German trenches but I cannot say what the truth there is in the statement. If true, he is a good souvenir.*'

In February 1916, Mark Russell, referring to German shell fire recorded that:

'*We are close up to the line a few kilometres away, and souvenirs come over occasionally*'

The 'Audit boys' often collected souvenirs including buttons taken from German greatcoats. Gilbert Williams saved a German helmet and Will

Davis acquired part of the framework from a German taube* and Harold Watts planned to bring home a nose fuse from the Dardanelles for a paperweight as he was not allowed to send home a Turkish shell.

In order to give those at home a sense of what they were going through, some men chose to reference Paddington. Jack Symons, a regular correspondent described shellfire and wrote,

> *'to give you an idea it's like sitting at Paddington and hear[ing] the engines screech'.*

For Stanley Frost on the other hand his regular trips to the same trenches in the same district were getting 'almost monotonous as using a season ticket.'

References to colleagues lost in the war are common throughout the collection. Many 'Audit boys' mourned the death of the hugely popular figure of Monty Pond in particular and E.H.C. Chamberlain, an early casualty for the Audit office, was remembered as 'one of the best' along with H.W. Cronin and R.W.S. Court. Letters also frequently commented on news of promotions gleaned from the GWR grapevine. Arthur Smith enjoyed providing a tally of recent promotions within the ranks of the Audit office, including his own. Arthur Barron was equally pleased and wrote in July 1917:

> *'I think our chaps are doing well don't you, so don't be surprised to hear one of these days that I have been made a Sergeant…'*

Details of injuries and wounds, treatment and convalescence in military hospitals at home and abroad, transport on hospital ships all feature in the letters. 'Fatty' Hyam for instance wrote whilst back in England after recovering from shell shock,

> *'I hope you will excuse the writing but I can't keep still, sometimes I feel in the pink and then I get a relapse'*

Aside from the prime reason of keeping in touch with their colleagues or thanking for gifts or the GWR Magazine*, some men, like Stanley Frost, wrote specifically to the office to request privilege orders* to allow them free travel as soldiers on convalescence.

Gifts for those in khaki

The Paddington Audit office frequently sent out parcels to the men. E.H. Brackenbury listed the contents of what he received in a letter from November 1915,

> 'I received a parcel from the GWR the other week containing: Tommy's cooker*, tin of sardines, tin of cocoa and another which I had to divide between an erstwhile relief signal man at Portishead and myself, waterproof wallet and khaki handkerchief.'

Other men received parcels of socks, scarves, cigarettes and chocolate. The Great Western Railway set up a committee at Paddington station to encourage and process these collections. The company did this because of the large numbers of GWR men, including clerical staff, that had joined the four companies of Royal Engineers for service abroad and different organisations had been collecting gifts for distribution to the Regular Army and Territorial Forces. Those at the front frequently wrote back to the office thanking them for their gifts or even put in special requests, like Gilbert Williams in August 1915,

> 'Awfully kind of you to offer to send me some cigarettes. We get issued with some periodically but it's very poor stuff we get. If you could send me a box of Abdulla you would be making me feel as if heaven had opened its gates to me.'

Or Monty Pond who politely wrote in a letter from October 1915,

> 'Some chocolate or anything of that sort would be very acceptable.'

Importantly, L.W. Sharpe pointed out in December 1915

> 'I can speak for most chaps out here and say that nothing do we enjoy more than a decent English fag and some good old 'Blighty' chocolate…it's a reminder that we are not forgotten.'

Some office members sent out the GWR Magazine too, as did friends and family.

It appears that throughout the letters that the men were always keen to lay their hands on a copy of their magazine if they could. Seemingly, one could take the man out of the GWR but not the GWR out of the man.

First contingent of G.W.R. Regimental Company of Railway Troops R.E., leaving Paddington Station.

The Roll of Honour

The Audit office raised enough money through collections and the sale of Christmas cards, to create a temporary roll of honour for the office at Paddington to commemorate those who had fallen in battle by August 1915. Photographs of the Roll of Honour were sent out to several of the 'Audit boys' as their correspondence reveals. By this stage the Audit office had sent 103 men to the forces out of a total of 322.

The Audit office

In peace time the 'Audit boys' worked in the Audit Accountant's office at Paddington in a range of different roles from insurance, accounting to ticketing for the Great Western Railway. The office was made of up of Agreements, Passengers, Goods and Parcels & General departments.

During active service in the First World War these 'Audit chaps' were to be, in the words of A.E. Kirk, 'scattered about doing their bit.' As a result this has provided us with an astonishingly vibrant collection of letters which really must be viewed as a whole. The correspondence represents a group of male work colleagues and friends bound together by their common connection to the Paddington office for the GWR who cared about each other and longed to be home.

Transcriptions

The authors have made minimal changes to text of the original letters. However, in order to make them easier to read we have added punctuation and corrected obvious spelling errors. For convenience, some abbreviations and additional notes are explained within the text and a glossary is included. All words which appear in the glossary are asterisked once. The term 'bobbing' has defied definition as it suggests a range of meanings depending upon the context of the letter. We have indicated where lines were censored. In a few cases we have omitted text caused by damage to the original or repetition within the letter. For this we have used the convention of three dots. Finally, readers need to be aware that in some cases, the date of the letter or location of the correspondent has not been specified.

Acknowledgements

The authors would like to express their thanks to their editor Lisa Thomas at Bloomsbury and Elaine Arthur at Steam, the Museum of the Great Western Railway.

They would also like to thank Ed Field and Hester Vaizey at The National Archives for their wonderful support and without whom this book would not have been possible.

Thanks also go to the following people: for C.H. Chris, Lotte and for K.P. Tom and Marla, Robert, Barbara and Sarah – always

GLOSSARY

❖

AI or A1 In the context of the letters this was usually used to mean in good health. However, it was also used refer to a specific military category of fitness, namely the ability to carry out full active service overseas.

AIII or A3 Soldiers who had returned from the front, who were not physically fit for fighting.

A.P.C. Army Pay Corps (non-fighting troops).

A.S.C. Army Service Corps (non-fighting troops)

A.M.F.O. Assistant Military Forwarding Officer

A.D.R.T. Assistant Director Railway Traffic

Bordon, Bordon camp See 'Longmoor'

Bully beef This was tinned beef, like corned beef and the staple of the British soldier's diet.

Commissariat A military department in charge of food supplies or equipment.

Derby Scheme Lord Derby's Scheme was also referred to as the 'Group System'. It was a voluntary recruitment policy in Britain created in 1915. The idea behind it was that men who voluntarily registered would be called to serve in the forces only when necessary. Men were classified according age and marital status, and single men were to be called first.

Dodging the column Avoiding working or in this case, avoiding going to fight.

Flapper A young, single, independent woman.

French leave A leave of absence without permission or without announcing one's departure.

Furlough   Leave of absence.

Green envelope   Soldiers were issued these once a week and they could be used to send letters about private, personal matters only. However, the contents could still potentially be censored.

Group system   See Derby Scheme, above.

GWR or **GW**   Great Western Railway.

In the pink   The best condition in terms of health.

Iron rations   An emergency food supply carried by servicemen in action.

Jack Johnson shells   German heavy artillery shells, which were very powerful and named after an American boxer of the time.

L. & N.W.R.   London & North Western Railway.

Longmoor and Bordon camps   Military training camps in Hampshire, England. Longmoor, and later part of Bordon, became the training centre for all Royal Engineers railway, road and as well as inland water transport men. Over the course of the war, nearly 1,700 officers and 66,000 other ranks were sent overseas from this base.

Magazines, mags   The Great Western Railway Magazine published from 1862-1949. For more information see the Introduction.

Maxim gun   A type of machine gun.

Mess dugout   A rough shelter in a trench, or cut into the side of a hill or a bank, for officers to eat or take a break.

M.F.O.   Military Forwarding Officer.

Orderly room   A room in a barracks in which company, troop, or battery records were kept. It was used for company business.

Picquet or picket   A small advance group of soldiers or boats used to keep watch.

Privilege orders   A warrant or pass for free train travel on specified journeys for GWR staff in the forces and their families.

Railhead   The nearest point to the front where men and supplies travelled by train. They were then taken to the battle line by motor vehicle or horse.

R.E.   Royal Engineers.

R.F.C.   Royal Flying Corps.

R.G.A.   Royal Garrison Artillery.

R.T.E.   Railway Transport Engineers.

R.O.D   Railway Operating Division.

This was a division of the Royal Engineers and largely made up of railway employees who combined their railway expertise with military training. F.E. Andrews for example outlines his role for this division, in a letter dated 16th October 1917.

R.T.O.   Railway Transport Officer, usually a company Captain stationed in the railhead area. He organised the movement of supplies, goods or men in the district to the front line.

Reveille   A trumpet call used to wake the soldiers.

Sapper   A soldier employed in the construction of fortifications or trenches.

Sap   A trench or short tunnel.

Self Help Society   This was a GWR collection fund that paid benefits to its members. Members paid a weekly subscription and could get various payments from the Society in times of need.

Smoke helmets   An early form of gas mask used to protect soldiers against poisonous gas. The mask was made of chemical absorbing fabric and which fitted over the entire head, like a hood. Sometimes referred to as a respirator.

Taube   A pre-war German plane which came to mean any German aircraft during the First World War.

Tommy's cooker   A portable cooker which was powered by a block of solid alcohol for fuel to create a smokeless fire. It proved to be fairly useless.

Top boots   Tall rubber waders or gum boots designed to try and avoid the problem of trench foot.

Uhlan   In this context, Cavalry regiments of the German army.

W.A.A.C   Women's Army Auxiliary Corps.

Whizz bangs   A German shell. The name comes from the sound a shell made when fired from a field gun.

ONE

AUGUST 1915

'It seemed as though hell had broken loose,
shells were falling like summer rain'.
EDWARD HENRY CECIL STEWART

These words from a letter written by E.H.C. Stewart to the Great Western Railway Audit office at Paddington capture the actuality of life under fire. Stewart's letter was included in the first office newsletter dated August 1915 which opens the collection held at The National Archives in Kew. Another letter from Montgomery Pond gives us a clear idea of what was really meant by the office newsletter. He wrote that he was:

> *'very pleased to hear about the collection of letters and photos from the troops that you are sending round the office.'*

The Paddington office also gave an open invitation to those who wanted to write or send gifts to those away on active service:

> *'Those desirous of cheering up our comrades can be put into touch with those forwarding parcels.'*

It is clear that the August newsletter was actually the second in the series, as the text mentions that the first had 'been favourably received' and thanks were 'due to those who kindly lent the letters and photographs' according its editor, Herbert Hunt, or 'Bertie' of the Agreements department.

In August the Audit had news that E.H.C. Stewart had been erroneously reported missing and heard of the death of colleague Sergeant E.C. Chamberlain of 13th (County of London) Battalion of the London Regiment (Kensington). He was one of the first to be killed in action from the Audit office and recorded in the Great Western Railway, Roll of Honour. He died on 9th May 1915 almost certainly in the Battle of Aubers Ridge. E.W. Bratchell was shocked to hear about it and his own experiences in France at Neuve Chappelle prompted him to write:

'I occasionally wish heartily to be on the old job again, the quiet life will do for me after this.'

The letters collected here cover the period from June to early August 1915 included word from Harold Watts in the Dardanelles. Other men wrote from France namely, R.A. Dyer, Billy Hastings, R.C.S. Frost, W.J. Martin, G. Williams, A. Smith, F. Ferdinand, M.P. Pond, F. Hull and A.E. Rippington from England. Lance Corporal H.G. Langford of the Berkshire Yeomanry sent a colourful postcard from Egypt depicting a lemonade seller and declared that he had managed to avoid the casualty list so far and thought that Cairo ran 'a close second to Paris'.

In contrast, Fred Hull described what it was like to be in the heat of battle on the Western Front.

'I am very sorry to say we had many casualties, thirty five killed and hundred and thirty eight wounded and I can assure you it was an experience I shall never forget.'

Stanley Frost penned a very detailed letter that described life in the trenches, at times somewhat lyrical in tone,

'at the back of our trenches is ripening corn and plenty of wild flowers in bloom'

Indeed, many of the letters in whole collection comment on the landscape of war. Unusually, R. A. Dyer, who still claimed to be 'whole-skinned' and hoped to 'come home the same way', wrote an entire letter about pigeons. Back in Ealing during peacetime he bred and raced them. He had a job connected with birds whilst serving with the 2nd Bedfordshire Regiment.

Montgomery Pond described his journey to his railhead in France, the office, never far from his thoughts. He said it was

'a glorious trip, the scenery being very fine, almost as good as our office outing, only not quite as comfortable travelling.'

Harry Beaumont managed to convey a sense of the sheer scale of his sea journey to Bombay accompanied by liners filled with Australian, New Zealand and Indian troops, 'it may truly be sung that Britannia rules the waves.'

'Fatty' Hyam wrote from his Remount Depot at Shirehampton which was used for horses received at Avonmouth. This base was used for training and provided horses to other army units. He noted that 'we have about 10,000 a week come in of horses and mules and some of them are fair devils, so wild and timid.'

Finally, Fred Ferdinand made a very interesting observation which revealed a sense of disconnect between impressions of the front at home and the realities of war which must have added to the sense of estrangement that many experienced when they returned home:

> *'By the tone of your letter you do not quite understand our mode of living, there is just a small camp arrangement, a few wooden huts, there is no such thing as going to a café for food unless of course it is for our own special enjoyment.'*

Here follow the letters which appeared in the Audit newsletter for August 1915 covering the experiences of those men who were amongst the first to enlist. They provide a powerful insight into life under combat and beyond.

A.E. Rippington, undated, England.

Dear Ernie,

Thanks very much for your letter and kind wishes. My wounds are getting on all right and they have discovered eleven in all. It is hard not to be able to get up, but I suppose a month will soon be slip by. My people came to see me yesterday and the day before.

You ought to see my face. They cannot shave me because I have scraps of shell sticking in, and as I had not had a shave for about a week before I was wounded, I look a pretty picture.

Well old chap, I am glad I am wounded to get out of that hell, and if you ever meet a chap that says he wants to go back call him a liar.

If you could manage to come down at any time I should be delighted. I have not received any letter from Dalton but perhaps will get it later. That will be the time old chap when I look into the office on my way home. We'll manage to get a drink then. Well I must close now and I expect you will have quite enough trouble to read what I have written already. Hoping to be with you all,

Your old pal, Rip.

A.E. Rippington, undated, England.

Dear Mr Wiggs

Please convey my deepest thanks to those kind friends who contributed to the watch, and for their kind wishes. The watch will more than replace the one I lost, and serve to remind me all my life of the kind treatment I received from my colleagues. Hoping to be with you all again soon,

Yours sincerely,
A.E. Rippington

H.G. Langford, 12th May 1915, Cairo, Egypt.

[H.G Langford sent a postcard called the Lemonade Seller *from Cairo. This is what he wrote on the reverse]*

Dear Mr Earl and friends of the Audit,

Still out of the casualty list, have seen plenty of Australian boys who have returned from the front. This city is a very gay place, runs Paris a good second I know. Kindest regards to all.

Yours sincerely,
H.G. Langford

[See colour plate: Lemonade seller.]

E.H.C. Stewart, undated, France.

…As long as you kept your head down you were comparatively safe, so as it went on, this was where I had my first escape. I was on sentry duty for a couple of hours, from 1am to 3am and was instructed to keep a sharp look out. I did not care for the idea of keeping my head above the trench and looking for beastly Germans, however it had to be done, it was quite uncanny to watch the enemy trench which appeared somewhat like a black wave and only sixty yards in front, then you would suddenly see the flash of their rifles and machine guns immediately after would come the report and nasty thuds on the sandbags which you might be resting against. I fired about five shots at their flashes (the only target to aim at) then another two shells which lodged in the parapet either side of my head leaving about 2 to 3 inches between me and certain death. I thought that near enough but it turned out that it was to have something nearer than that. Our casualties here amounted on the average, to about two per day killed, of course, we thought it terrible at the time at least I did.

Early April saw us relieved by another division and we were sent a few miles back for a well-earned rest, which consisted of physical drill and a run before breakfast. The remainder of the morning being spent in platoon drill musketry drills. After dinner we put the 'cap on' our rest (why so called I do not know) by having a route march for two hours. We spent a few days like this and were dispatched with all possible speed to Ypres, here we went in to support the Canadians and spent a most unpleasant eight days, during which time we lost several hundred men, nearly all my friends who came out in the same draft and were killed or wounded, we had to retire, the best part being that the Germans did not find this out until two days after when we were more or less safely bivouacking in a very pretty wood. We stayed here for about a week; then we got to work again, digging reserve trenches just behind the front line, building up parapets which had been demolished by the enemy's high explosive shells and such like, working all night and getting what sleep we could in the daytime.

One morning we were awakened by the most awful din, it seemed as though hell had broken loose, shells were falling like summer rain. And people have often told me in the course of conversation it was raining shells and I admit I took it with a grain of salt, could not be possible I thought, but such I was surprised to find was possible and actually taking place there about 3.30am. This bombardment started and about half an hour later, I, with three others, were ordered to start reinforcing. We went up in fours, it being considered safer that way, half a mile over open ground we had to do, this being swept continually with shells, to give you a slight idea I can say the previous night, just in front of our reserve trenches was a beautifully green field, and the next morning it was as much as one could do to see any grass at all, simply one mass of craters, varying in diameter from ten to twelve paces.

I had gone about half the required distance when a shell fell only a yard from where I was, the force of the concussion *[explosion]* pitched me several yards to my left and I came down rather heavily, however I reached the first line without any further mishap, where we had to stay until midnight when we had to be relieved again owing to not having enough me to hold the trench. Our honours were one V.C. *[Victoria Cross]*, two D.S.O. *[Distinguished Service Orders]*, one Military Cross and one or two D.C.M. *[Distinguished Conduct Medals]*.

The next day I paraded sick, my back paining me so much that I could not stand straight for a week after. I am now back with the regiment who are on the line of communications. We are having leave shortly and if possible will pay a visit to the Audit office…

Yours truly,
Rifleman E.H.C. Stewart

E.H.C. Stewart, 28th July 1915, France.

Dear Sir,

Thank you very much for the nice letter, which I received from you yesterday…

[Lines censored]

I hope to look through the Guard Book one day, it should be very interesting. I was rather surprised at the number of names on the Roll of Honour, many thanks for sending it out to me. I do not remember if I told you Sergeant A. Maggs who worked in the Goods Audit, is at Rouen Camp, trying to get over the effects of frostbitten foot, which he received last winter. Kind regards,

Yours sincerely,
Rifleman E.H.C. Stewart

R.C.S. Frost, 6th July 1915, France.

My Dear Standew

Many thanks for sending on the magazines, the last of which I received this morning. I intended writing before but we don't get much peace on this job, and the time goes by so quickly. Fancy it being July and still we are pounding away at the Huns, or very often it is the reverse, worse luck! I suppose it is no good, applying for a fortnight's leave!

However I am glad to say I am keeping fine, and still going strong, like a certain brand of whisky. I have been in the trenches at four different places on this front, and on one occasion we were in for fifteen days except for a days' rest after the first week. The second period was unexpected as an attack was made by the British, and we occupied the reserve trench at that time.

I was in the firing line all last week and came out on Sat. night. It was rather a hot place; the enemy being only hundred yards distant, and on Friday night we heard a cornet being played in their trench. For the past two months the R.E.*s have been busy with mines, some of which were exploded last week, to destroy similar work which was being done by the Germans. Just after the upheaval, which I might say was like a miniature earthquake, and made us afraid the parapets of sandbags would collapse on us, the British bombarded with artillery, which wasn't very pleasant for us considering the closeness of the lines. But our people got the range very well so no damage was done to us.

This trench of ours is a model in its own way, being fairly safe, and connected by good communication trenches. The Commanding Officer's house of white sandbags is fitted with window, curtains, and window box with pansies in it. It is furnished with table and chairs also a large mirror. Of course this is quite a 'one occasion' affair and don't imagine we are here town planning with model dwellings etc! But it will show you how soldiers can adapt themselves to circumstances. At the back of our trench is ripening corn and plenty of wildflowers in bloom.

We have also canaries in cages in the trench! But these are used by the miners for testing the air in the mines after the explosion, to see if it was possible to finish off their job. *[Censored line]* captured from the Germans a short time ago and during the stay we were kept busy with sandbags etc. and at night of course had to especially watch the enemy.

When in the reserve or support trenches fatigue work has to be done every night, such as carrying food, ammunition, material for the engineers etc. to the firing line, so you can guess it is nothing but continual 'bob work *[odd jobs]*.

I saw Williams and Hull last Sunday week, and they were both well. I am very sorry to hear about Chamberlain, also George Shipley's brother Sam, who I knew very well.

Do you ever hear anything of Martin? I haven't for months! Well I must bring this to a close. With kind regards to Messrs Hunt and Taylor and all old friends in the Agreements department…

S. Frost.

R.C.S. Frost, 15th July 1915, France.

Dear Mr Hunt

Many thanks for your welcome letter volunteering so much interesting news of friends at the office. I wrote to Standew just before receiving your letter, but no doubt a few more lines will be acceptable.

Beaumont seems to be doing the best of us all. I saw Williams and Hull about three weeks ago in a small town near here. Of course the Seaforths and Argylls *[Regiments]* always move about together, but we don't meet very often. I am glad to hear the old section is still in being, and not like the German Empire is fast becoming a thing of the past! And hope your three survivors will be allowed to keep the flag flying until the wanderers return.

I have been in the firing line several times, and at four different places, besides being in the support trenches at others. I hear this is called a mobile division which accounts for our gipsy life in France.

Our last turn in the firing line, for six days and six in the reserve was the most exciting of all.

It has been a quiet place for two months, until two days after our occupation, when the British exploded mines under some workings of the Germans near their trenches, to prevent them blowing our trench up. Well! That woke them up and the following Saturday they retaliated by opening rapid fire early in the morning.

However we were ready for them and quickly replied, so they then bombarded us, which to say the least of it was a noisy business. That eventually ceased and rapid firing was quickly in process again, followed by another shelling, which our guns again put a stop to. The whole affair lasted an hour and ten minutes, and although we believe an attack was intended, the Germans didn't leave their trench, opposite to us. After putting our trench in order again which took some time, as the parapet was blown down for about three yards near me, and a shell burst amongst a lot of beef tins, scattering them and the contents in all directions, besides the bottom of the trench being littered with hundreds of empty cartridges, we proceeded with boiling water for tea, also to show the Huns by the smoke that we were still there. Only a hundred yards separated the two trenches, so it was always a case of 'bob down' and the enemy were good shots, as we found out to our cost when they smashed the top glasses in two periscopes within half an hour one morning.

At present the division is resting, and I and two friends have erected

a wee bivouac under an apple tree on a farm. It is quite cosy, in fine
weather, but last night it was raining hard for several hours, so we had
to beat a hasty retreat to an old barn. There is plenty of fruit about here,
but the water supply is very bad.

Last Sunday morning we enjoyed our first <u>hot</u> bath since our arrival
here. An old disused brewery has been turned into baths for troops,
also under clothing is washed and disinfected, and kilts ironed there.
Fifty tubs are provided for washing in and two large vats filled with cold
water to plunge into afterwards.

I have not got any stripes yet, but have been studying signalling
lately, so expect soon to be in the signal section...

'Frosty'

R.A.W. Dyer, 26th May 1915, France.

Dear Mr Wills

Sorry I have not been able to write to you lately but no doubt you have
guessed that we have had a good hard time lately. I have not received
any papers *[racing papers]* from you lately but it is probably because I
am with the Battalion now. I have sent my above address to the Quarter
Master Sergeant and asked him to forward all my letters on so I may get
them in a day or two. I am keeping pretty fit and well although I got a
soaking at the beginning of last week that has left its mark on me. I am
now on a job in connection with the birds and it makes me laugh to hear
some of the chaps talk, they think they know everything and tell me I
know nothing, but I just keep quiet, little do they know that I have raced
as many birds as probably they have ever seen because none of them
have ever done any serious racing with clubs or Federations. Fancy old
Smales wanting to be remembered to me, is he still keeping on with his
birds? I had a letter from Doctor Derbyshire a week or two back and he
told me the Ealing Club had got up a programme that will give a few
old stagers a chance to show themselves again on the West Route. Yes,
I have been in the two rough houses since N. Chapelle, *[Battle of Neuve*

Chapelle, 10th-13th March 1915] but am pleased to say I am still whole-skinned and I hope to come home the same. Have you managed to find a suitable new house yet? You might let Billie Dawson know I am still alive and tell him I will write him at first opportunity. Must close now,

Kind regards to all at the office and to Mrs Wills,

From yours very sincerely, R.A.D

32.

DYER, PRIVATE R. A. W. (14833), 2nd Battalion, Bedfordshire Regiment, attached to Signal Company, 47th Division, British Expeditionary Force. Before enlisting, in August last, he was a clerk in the service of the G.W.Rly. Co. Audit Office, Paddington. Has been in France for some time, taking part in the Battle of Neuve Chapelle. At one time he was a member of the Ealing Central H.S., and flew up to Rennes in partnership of a friend, and at the time of enlisting was an hon. member of the society. Private Dyer receives *The Homing Pigeon* every week from his friend, Mr. J. G. Wills.

R.A.W. Dyer, 4th July 1915, France.

Dear Mr Wills

Sorry that I have not written you for so long but I do not get so much time for writing now as I used to. I am not sure whether I have sent you this address before, but if not you will see where to send in future. The last papers *[racing papers]* I received from you was about three weeks ago and I thank you for them. It is nice to have them sent out because I can see just how things are going. Hard luck having the racing stopped altogether, but the Hounslow Club managed to get three races in and I only know the result of the first one and Piercey won that with one of the birds he had off me about four weeks before the race, he came over and took several of mine. He won the pools as well so he didn't make a bad start. Did you manage to get any races in? Dad told me you were moving to Hanwell, have you shifted yet? I suppose as soon as you can get settled down up will go the loft and breeding will go on with a rush. I am working with the Royal Engineers now, and most of the work is with horses and as you may guess I like it alright and although when I came here I could not ride, I have got on famously and can ride quite alright now. How are things going at the office, still no much to do I suppose? Have any more fellows left for the army lately? I notice poor old Joe Chamberlain of the Statistics department got killed, he was a Sergeant too. How are Mrs Wills and the youngster getting on? A1* I hope. There are still three birds at home, two cocks and one hen so if you want an odd one you had better go up and look at them or if you know anybody reliable that wants one or two you might be able to get rid of them for Dad.

Everything has been pretty quiet along our front lately but I expect we are waiting for some of the ammunition that Lloyd George is getting ready for us. Tommy Sharpe from the Goods department that joined with me is still alright. He is an Officer's Servant now but of course he is still with the Battalion. What is your opinion on how long the war will last? Anyhow roll on when I can get back to Ealing again.

Yours sincerely, Ron

F.H. Ferdinand, 14th July 1915, France.

Dear Mr Goff (Agreements)

[F.H. Ferdinand also sent a portrait photograph with this letter. See colour plate Ferdinand]

I have to write and thank you very much for your most interesting letter, which although about eight days in transit reached me last evening, it having been forwarded to me from Calais by my brother. You seem to have got a very vague idea of my address and consequently the letter in question went to G.H.Q and numerous other places, eventually being handed to my brother at Calais. Incidentally I might mention that the address was practically obliterated by blue pencil remarks such as 'not here', 'not known' etc. so for future occasions, please note 'as a special case and without prejudice' (sorry I forgot for the moment) I suppose you think it's about time I had forgotten those beautiful sentences so frequently used in the past. Anyhow my address is: Sapper F.H. Ferdinand, No. 87725, R.E. Attached Military Forwarding Officer, B.E.F., Havre, France.

By the tone of your letter you do not quite understand our mode of living, there is just a small camp arrangement, a few wooden huts, there is no such thing as going to a café for food unless of course it is for our own special enjoyment. Of course a little light refreshment goes down a treat. Poor old Dick Gilson has had some stirring experiences.

All the chaps that came out here from Paddington with me have been shifted to various places, one to Rouen, one to Boulogne etc. and now I am pleased to tell you that I am getting on nicely here and am now in the Office.

When the photos of the Roll of Honour have been completed I shall be very pleased indeed to receive one, it will be of great interest to me.

I ask you to remember me to Mr Cox and Mr Clark, and tell them that I should not feel at all annoyed at having to settle down to the old Agreements section again.

It seems ages since I had anything to do with the office, but of course, under the circumstances, I much prefer to be here. Well cheer up old chap and keep the 'pile' low. Kind regards to all,

Yours very sincerely,
Fred Ferdinand

R.F. Hull, 19th June 1915, France.

Dear Gerald

Many thanks for letter which was somewhat a surprise to me. No the news was quite fresh as I do not hear from anybody in the office.

We have just come from the trenches where we were for seven days and had a most awful time. We were three days in the Reserve and put in the firing line where we took part in an attack and were also under a very heavy bombardment.

I am sorry to say we had many casualties thirty five killed and one hundred and thirty eight wounded and I can assure you it was an experience I shall never forget. Anyhow Williams, Kemball and myself came out quite safely.

I have seen Frost out here, of course his battalion *[8th Argyll & Sutherland Highlanders]* are in the same brigade also, as a matter of fact, they were in the firing line the night we came out. I received a letter while I was in the trenches from Mr Slater. Yes, I heard about Chamberlain, jolly sad was it not, if you do hear from Dick James you might pass any news on to me...

Shall be glad to hear from you. I could write more, only am a wee bit tired after seven days in trenches.

I am yours sincerely,
Fred Hull.

E.W. Bratchell, undated, France.

Group taken at Malta including Pte E.W.Bratchell
3rd. Batt'n London Reg't. (No. 3 Back Row)
We regret to hear that E.W. Bratchell has again
been wounded by Shrapnel in the ear while fighting
in France. He has satisfactorily undergone an
operation and the missile removed.

The newsletter this month circulated this group photograph which included
E.W. Bratchell

Dear Burgie,

Was very glad indeed to get your letters although, your news in regard
to Joe *[Chamberlain]* comes as a shock. It was the first I had heard of him
since he arrived in France in spite of the fact his regiment being quite
close. Am afraid the 9th and few days following were rotten days for a
good many battalions, our lot as much as any. We have been 'in' since
the 8th and have had a fairly trying time we were reinforced during this
week, not before time as we were down to our last two hundred. Can't
tell how sorry I am to hear about Joe as you say he was 'one of the best'.
I hope you chaps have not been annoyed at my not answering your
very welcome letters. I don't pride myself much on writing good yarns
though and opportunities are also hard to find. As you know I had a bit
of a knock at Neuve Chappelle but have quite got over that and am now

in the best of health and spirits. I came across Len Phillips and Peter Hawes in different drafts of the London Scottish while down at Rouen both of them have now had some experience on the job I expect. Thank Mr Drewe very much for making enquiries, tell him I occasionally wish heartily to be on the old job again the quiet life will do for me after this. No I did not get Dick's magazine or letter expect it went astray while I was in hospital. Thank him very much for sending them will you. Had a game of football about two weeks ago with R.G.A.* Battery, the pitch being a serious drawback. I think it was a cabbage patch. Still we managed to get a good game in and most important of all, won. The weather here has on the whole been very good just lately only getting an occasional day's rain. Last night we had a sharp thunderstorm, a new experience it had at least the effect of shutting all the other disturbances of our rest up so we did not grouse. Much obliged for all the information re the other fellows. Am glad most of them are getting on so well. Peacock seems to have come out top dog. The job alone from other examples seems to be a paying one, leaving out the holiday in Scotland. Well must close my epistle.

E.W. Bratchell

W.A. Hastings, 11th July 1915, France.

Dear Effie, *[F. E. Lewis]*

Very pleased to receive your letter, like yourself I find my correspondence voluminous for me at times, especially since I have taken on the duties of Platoon Sergeant which takes up more time than one realises at first. We are still in the trenches and have been in action twenty four days consecutively and I don't know long we shall keep it up. Had a dirty time yesterday morning dodging damned great bombs the blighters were presenting to us without exaggeration they were eighteen inches to a two feet long and made a hole about ten feet deep and fifteen feet diameter at least we did not wait to see them burst. They can be seen descending through the air and then a scoot is made to get as far as possible round the corner, the iron and dirt seem to be falling for a minute afterwards, they are disturbing. Dicky Gilson has not been with us the last twenty four days, he broke his glasses and would not buy new ones (went to the doctor and all that and worked the oracle and was left behind with the Transport, don't know whether he worked the ticket properly and got a safer job farther back, should not blame him if he has, his nerves have been in a shocking state, he'd brood a lot as you know that is absolutely fatal when you have a dirty job on like this.

I have not seen either Frost or Kemball out here, do not seem to meet anybody fresh as we are always in the same district and relieve the same crowds generally.

Our pals the French in my opinion scrap jolly well except in the isolated instances which are given undue prominence by our chaps by prejudice probably. The casualties have certainly been enormous but a lot of them are a week old and one cannot form any opinion of what is going on by the lists, and I should not be allowed to say what I thought of our doings lately. Cronin is still with the 5th Bedfordshires and not out yet, I think not likely to be in all probability. Only wish we could repeat our swimming performance off Penarth 'specially the Wednesday evening ones. Have heard rumours of leave being given shortly but do not rely much on it, have been offered a Commission in this Battalion and I may take it up if my papers go through satisfactorily.

Kindest regards and wishes to Mrs Lewis,

Your old Pal, Billy

E.W. Jackson, 26th July 1915, France.

Dear Mr Taylor

Many thanks for letter of 23rd. Good, getting over the half yearly without bobbing.

Yes the Registration bill is satisfactory, if late. Also the War Loan, but the rate of interest is too high, it has played hell with people's others investments, fancy Great Western stock below par, it is wicked. I can see it is a little better now. *[Censored lines]* I ... saw a short paragraph in The Express about Crossely, it was very sudden, still he had been ill on and off for years had he not? Thank you for Symon's card and message, apparently by his badge he is in the King's Royal Rifles, but I don't know. *[Censored lines]*

Am sending this through Dawson to save precious green envelope*.

E.W.J.

M.P. Pond, 31st July 1915, France.

Dear Mr Hunt

Many thanks for your long and interesting letter which I was very pleased to receive. I am sorry I have been unable to answer it before but I have been constantly moving about from one place to another lately, and have had no opportunity of writing letters. Well I am very pleased to say I am feeling very fit and well, and quite enjoying the life. When writing to you last, I was attached to the 4th Division and was stationed at a small village where we were living in tents. We were stationed there about six weeks. Just over a week ago I was transferred to another place about eighty miles from the other one. I travelled by motor lorry with the Supply column and it took us all day from 7.30am till about 9 o'clock in the evening to do the journey. It was a glorious trip, the scenery being very fine. Almost as good as our office outing, only not quite such comfortable travelling. We put up for the night in a small village, sleeping in the lorry with some empty petrol cans for a bed. Next morning I was taken to the railhead where I was stationed until yesterday being only in that place just a week. While there we were all still sleeping in tents, but I was fortunate enough to have my meals with the Post Office Staff so have had a rest from being my own cook. Yesterday afternoon, just as I was going for my tea, I was sent for and told to pack up my things and catch a train to another railhead as I had to take charge as the A.M.F.O* for three Divisions there. As there is usually a man attached to each division, this was rather a large order.

I only had about twenty miles or so to go, but it took from 5 o'clock till after 9pm to get there. These French trains are very rapid.

I am now attached to the 51st (Highland) Division, the same division as Williams, a number of his lot were here today, but he was not with them. We shall probably only be here for a few days and will then move to another village further on. I was very surprised to hear of Mr Pritchard's death. I also heard that Mr Crossley is also dead. We are having glorious weather here at present and very hot at times. Glad to hear you are having a soft time on the old section.

I was very pleased to hear about the collection of letters and photos from the troops that you are sending round the office and will certainly send you a photo later on. I have has some taken but have not received them yet. Have you heard from Ferdie or Gray at all? We all had our photos taken at Longmoor before we came out here a group of six. Unfortunately, I only had a few copies and they have all been sent away. Ferdie and Gray are still at the Base, I believe, but Arthur Smith is at one of the railheads somewhere. Well I don't think I can tell you any more news at present. Will write again later and send photo.

Kindest regards to all.

Yours sincerely,
M.P. Pond

A. Smith, 3rd August 1915, France.

Dear Sir,

I was very glad to get your letter some weeks ago. It is always nice to get some office news out here. I was glad to hear that Hull and Kemball had been promoted to Corporals. *[Lines censored]*

I was sorry to hear the sad news about Chamberlain and Stewart. A photo of the Audit Office Roll of Honour has been sent out to me. It is a good one. A few weeks ago I happened to be attached to the 51st (Highland) Division, the Division in which Frost is or was…

Since my last letter I have been promoted to the rank of Lance Corporal. I get three shillings and six pence per day now.

The other day a German taube was over here and one of our men met him in the air – a maxim gun* duel ensued but neither came to the ground here. We have had one or two visits of taubes recently – one was over here yesterday morning early. Our Anti-Aircraft people did pepper him.

The Military Forwarding Establishment has undergone a re-organisation as far as railheads* are concerned. We do now come under the Railway Transport Establishment and our Superior Officer at a railhead is the Railway Transport Officer. It is a very good department to be in. The bases are still under the same system I believe.

I had a letter from Brackenbury a short while ago. He is stationed just outside Rouen. When walking down one of the principal streets of Rouen one evening, he met Ashfold so naturally, after overcoming their astonishment at meeting one another, they had a chat. Among other things the Self Help Society* was discussed by them and Brackenbury kindly told me that if I were a member I should have to apply for my five shillings or some such amount but I am not a member. As far as I know Ferdinand and Gray are at Boulogne. I know the latter person is here because I recognise his hand writing in letters from A.M.F.O.* Boulogne.

I am pleased to say I am getting on alright with work and everybody, also am enjoying good health. Kindly excuse writing, we don't get chairs and tables out here.

Yours obediently,
A. Smith

H. Beaumont, 29th November 1914, SS. *Grantully Castle.*

[H. Beaumont was travelling on a troop ship sailing in convey out to India]

Dear Mr Wheeler

Just a few lines to let you know of my whereabouts. This is our fifth
Sunday at sea. We left Southampton on Thursday October 29th shortly
before midnight and our convoy of ten huge liners each with about 1700
to 2000 territorial troops on board assembled in the English Channel
early next morning.

We were escorted by British warships as far as our first port of call–
Malta, the French warships to Port Said. After staying one night there we
proceeded through the Suez Canal. We lay off the Port of Suez six days

waiting for another escort then on through the Red Sea to Aden where we stayed four days waiting for our Japanese escort. When it arrived it brought with it an immense convoy of over <u>80</u> huge liners transports filled with New Zealand and Indian troops. This, in addition to a convoy of 35 vessels that came into Suez whilst we lay there. So it may truly be sung that 'Britannia rules the waves.'

It has been a most delightful and interesting voyage and the weather is now so hot that hundreds of troops are compelled to sleep on deck nightly as the heat is much too great below. We landed two cases of fever at Aden. Fortunately it does not appear to have spread any further so far.

We expect to reach Bombay on Wednesday next, December 2nd then three or four days' train journey to Fyzabad, some distance north of Lucknow. Shall be very glad to get there, as five weeks on board a crowded troop ship with very little opportunity for exercise is getting rather irksome, especially, when we get no 'Daily paper', only a little wireless war news, occasionally.

I am glad to say that I am wonderfully fit and well. Our food has been wholesome and plentiful. Trusting you are well, with my best wishes for as Happy a Christmas as is possible under prevailing war conditions,...

Believe me, yours faithfully, H. Beaumont

Will you also convey my respects to Mr Price please?

G. Williams, 4th August 1915, France.

Dear Mr Hunt,

I suppose you know that Frosty's Battalion is in the same Brigade as the 6th, but even then I see very little of him. As a rule when he is in the trenches I am out and vice-versa. I have seen him once or twice.

Hard luck about Crossley. Anything due to me from the Self Help, you might send to *mater*, Mrs H. Williams, Yarrow Cottage, Burnham,

Bucks… Also when you send home the money, you might send a note explaining.

Awfully kind of you to offer to send me some cigarettes. We get issued with some periodically but it's very poor stuff we get. If you could send me a box of *Abdulla* you would be making me feel as if heaven had opened its gates to me.

Yes I am keeping a regular correspondence with Jackson. He seems to be keeping very fit. His only objection seems to be that he has to rise at 5am in the morning still he is on a good job, Quarter Master Sergeant.

I'm not in the Machine Gun Section. I was only attached to them for a few days, so my address is 12th Platoon, C. Coy, instead of Machine Gun Section.

Our division along with one or two more has been taken from the British front in Flanders and has taken over part of the French line some seventy miles south of where we were before. The battalion is at present in the trenches and from the front line, we cannot see the German trench in front, it being over the brow of a hill. My company is in reserve, and our dugout is perched on the top of a wooded hill at the bottom of which is a marsh, which seems to be the breeding place of millions of mosquitoes, and by Jove they do give us hell. We have a jolly fine view from our dugout. There is also a spring of the finest water I've had since I came to France.

Will chuck it now, with kindest regards to all the boys,

Yours very sincerely,
Gilbert Williams.

T.H. Watts, 18th June 1915, Dardanelles.

Dear Arthur,

I expect you are wondering why I have not written, but it is an awful effort to get all correspondence off, and be on active service at the same time. I can't say that I am enjoying myself out here. It's awfully hot, and we are eaten up by millions of flies. Life in the trenches is not a picnic either we have about four or five days out of them and eight or nine in them. When we are out supposed to be resting, we have to go on working parties, digging etc., then wherever we are, we are always under shell fire, so it's not much rest after all. The last shell we had in camp, there was four killed and seventeen wounded.

We have been under fire for three months now, and we should like a rest as the strain is tremendous on one's nerves. I don't think the troops in France get it quite as bad. Then again, the only comforts we have are sent from home, as the country here is quite barren, and we cannot buy anything in shops, I would give a quid for a pint of beer down the club. Our food consists of half a loaf of bread per day, bacon and tea for breakfast, Bully beef and biscuits for dinner and jam for tea and cheese. Lime juice is served out about four times per week, that is a drop is put into a dixie of water and a cup full served out per man, and rum is served out twice a week (sometimes) that is about four table spoonful each.

We live in a trench and it is a mercy it don't rain otherwise we'd be washed away. The fighting just lately has been terrible. Our shells knock the enemy all ways and the sight in the trenches that we take is awful. We wear our respirators because of the awful smell of the dead. I'll never get the sight out of my eyes, and it will be an everlasting nightmare. If I am spared to come home, I'll be able to tell you all about it, but I cannot possibly write as words fail me. I can't describe things.

Wouldn't it be nice to be at Walmer again and you come down and see me again, I did enjoy that time, and also seeing Billy Dawson and Richardson. There seem to be a lot of French troops out here, but there seems to be no relief for us. Nobody loves us now Churchill has gone, we are nobody's pets. It's the army first here, except when there is work to be done, and then the Naval Division have to do it. You know both my brothers have commissions in the 4th Bedfordshires and are at Dovercourt. My wife tells me she has sent me three boxes of stuff, I received one box, and I fear that one transport has been floundered [sunk] and another has been torpedoed, so I expect that is where my other two boxes are. It's awfully disappointing because I do look forward so to a bit of chocolate and a few biscuits from home. We get cigarettes and baccy served out to us, but it is too hot to smoke much, so that I don't miss that so much. I get a bath in a biscuit tin when I can, but when in the trenches I have to go all the time without a wash, so you can tell I am used to being dirty.

How are they all down the club, and is Emmie still there, and is she better or not? Is Paice going to Looe this year? And where are you spending your holidays? Lord how I'd like a holiday, I am so tired and would give anything to get away from this continual banging.

Please remember me to all fellows who are left in the office...I can't write to all separately, also for details of my experiences you must wait until I get back, if ever I do, of which sometimes I despair.

The papers tell you pretty full accounts, although they are rather anticipating events as to our advancing. Now I must close old chap, and thank you very much for all your kindness. Wishing you all the best

Yours very sincerely,
T. Harold Watts.

W.J.E. Martin, 2nd August 1915, France.

Dear Joe

Just a short note as promised to let you know I am alright and in good health up to the present. We had a decent trip on the boat and I don't believe anyone was seasick. We have not been in the firing line yet, though I don't expect we shall be long now, anyway I hope not. The weather is pretty well the same as in England, but the people and streets etc. are a mighty lot different. The roads are absolutely awful they are either cobbles or chalk, and when it rains there are young rivers in the streets. We go on very much the same as we did at Marlow *[training camp in England]* as regards training. Our food is pretty good too and we get plenty of it. I reckon we are about perfect now for fighting and hope they don't keep us hanging about here very long. Well Joe, I can't tell you very much as we are not allowed to so I may as well close. Please

remember me to Mr Davies and Mr Goodall and all the others enquirers
and give them my best wishes,

J.W. Hyam, undated, England.

Dear Bertie,

Many thanks for letters and fags both were very acceptable as you can
imagine for it bucks one up to hear from old associates. I also had a
letter from 'Tinker' Taylor who told me Gwen has left the Great Western
Railway Company. I will write to Ferdi *[Ferdinand]* and ask Frosty if you
give me his address. I can imagine how lovely and empty the old room
looks, fancy more flappers eh, quite a selection as you say. I will just
give you an idea of our work here day by day. Reveille* 6.00am, stables
at 6.30-7.30, breakfast till 9. Then exercise ride one and lead two or
three *[horses]* for one and a half hours, then groom them until 12.15, then
we water and feed and go to dinner till 2.30 then sweep up …
[Letter damaged]

Bed *[horses]* down at 4pm then water and feed at 4.15 to 4.30 and
hay up at 5pm, only we take it in turns to do that and we have stables
like this. *[Fatty has drawn a rough sketch of the stables which house the
horses].*

We have six and seven a side which leaves us four horses each.
Of course, sandwiched between this is probably a visit to Avonmouth
Docks to fetch horses or take ours to the station for we only keep them
for a week at the time just to knock the mud off and feed them up so as
they get their shore legs and look a bit shipshape again. We have about
10,000 a week come in of horses and mules and some of them are fair
devils, so wild and timid.

I may come and see you Saturday if I get the weekend off…

OCTOBER 1915

'It's all wrong to call them men, as they were mostly mere boys.'
Dick Gilson

Dick Gilson described his experience of coming under machine gun fire, witnessing men or boys around him being killed or injured while he miraculously remained unhurt. Yet these letters do not all focus on the heat of combat. The nature of the correspondence received by the GWR Audit office between August and October 1915 was effectively captured in the words of Dick James, who wrote from France,

> *'Well the old Brigade has had some pretty varied experiences in this land of stinks and bad beer.'*

The letters sent at this time were often lengthy and described the minutiae of army life. They seemed keen to reassure those at home that they were doing as well as could be expected. After his training at Longmoor and arrival in France Arthur Smith wrote

> *'I find the life much rougher from that which I have been used to, but it is a fine experience all the same.'*

Two photographs *[see colour plate]* sent by Jack Symons provide an insight into his training before he was sent abroad. In the top photograph he and his comrades are seated in deckchairs apparently enjoying the English countryside. The bottom photograph shows eleven soldiers, one dressed as a waiter, presumably for comic effect. In the foreground a bottle of wine has been placed on a metal tray with a bouquet of flowers, the soldiers had staged these items especially for the scene.

These photographs are some of the many sent to the Audit office. When viewed with the correspondence they provide greater insight into the lives of the 'Audit soldiers'. For example, we know that these photos were taken during Symons' extended period in UK training camps and a letter sent at the same period said:

> 'Well I shall not be sorry to leave here, but honestly I would sooner take my chance across the water than move to another station in England. I am fairly fed up with soldiering on this side of the water.'

These words are not in keeping with the jovial photos of Symons and his comrades. Symons said that he disliked training so much that he would rather leave its safety and go abroad. The photographs contradict the way in which most Audit soldiers described their training as consisting of hard, monotonous and dirty work; one can safely assume that these were taken during a fun moment on a rare day off.

Many soldiers used photography to record their experiences. It was not unusual for a soldier to carry a small Vest Pocket Kodak that measured about 1 by $2^{1}/_{2}$ by $4^{3}/_{4}$ inches. Symons probably used one, even though it was forbidden to carry cameras after 1915, soldiers often flouted this ban. E.F. Henderson, who had completed his training and was writing from France, was seemingly home sick and wondered about the logistics of his return home after war:

> 'I have been wondering if, when the war is over, the GWR will do anything to expedite the discharge of their servants from the army. Because I should like to settle down again as soon as possible. After all is said and done there is no place like home.'

On the other hand E.W. Jackson considered the possibility of conscription which suggested that he had some access to current newspapers,

> 'The recent speeches seem to lean towards the idea of compulsion, but I don't believe the people would have it, even if it were law, if a large number of men started passive resistance and refused to go, what would happen?'

With regards to the fortunes of the Audit soldiers, in the typed office newsletter staff in Paddington heard that:

> From the last big fight information is now coming to hand.
> We regret to hear that Lieut. C.D.Mayo of the Royal Scots
> Lothian Regt. is reported wounded and missing.
> Billy Hastings writes from Gosforth Hospital. Newcastle on

> Tyne, the card is included in this issue, that he has
> a fractured skull. We wish him a full and speedy
> recovery. Billy is one of the best of sports, and we
> hope he will soon get his Commission.

One author stood apart both for his geographical location and his personal experience of war. Sergeant Harry Beaumont arrived in Rawalpindi, India, and after about 10 months there had established a comfortable routine:

> *'Am having the time of my life out here… we have Cinderella dances about three times a week, whist drives, racquet and tennis parties and have most enjoyable times.'*

His letter was bleakly contrasted by others such as that from Dick Gilson recounting battle in France:

> *'It was horrible suspense, as I seemed to be the only man untouched, all around me, and being personally acquainted with each man made matters worse'.*

After being away almost a year, George Shipley wrote his first letter to the office, in reply to letters of condolence sent after the death of his brother:

> *'First of all I must thank you and all others who sent me their kind letters of sympathy in regard to my brother Sam. We all felt it very much at home and it was a great shock to our parents…'*

He went on to say 'I expect you heard I got married a week before I left, a lot of us did the same thing.' Getting married shortly before going off to fight was not unusual. This was probably due to the heightened emotions experienced by many as they set off for war, coupled with thoughts that they might not return, which caused some to seize onto the things they valued most with a sense of urgency. Later on, the Audit Office heard that that George Shipley had died of disease whilst serving at sea.

A. Smith, 4th April 1915, France.

Dear Sir,

I have now been out in France a fortnight. I am getting on quite well in the army. Food is also good and plentiful. Of course, I find the life much rougher from that which I have been used to, but it is a fine experience all the same.

We were at Longmoor camp for a week where we were equipped and put through elementary drills. We slept in a big hut there and had a sack of straw and three blankets each. The huts… were called Apple Pie and they are about a mile from the camp, so we had to be up about six every morning in order to march down for parade at the camp. The parade was at 7.15am. Some mornings we had an hour's drill before breakfast. It was about 11pm I should think, when we arrived at Longmoor on 31st March, and consequently we went straight to our hut. No light was provided so we had to fish about for our beds in the dark. Fortunately it was moonlight, and after some time a lantern was brought. We were only too glad when getting up time came the next morning. It was before six. We were marched down to the camp and were inspected by the Sergeant Major and after waiting some time went into breakfast. Roast sausage was the chief item on the menu but to our amazement no knives and forks were supplied for us…Well, the only thing was to convey the sausages to our mouths with fingers.

The nearest thing to a knife and fork that some had was a pair of nail scissors so these were used. Personally I did not know whether to feel shocked or to laugh at the situation; it ended in the latter. We Audit fellows got to one table and we had to have a good laugh before we could eat much. It was a hopeless situation to be in. Don't let this discourage anyone from coming but I warn him to bring a knife and fork with him. After the first day we were issued with kits and we treasure our knives and forks now. We came across on the mail boat *Hantonia* from Southampton to Havre… We had to sleep in huts there on the docks but the sleeping accommodation was better. We Audit fellows were able to keep together till last Saturday night, when Pond and I were sent off to different railheads. He is at 3rd Corps Railhead. We had to travel in horseboxes and during night time. We travelled in this manner Saturday, Sunday and Monday nights. French shunting is severe and we were shaken up. Saturday and Sunday we were about 30 in the trucks, Monday 17.

We were fortunate enough to get out at every town at which we stopped during the day. On Tuesday night another young fellow and I were stranded at a station somewhere in France, and we were instructed by the military authorities to sleep in the goods shed. We had to sleep on the deck of the shed and shunting was going on during the night. This was about the limit, I thought.

I arrived finally at my destination about midday last Wednesday. Now I live in a truck at a small French station…I deal chiefly with gifts and comforts sent to the troops…We are out in the country. I think this railhead is about seven miles from the firing line. Can hear the guns and see the star shells at night. I must ask you kindly to excuse me for writing in pencil because I have no pen and ink here. Would you mind letting this letter be treated as to the whole of the statistical department, please sir.

With kindest regards to all. Arthur Smith

A. Smith, 3rd June 1915, France.

Dear Sir,

Many thanks for your reply to my letter. I was very pleased to get it. This life certainly has the effect of making us do things for ourselves, which, as you say, is very good, although I believe we shall all appreciate the time, when it comes, of being relieved of some of these domestic duties. One thing I am sure of, we shall all greatly appreciate the comforts of civil life. We seemed to take them as a matter of course, but we realise now their value. Don't let these foregoing remarks lead you to suppose that I am unhappy or discontented; on the contrary. They are statements of fact. I like my work very well and am getting quite used to this place. The country is looking very pretty round about and the weather has been fine for some two or three weeks, although the temperature has been very changeable.

I am still living in a railway truck and have got a Corporal and another Sapper with me. We get on quite alright together. Our food continues to be good and plentiful and we are quite as comfortable as circumstances will permit. This seems one of the best railheads by all accounts. I have heard from Ferdinand recently and he informs me that Brackenbury and Gray have left Havre docks and are working at the depot in the city.

All the representatives of the Audit are separated now. Some of us had hoped to keep together. I see from the newspapers that Zeppelins have dropped bombs on London at last. By all accounts they don't seem to have done very much damage considering 90 bombs were dropped, or said to have been dropped.

The recruiting spirit seems to be very high again. Have any more gone from the office?... I am sorry it is not more interesting, but thought you might like to know that I am still safe and sound.

With warmest regards. Yours obediently, A. Smith

R.F. Hull, 1st June 1915, France.

Dear Sir,

Just a line to let you know I am at present in France and have tasted a bit of warfare. We have been in the trenches for three days, fatigue work (burying dead and helping engineers dig trenches) for eight days and are now resting a few days before going back to the trenches.

My first experience of the trenches was not very pleasant as the first day we were under heavy artillery fire all day. The second a bit quieter but the snipers were busy at night. As regards the snipers they get right behind our trenches and wait until dark and fire on men in the trenches...

R.F. Hull

E.H.C. Stewart, 11th January 1915, Hayward's Heath, England.

Dear Sir,

I have thought that you might be interested if you knew how I am getting on.

I have been here for nearly eight weeks, and am billeted in empty houses; we are used to it by now, but at first it seemed very hard after the comforts of home. We have to turn out of bed (so called) at 6.30am, shake our blankets and clean rifles by 8am, then comes breakfast; we generally parade at 9am and march about five miles, after five minutes' rest we start sham fighting or practising the attack, the worst part of this is what we call 'belly flopping', that is, we advance about 25 yards, and then lie down to take cover, and now that the ground is absolutely soaked, and you have to lie in half an inch of water at times, you can guess what we think of it, by the time we get back to billets we are quite ready for our dinner, 'skilly' *[thin soup]* seems to be the favourite menu here; in the afternoon we usually do rifle drill, or for a change we go firing on the range; now and again in the evening we have night work; it is quite exciting sometimes. 200 men from the battalion have been detailed to join the Expeditionary Force overseas; they leave here next Saturday. We go to Crowborough this week to undergo a course in musketry: if we pass this test, we have to hold ourselves in readiness for anything.

I should like to be remembered to all in the Agreements: I wish you the compliments of the season.

Yours faithfully, E.H.C. Stewart

E.W. Jackson, 19th June 1915, France.

Dear Taylor,

Many thanks for letter dated 14th. So there are as many as 102 from the office serving somewhere; that is a good record. I suppose what little chance of promotion we had will have gone west through our being away so long, if ever we get back... No doubt you are right about the Zeps mistaking the sea for the Thames; still it helps recruiting if they come regularly and it does not affect the military situation. Am glad to hear you are having a somewhat easier time at office than you have had the last 20 years...

I have no news beyond what you see in the papers; we have moved about 20 miles north of where we were, and are in the country now. I sleep in the wagon now and not in a billet, but that is no hardship this time of year. We still get plenty of food; our men have not missed a meal since they landed on 2nd November, which speaks well for the organisation.

The general opinion is that we can push them (the Boshes) back when we want to and the word is given, but apparently the time is not yet. Perhaps Kitchener means to crumple the Germans up when he is ready like he did the Devonshires at Omdurman. Was sorry to hear about poor little Phillips. *[Censored]*...The Kensingtons have caught it badly.

The Belgian beer, it may interest you to know, is not quite as bad as the French... I am pleased to say I am very well, the outdoor life agrees with me; all our men are getting fat, as I am... *[Censored]*... Well, I fear my letters are very dull, but my routine is the same each day, so don't gather much information. Am rated as Warrant Officer now, and wear crown, and no stripes, but no more money, as yet. I remain

Yours sincerely,

E.W. Jackson

E.W. Jackson, 29th June 1015, France.

Dear Taylor,

Just a line to let you know I am still alive and well, and to thank you for news of my S.B. *[possibly stocks and bonds]* book contained in your interesting letter of 22nd. Much obliged for congrats re: Warrant Rank, it is quite an empty honour, except for 6d a day extra pay. Also we wear the crown without any stripes and are entitled to be addressed as Sir. No I have not met Pond yet, our railhead is about 20 miles from his, so am not likely to unless he comes out. Am very sorry to hear Hayward has lost his son. The old man was always quite decent...yes, Gilson wrote me he was 1st Corps am surprised Cole is Regimental Quarter Master. I could see nothing in him. Still in these new Scotch mobs I expect they are at their wit's end for officers and Non-Commissioned Officers, and as they had to recruit that and the 6th Seaforths in London, they are not much cop.

Of course anybody who is not too old (like myself) can have a temporary commission nowadays in Kitchener's army, so that is no very great honour. I see Miss Salmon, 30 Bishops Road, has married an Officer, in yesterday's Times. *[censored]*

It is pleasing to see our office chaps doing well on service, but they always do at everything, don't they, once they get away from the office?

... We have been quiet here lately. Most of the Germans seem to have gone to the other side to give the Russians a smack. We expect them back shortly, and are prepared for a romp with them (blast them). How are the Moores? Tell S. Moore I could do with an evening at the Palace theatre very well, just now.

Please remember me to... Hunt and kindly thank him for message re: financial matters...

With kindest regards...
E.W. Jackson
PS I suppose you are having a bit on the new loan. It has knocked the stock market to blazes, I see. Fancy GW stock below par!

R. Gilson, 12th May 1915, France.

My dear Mother,

Have just come through a particularly nasty period. We went into the trenches on Wednesday night and on Sunday morning at 5am our Artillery commenced bombarding the German trenches and after 20 minutes had elapsed we went over the parapet. My goodness what a reception the Huns had in store for us, they simply swept the ground with machine gun fire and shrapnel. Poor old 'C' coy. caught it hot and Neuve Chapelle seemed to be a fleabite compared with this. It was found impossible to make any advance in our quarter, so I dug myself in and awaited events. It was horrible suspense, as I seemed to be the only man untouched, all around me, and being personally acquainted with each man made matters worse, in fact, it's all wrong to call them men, as they were mostly mere boys.

About early afternoon I was hailed from the trench as to whether it was possible for me to get back. I replied in the affirmative and decided to run the risk of getting potted on the way. So I commenced crawling on my stomach until about a few yards from the parapet, then made a spring and rushed headlong over the top, nearly spoiling the features of a few who happened to be in the trench and were not expecting me. We were relieved that afternoon, but some of the fellows did not get in until nightfall and these experienced another bombardment... Billy Hastings is quite fit and the only pal left. We have been resting since and getting information about the *[illegible]* but by all reports we shall be up again soon. No rest for the wicked it is said, and if true we must surely be a bad lot.

What a terrible thing about the Lusitania, and with so many Americans aboard. Should imagine there will be more trouble. Have received box and letter dated 6th and am most thankful for everything you are all doing for me. *[censored.]*

As regards the pads, *[masks of cotton pads which served as gas masks]*, all we were served out with were made 'on the spot' and consisted of a piece of gauze and tape and were steeped in a solution of bicarbonate of soda, prior to this charge. I lost all my belongings except the Gillette *[razor]* so should be glad of a few toilet requisites when next you are sending a parcel. Do not trouble about towel and perhaps Frank would get me a shaving brush. Must now close. Much love to all.

From your affectionate. son, Dick

G. Williams, 10th May 1915, France.

Dear Mr Hunt,

Thanks very much for magazine, which arrived from England, all OK. You'll of course see that the 6th Seaforths have at last broken their neutrality. Yes, we've been in this foreign clime over a week now. We came straight from Bedford to a certain English port, where we went right away on to the transport and then to the field of operations.

We have not been in the firing line yet, but are acting as reserves. We are billeted in barns, quite within the sound of the guns. May be called up any minute.

Last time I came to see you, you asked me how I went on for cigarettes. Well I was all right then, but now I could certainly do with a few. There is not an English cigarette to be had for love nor money, and the French ones are, well, French. Hope you will excuse my cheek in asking, but we haven't been paid a brass farthing since we came here. Will write again, when there is anything interesting to tell...

Kind regards to all...

R.C.S. Frost, 22nd May 1915, France.

Dear Mr Hunt,

... I am much nearer the front now, and we moved here last Tuesday. It was a long march and of course done at night, and our present billet is a farm (or the remains of one) in a large village about ¾ mile from the trenches, more north than we were before, and nearer the Belgian frontier.

It is an awfully desolate spot and constantly under shell fire. This morning I was trying to get a sleep on the grass, when a shell burst in a tree, not fifty yards away, and sent a shower of leaves to the ground. Fortunately no one was hit, another burst in the same field ten minutes afterwards, then I thought it was time to shift! So went into a barn. There are a number of dugouts around, but they are so cold, and you might get buried inside. The farm is a vile place, with a lot of stagnant water around, and a lot of German soldiers are buried here. The barn where we sleep would be improved if a shell struck the roof, and ventilated it, in our absence! As the smell inside is bad, and makes it nearly necessary to wear a respirator! The rats seem to object to our company as they often have a free fight on top of us.

Last night was my first experience in the trenches, and we returned to billet this morning. The din is simply awful, and just lately the big guns have been giving the enemy 'beans' every night. I am glad to say we had no casualties, although the rifle fire was heard at times, especially on our left, where the Germans made an attack on the Indian troops. The British gun fire was simply terrific, all night, and the Germans did not reply very much. It was fine to watch the flashes of our guns at our backs, although the screaming of the shells overhead is at first rather 'scaring' to say the least of it!

However the news we hear from day to day at this part of the front is very cheerful and encouraging. Yesterday I came across an Indian soldier who could speak English very well, and he thought another month would see the war over, also a German officer captured near here said it could not go on very much longer. I for one hope these remarks will prove correct!

The church here is practically demolished, just some of the walls and tower standing, and the churchyard is in a bad state. Great holes have been made and bones exposed. In these holes is water sufficiently deep to drown anybody. Great stone vaults have been opened, and coffins and bodies can be seen.

Of course the place here is not inhabited except by soldiers. I have been through some of the big houses, and plenty of good carved furniture, pictures, fittings etc. still remain in them. I also have been in some of the gardens, and roses just coming into bloom can be seen in great numbers. I should like to see them at home!

Sincerely yours,

S. Frost

M.P. Pond, 12th June 1915, France.

M. P. POND, clerk,
Audit Office, Paddington.

M.P. Pond, taken from the GWR magazine. Copyright, reproduced with kind permission of Steam, The Museum of the Great Western Railway.

Dear Mr Hunt,

I was very pleased indeed to receive your letter. I have been moving about a good deal, and it was sent on to me from one place to another and only reached me two days ago. Well, I am pleased to say I am feeling very fit, and am quite used to the new life and enjoying the change. We had a rather rough journey coming across, but I stood it alright although it upset a good many of the others. We travelled from Southampton. After spending about a fortnight at the base along with Ferdie and the rest of the Audit boys, I was sent up to one of the railheads… The railheads are the nearest points the railway can run to the firing line and the supplies are then taken on by motor lorries to the trenches. Of course, some of the railheads are only about two miles from the trenches. The one I was at first was only a quite short distance away, and strangely enough Mr Jackson was in the division to which I was attached but I never had an opportunity of meeting him…

The work consists of checking out the goods for the troops from the supply train onto A.S.C*. motor lorries and also in despatching all the kits of dead and wounded officers and men to the base, where they are being sent to England. We also have to deal with the newspapers for the troops and get all the daily national papers one day late.

At the first railhead I was at, we could hear the guns going day and night. The flashes from them and the star shells could be seen for miles around… There are also plenty of aeroplanes flying about and we very often watch them being shelled… We have been living in large railway wagons which we fit up with cupboards and tables etc. and make ourselves fairly comfortable. At present I have to do all my own cooking. They feed us very well indeed. The only thing that troubles us is the French system of shunting. I shall never forget the journey from the base to the railhead. It took us three days to come up, travelling only at night. They brought us up in wagons; there were 32 of us in one wagon. In the morning we were standing drinking tea out of our cans, when without the slightest warning we were shot from one end of the wagon to the other, tea and all. On another occasion I was shot clean out of bed in the middle of the night…

At the last railhead I was at, we had a taste of the German gas. Of course we were some distance away from the fighting, but it affected nearly everyone's eyes on the railhead. It made them smart and water for a very long time…

I am kept very busy here, but am out in the open nearly all day… I do not get very much time to myself. Many thanks for your offer of the cigarettes. As you say, I am not a great smoker, and as we get about 50 with our rations every week I have more than I know what to do with. Thanks all the same. Please remember me to all the section…

M.P. Pond

H. Beaumont, May 1915, Rawalpindi, India.

Dear Bertie,

Just a few lines to let you know how I am getting on. Am having the time of my life out here.

… I have been exceedingly fortunate in seeing so much of India in a short time. I shall never forget my trip through the Khyber Pass which has since been the scene of hard fighting, one consequence of which we were hurriedly moved from Fyzabad to Rawalpindi in readiness to reinforce.

You would scarcely credit the feeling of disappointment that exists among the few British regular regiments left in India, over not being ordered to France to take their share in the war. The same feeling also exists in the Territorials… A dragoon left a few weeks ago to replace heavy casualties among the Norfolk regiment at the Gulf.

As the hot weather commenced the latter part of April, and as many British troops as possible are always sent to the hills (being almost unbearable on the plains), we are fortunate enough to go, and had a three days' march and climb to this place 8,000 feet up. Well I never in any wild stretch of imagination ever dreamed that I should be soldiering in the Himalayan mountains.

Kuldana, although 8,000 feet up is on the lower Himalaya, and from my bungalow, which is situated on the edge of a steep precipice, I can see lovely views which words fail to describe, a perfect mixture of Devonshire, Scotch and Alpine scenery. Although seemingly only a few miles off, the higher snow clad ranges in full view are from 100 to 150 miles away. I have about 1½ miles trek to our Sergeant's mess, through beautiful scenery, lovely wild rose bushes climbing up giant pink trees, smothering them in roses, maiden hair fern and all kinds of pretty flowers in the woods. The climate is perfect, lovely English summer weather, with delightful mountain breezes. The heat in India has not distressed me in the least, not even on long arduous marches. I am feeling splendidly fit and well, and trust I shall continue so. We have no end of gaiety; all the married families of the Yorkshire regiment are living in our barracks under our charge, (as their regiments had to remain behind at 'Pindi, and are being bitten to death almost with mosquitoes.) So we have Cinderella dances about three times a week, whist drives, racquet and tennis parties and have most enjoyable times.

I wish May and Eileen could take an aeroplane trip of a few hours and get to me, it would be ripping for them. I should be glad to hear that you had called to see them on your promised visit of months ago when I was home, they would be awfully glad to see you both. Do drop them a card old boy. Fancy it is 10 months ago today since I left to go to camp, what a lot has transpired since then. I was in the 8th Middlesex 12 months ago, and I see they have lost heavily in France, funny I should have left them, and joined the 6th East Surrey and to pass them at Gibraltar... on my way to India.

On the whole I am enjoying life in India immensely; I am acting Company Sergeant Major now, and expect to be promoted to the rank shortly. We are all 'Tommies' now. Trusting you are both fit and well. Remember me to Stacey.

Yours sincerely, H. Beaumont

G. Williams, 22nd May 1915, France.

Dear Mr Hunt,

Very many thanks to yourself and the other gentlemen for the cigarettes, which reached me before the letter you sent me. By Jove they were a treat. Am pleased to hear that the enemy in your midst is at last receiving attention. It is certainly not before time.

Went into the trenches Wednesday evening and came out for a rest last night. Am pleased to say I was not a wee bit nervous when I went in. In fact, I was sorry we were only in the first line of support trenches, and not in the fire trenches; but I suppose our turn at popping the devils off will come.

About all we had to do was make ourselves comfortable and dig in for protection against shell fire. We had a hell of a shelling yesterday afternoon, but nothing to what the Germans are getting. Our guns are at them all the time. I reckon our artillery is vastly superior to theirs, here at [censored] anyway.

Well that's about all the news so will shut up, kind regards to everybody.

Yours very sincerely, Gilbert Williams

A. Smith, 2nd July 1915, France.

[Extracts]

… I was sorry to hear of Chamberlain's death. A parcel for him actually came through our hands at the railhead some time ago. Am glad Mr Pond has written to the office. I suppose his account of our travelling amused many. He and I travelled together for three days while on our way to different railheads… I am in a truck all alone now. I do not prepare any of my own meals now I am alone but get cooked food from the labour party. If anyone takes his ration of meat and bacon down to them they will cook it for him. It takes too much time to prepare one's own meals when alone. I am quite as happy as circumstances permit. This is a very pretty place. At the back of the truck there are cornfields which are delightful at present and make the scenery very pretty in daytime. At night I can lie in bed… and watch star shells go up at the firing line. When it is very dark we can see the flashes from the guns. Needless to say we hear them quite plain. The vibration makes this old truck rattle sometimes. This is quite an interesting railhead and I think the nearest to the firing line. Some shells were dropped not far from here the other night. With warmest regards to enquiring friends…

Arthur

J.G. Symons, 30th June 1915, Belhus Park Camp, England.

J.G. Symons, date and place unknown.

Dear Bert,

I enclose photo as promised; would have sent it earlier, but only received them today. You will see by it how they like to get at the innocents, anyway it's all in the fun of camp life during spare time. The order for Shoreham was cancelled all of a sudden, but at midday today it was all bustle, for we have just received orders to be prepared to move to Colchester at a minutes' notice. I have been on the sick list since last Saturday and will be so for a few days more. We had a long march last

Friday round Upminster and Romford, and when we returned to camp in the evening I had a blister about the size of half a crown under my right heel. I went to hospital Saturday morning and they cut it clean off, result left raw skin and Johnny can't put his heel to the ground. I do the rounds of the camp with one boot and one shoe on, and everywhere I go the sergeants whistle the old line 'army duff.'

Well I shall not be sorry to leave here, but honestly I would sooner take my chance across the water than move to another station in England. I am fairly fed up with soldiering on this side of the water.

Did you see in the paper a Fulham youngster, 19, has got the V.C.? [Symons is referring to Corporal Edward Dwyer, who was awarded the Victoria Cross.] Well Bert one to Fulham and I shall try and make it two if ever I can get a chance.

Give my kind regards to all and accept same yourself…
Jack Symons

G. Shipley, 6th August 1915, at sea on route to the Dardanelles, Turkey.

Dear Nic,

First of all I must thank you and… the others who sent me their kind letters of sympathy in regard to my brother Sam. We all felt it very much at home and it was a great shock to our parents naturally, but it can't be helped, as he was killed in a good cause.

I suppose you have heard how we left Bedford early on Sunday 18/7/15 and had a lovely trip down the old firm to Keyham, we were well laden and I was glad to get aboard and get to my berth in which I am very comfortable with two other Warrant Officers. The men and Sergeants are on the troop deck and none too comfortable but are jogging along alright now.

The first part of the voyage the sea was very quiet, we passed Gibraltar in a fog at night, so couldn't see it. We then skirted the coast of Algeria and had a pleasant run to Malta where we stopped a full day.

The higher officials went ashore for a few hours (including myself) and had a good time. I cannot mention troops or ships so refrain from doing so but there was a hell of a lot.

Our next stop was Alexandria for three days, where we had another look round including a route march for the Battalion. The sea is fairly rough at this end, rather surprising, but a lovely colour, light blue at day and dark at night. All lights out at 8.00, perfect darkness, there is no twilight to speak of, being dark at 7.30pm.

We then wondered where we were off to but eventually reached Port Said, stopped a day, went ashore, and off we go to the Dardanelles which we expect to reach tonight.

Our kits have been left behind in Egypt and all we have got we stand in. We are now passing through the Aegean sea, full of rocky islands, very much like the highlands of Scotland. Bullen has just lost his helmet over the side, but is otherwise well…

I am in the best of health at present and hope to go through alright. I expect you heard I got married a week before I left, a lot of us did the same thing, it was quite a common occurrence.

Our old boat is a captured German liner and is full up but we have got a Greek crew with a few Portuguese thrown in and so are a mixed lot, especially with Welsh men aboard. How are things going at the office, I have been away nearly a year… I shall be glad to hear from you now and again just to keep in touch… I must close now as they say a mail is being collected before we land…

Yours sincerely, George

A. Smith, 8th July 1915, France.

Dear Charlie,

… I expect you have heard a great deal about me from one source and another so I will not bore you with past experiences. This is an excellent railhead. I can lie in bed (no ordinary one) at night and see the star shells going up. I get on well with my work and like it. It is mostly clerical... I have a man to assist me during the day and at night I have the truck on my own. Very nice too. The country is looking extremely pretty now. I go for a walk sometimes and it is very enjoyable.

The other week I had to go to see our representatives at a place about four or five miles down the line. While there, I saw an ambulance train loaded –it is an awful spectacle– the wounded were mostly Indians. The Red Cross trains are fitted up beautifully. However, after viewing this sight I had a nice walk back along the river back to here.

I am able to attend church on Sunday mornings before work begins. I go to the English church when possible but the French is most convenient as regards distance and time so it is generally there.

Kindest regards to... all in the office. Arthur Smith

E.F. Henderson, 28th September 1915, Base Camp, Boulogne, France.

Dear Mr Welsh,

Just a few lines to let you know I am getting on alright in France... We have a very nice camp (canvas) and are pretty comfortable. We are right on top of the cliffs and have a fine view of the sea, and the cliffs of England on a clear day... There is a fine beach where we have some good swimming from. There are a nice lot of fellows around us and we have some good times. The French towns are very poor compared with the English towns. One soon picks up enough of the language here to understand and be understood...

Have you seen anything of the air raids? Expect you were all shook up a bit. I have been wondering if, when the war is over, the GWR will do anything to expedite the discharge of their servants from the army. Because I should like to settle down again as soon as possible. After all is said and done there is no place like home.

Give my kind regards to all at the office. Have you had many new changes in the way of working the accounts? I expect I shall find a difference when I return. The French railways are very poor, the best coaches I have seen do not come up to our suburban rolling stock. And as for the engines, well least said the better. Well I think this is all for now...

Kindest regards, E.F. Henderson

M.P. Pond, 29th September 1915, France.

Dear Mr Hunt,

This is to let you know that I am still going on alright and feeling very fit... I am now back again with my old division (the 4th). We have been moved to a very small village... a very quiet place with very few cottages. A lot of Scottish regiments had passed through there the day previous and had made things hum a bit, so when we arrived, all the cafés were out of bounds. It was a very dry job. They opened them to us a few days after though, but we could only get beer something like onion water. I was in that place for just over a week, and was then transferred back to my old division again. They were then stationed in a fairly large place with some very decent shops in it. We were at that place for about six weeks and were very comfortable indeed. Six of us managed to find a decent cottage where an old lady did all our cooking and washing for us. We were very sorry to leave there. About a week ago we moved to where we are now... Only one of the cafés is open, as the other one has all the windows blown out. There are plenty of aeroplanes flying about including taubes, and we often see them bombarded. One was brought down a few days ago, but fell in the German lines... How are things going at Paddington? I have not dropped across any GWR men lately...

There are three of us living in a wagon which we have fitted up as comfortable as possible although the rain comes through the roof in places...

M.P. Pond

E.W. Jackson, 19th September 1915, France.

Dear Taylor,

Many thanks for your letter. My field card was only intended to let you know I had received the magazine, and not as a reproach. Scarcity of news prevails here... The recent speeches seem to lean towards the idea of compulsion, but I don't believe the people would have it. Even if it were law, if a large number of men started passive resistance and refused to go, what would happen? I think we shall have to finish this job on the voluntary system, whatever happens after.

I had a very quiet five days in England and was really not sorry to be back here. I am sorry to hear of your back trouble, you want massage or rubbing, I should say.

So Cronin is married and gone out? I thought his engagement was off. Perhaps this is another lady though. I should have thought Court was too short sighted to have passed the army tests, but perhaps his eyes are better now than when he was in the office.

It is quite a good idea sending all letters from the front round the office, it also gives people another chance of wasting their time, like all seeing the minutes which the late W.A.B. stopped when he came to the throne of the Agreements department...

The regiment has still not been in any attack, save that on August 9th when we were in reserve and the people in front did their work so well that only two of our Companies and the machine gun people were required, as I think I told you before. I had a letter from Martin the other day. He expects to come over here today. Also young Williams and Gilson have written me lately, the last named is at Boulogne permanently...

As you say, winter will be on us soon; we have already issued blankets to the men, which were withdrawn in the spring. We are looking forward to five months in the mud. The regiment has lost 312 men who have obtained commissions, (this is from the 3rd Battalion of course). Not bad; more could have had them if the Commanding Officer had not objected to losing men in this way. So it is quite good for a corps which is not an Officer Training Corps like the Artists' and others. Many of the officers we see about now are not of very distinguished style and appearance so I am pleased to feel sure now our men who have been promoted are quite up to the average and above it.

I trust if all goes well to get home on leave again before Christmas and to find you are flourishing still. Please give my kind regards to Mr J. Wood… and others who are interested in my brilliant career and accept same yourself, from

E.W. Jackson
P.S. I hope you are keeping the work up, if I come back I shall feel less inclined for bobbing than ever! E.W.J.

R.C.S. Frost, 15th September 1915, France.

Dear Standew,

Just a few lines to thank you for the magazines for September. I have found a Caledonian railway clerk among the signallers so you will understand our magazine is also appreciated by him. Our cook also comes from the same railway, and has spent several years in signal boxes, and of course can read Morse code.

My last spell in the trenches was as a signaller and I occupied a dugout with three others. It was a cosy little place, with a small table for the instruments and a chair for the operator, and the room was lined with thin canes, and a blanket hung at the entrance… There was one part of the fire trench which was only 15 yards from the Germans, and it was hardly safe to breathe there! Fresh men were put in this part every 48 hours and they spent their time throwing bombs and hand grenades.

A German mine was exploded when I was in the signal section a short distance behind the trench. It was rather a shock to us all, and the candle was knocked over also a canteen of coffee we were preparing over a small stove. Fortunately the dugout roof consisted of tree trunks, so did not collapse.

At present we are in reserve, and billeted in a fairly large town. Of course the Huns have left their mark on the place, and the church houses and several large engineering works are in ruins. Our headquarters is in a fine chateau which has only a wing of the building damaged. There are well laid out grounds in which are grottos and waterfalls.

The last few times in the trenches we have been instructing men of Kitchener's army, and it makes one feel quite an 'old soldier' when answering questions and telling the tale!... With kind regards to all the old friends in the Audit, and accept the same yourself.

Sincerely yours S. Frost

R.A.W. Dyer, 1st August 1915, France.

Dear Mr Wills,

...I must thank you very much for... your letter of 8th July which I am sorry not to have answered before... It was hard luck not being able to keep birds at the house you relocated to at Hanwell, but I think you have done the best thing by not moving until the war is over, there will be much other opportunities then and you will be able to see better how things stand.

Fancy young Duckett obtaining a commission, he can't be older than 19 years old I'm sure. I know he's younger than me and I've only just left my teens...

You ask me if there is anything I want, well, you know what a big smoker I am and the weekly issue has gone to the wind in one day with me and as I don't get sufficient from home, because they don't want to encourage my heavy smoking, a few cigarettes would be greatly appreciated, that is of course if you can manage it.

...I hear old Walter Goldsack retires next week, lucky chap, I wish I was on the same footing, what say you.

I am getting on very well now with the horses; all the work is with horses here and I am getting quite expert at riding and I like it alright... Now old chap I think I must close...

From yours sincerely Ron

R.A.W. Dyer, 7th August 1915, 'Somewhere in France'.

Dear Mr Wills,

I must thank you for the cigarettes you sent me, I received them with your letter last night, and I was just on bankruptcy as regards fags, so you can consider you have saved my life. So you are going to have a *[pigeon]* kill off to reduce numbers, well, they'll come in handy for the homing pigeon fund, that is if you don't want them for yourselves. Dad has had my place lime-washed out, he says it looks quite smart again. I think there are only four old birds and two youngsters there now.

The bombs from the Zeps shook you up then, they make a nice little row don't they. I have heard them out here and seen them drop, and a piece of one of the bombs hit me and I was quite 500 yards from where it dropped, of course it did not hurt me, as it was spent. Even the noise from those bombs is not a quarter as loud as one I had drop near me last Saturday, it was a trench mortar bomb and although I was quite 50 yards from it the force of the explosion knocked me over. It was a licker to me that I did not stop a piece of it. They send up a flame about 20 to 30 feet high and make a hole in the ground about six feet deep. I saw one of the fellows last week that had specially enlisted for this job and although he is about 15 miles behind the firing line and never hears a gun fired or a shell burst he was grumbling because the sanitary arrangements were not what they ought to be, but perhaps after he has been in France a month or two he will realise that nowhere in France are the sanitary arrangements anything like as good as they are in England. I wish he would change places with me anyhow. He comes from Leeds but I don't know what his name is. He told me E.W. Jackson is up Armentieres way so I shall never get anywhere near him… I must dry up now, and don't think I shall have the chance to write again for a bit, you will see why by the papers in a day or two so.

So-long. Best of luck… Ron

R.A.W. Dyer, undated, 'Somewhere in France'.

Dear Mr Wills,

Thanks so much for your long letter. How did the army apply for the Company men you mention in your letter, was it through the 'fancy papers', fancy Jackson being one of them? I might tell you that it is a good job, if you can get it, as you will be well out of the sound of the guns, in fact about 10 or 12 miles behind the firing line, a private billet and not a lot of work and a good chance of stripes. I can't say yet what the money is but will try and find out. So if you do think of joining, now is your chance. By your letter it seems that practically all the eligible men from the Audit are out here, good luck to 'em. Now I must close, as I have no more paper so au revoir...

Yours very sincerely, Ron

W.A. Hastings, 11th August 1915, France.

Dear Effie, *[F.E.Lewis]*

I owe you an apology; I have to confess that I was home on leave and never got across to see you. Started letter with the best intentions in the world but the time was so mapped for me by other people I had not a minute to myself, did not even go to the office, as you know, and found that at the finish I had seen practically nobody. Had intended getting as far as Abergavenny but found it impossible, in fact it seemed like half an hour instead of six days. Hope you will forgive me, old boy, and I planned to make up for it (when the dust up is over we can settle down to it properly...)

Am at present in the front line of trenches but everything is fairly quiet, although we have had 54 casualties. Hear all sorts of rumours about being relieved for a long spell by Kitchener's army, Lord knows how much truth there is in it, we could do with a Garrison job in England or Scotland for a bit... The chap who gave you the information was not far wrong; think the Germans had a pretty good footing in northern France before the war and the people certainly seem bastard Germans in many instances. I would not trust one of 'em and they are the strangest crowd I have ever been unfortunate enough to strike... Well old boy, best of luck and health to Mrs Lewis and yourself.

Your old pal Billy

W.A. Hastings, 1st October 1915, Northumberland War Hospital, Newcastle, England.

[Hastings scrawled the following note on the side of his card:]

Dear Effie.

Shell fractured base of skull Friday 4th, going as well as can be expected.

Cheerio Yours Billy

E.H. Brackenbury, 6th September 1915, France.

Dear Sir,

I was very pleased to receive your letter of May 6th last, and although this reply is somewhat belated, it is not that I have forgotten about the existence of an Audit office at Paddington… The office at Sotteville has been finished… On the one side there was nothing but a sea of railway lines, several sets of which had been added since the beginning of the war, and there was the constant hissing of the locomotives –and they can hiss very well– on the other side was a very big field which stretched for about 500 yards down to the banks of the Seine, then on the other side of the river was a series of high hills on the top of one of which stands the statue of Joan of Arc.

We used to sleep in the office at night, and for our meals we had to cross all these lines to a railway truck on the other side. Our toilet was of the simplest. A bucket of water drawn from an engine had to suffice for the day. Altogether our life at [censored] was not uninteresting.

However the traffic there began to diminish, and after a time it became necessary to close the office entirely, with the result that we were transferred to Havre, where we are at present… Have no more news now, so with kindest regards to everybody.

Yours respectfully

E.H. Brackenbury

R. James, August 10th 1915, France.

Dear Burgie,

Thanks awfully for your letter, glad to hear that you are all serene and that the GWR is still flourishing without me, as a matter of fact I expect its better without me but still there you are.

By Jove! I had no idea that the Audit had shoved so many fellows into khaki, its fine. Well the old Brigade has had some pretty varied experiences in this land of stinks and bad beer.

We landed at Havre last March and after a freezing night under canvas on the heights behind the town we had a rather weird train journey up country. There were about 10 of us per cattle truck with a few wisps of straw to sleep on. Our horses were boxed six in a truck, three with their heads facing the 'engine' and three facing the rear of the train. Two men sat on corn sacks between their bottoms. If they kept the shutters closed they had a beautiful journey as it was so warm with the horses…

At about 2am the old caboodle pulled up and we thought we were in for a dreary hang about, however the order came down to bring out the dixies… and fall in for something hot. I took our one up and the liquid smelt so good that with a little judicious wangling we managed to get another one full. When we tasted it, it was simply gorgeous. Boiling hot coffee and rum as only Frenchmen can make it, you know how. Gee but it did go down a treat…

After about three weeks in this show we shunted up and got our baptism. It's a funny sensation being under fire for the first time but it soon wears off. One gets a rather nasty jolt when the first casualty occurs especially as it was in our case the finest fellow we had on the staff. He got a chunk of shell in the back of his neck and was killed on the spot.

We were in action at this place for about two months and took part in several bombardments, one of them being the one in which poor old Joey was killed. We had some pretty rough times but were very fortunate as regards casualties. Two months' action and 2½ days' rest, it doesn't seem much but that's what we got, and then at it again in a different part.

This show had been occupied by the Germs and then by the French from whom we took over. The filth and stench was too awful for words, one of our batteries striking rather unlucky in coming across Germs buried just under the surface when they started digging their guns in. The air was blue for miles…

The next action we had was a hell of a show. The staff were put into a huge Chateau which was under observation and fire from three sides. And they didn't half sling the lead about too. It's marvellous that we didn't get lifted skywards heaps of times, but still here we are. After a good spell in this show we came to rest again about 10 days or so ago.

We are having a good time here in the way of concerts, sports, boxing tournaments etc. The latter was great especially the bout between a Farrier Sergeant and a cook's mate. They biffed at one another until neither could stand, it was awfully funny.

Little Seedy Ellis has got a snip job at a base. He came up today with a draught of men. He is having the time of his life and looks it by the dark circles under his eyes…

I am feeling wonderfully fit and well and would not have missed coming out for quids. I suppose you saw in the paper that two of our boys have got the Distinguished Conduct Medal. They were in Major Lord Gorell's Battery; he is awfully bucked about it.

Well old man I must dry up. I hope you can read this disgusting scrawl, but will make that whiskered excuse 'active service conditions'. Please remember me to all the boys and tell Long Liz that I would give anything for a barrel or two of the club bitter.

Sincerely, Dick James

THREE

NOVEMBER 1915

'There are millions and millions of flies here
and they are all over everything.'
HAROLD WILLIAM CRONIN

In this month's edition of the Audit newsletter we hear from the recently married H.W. Cronin about the difficulties of fighting on the Dardanelles peninsular in terms of climate and terrain. In addition, E.W. Cowles wrote from St Patrick's hospital, Malta where he was transferred after contracting dysentery during his five week stint in the trenches of the peninsular. There were also two contrasting letters about hospital treatment, one from Billy Hastings at Northumberland War Hospital, Newcastle and the other from Second-Lieutenant Charlie Mayo, a wounded prisoner in hospital in Belgium. Mayo's father had lent the letter which had been typed out for circulation in the office. In this rather poignant letter his son wrote:

> *'I didn't get a very long run for my money, did I? It is rotten being out of the show, not that I wanted the war to last long, far from it, but while it was on I liked to have a finger in the pie, but it is no good grumbling and the best thing to do is to hope it will soon be over so that I can soon be home with you both again.'*

There were further descriptions of trench life in France and Belgium covering such evergreen themes as mud, worms and lice, to requests for cigarettes and, in the words of Gilbert Williams a longing for

> *'an extra-large Black and White* [Scotch whisky]. *We are getting little drips of rum here now and again…enough to drown a fly.'*

Comradeship was vital to them as ever and essential for morale. Arthur Smith, based at a railhead in France, was delighted to bump into a fellow GWR man because

> *'it was nice to meet someone who had something common with you in civil life, upon which we could talk.'*

Since the issue of this newsletter, a total of one hundred and sixteen had joined the forces. The latest recruits were good friends Mark Russell from the Audit Agreements department and Nick Boyce from the Passengers department to the Royal Engineers (Railway Troop) whose letters feature in subsequent editions. Russell had been the Honourable Secretary to the Roll of Honour Association and had carried out vital work for it.

F.E. Lewis, known as 'Effie' had joined the 2nd Middlesex Hussars and F.T. Turner the 18th County of London (London Irish) Regiment. Private F.G. Woodhams had been promoted to Lance-Corporal and Sergeant Maggs to Sergeant Major.

E.J. Cowles, 29th September 1915, Malta.

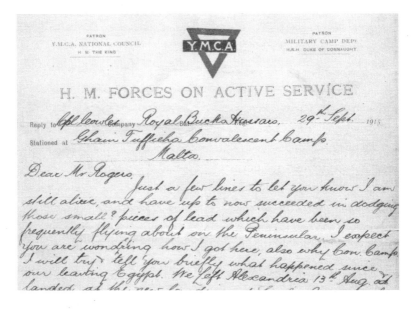

Dear Mr Rogers,

Just a few lines to let you know I am still alive and have up to now
succeeded in dodging those small pieces of lead which have been so
frequently flying about the Peninsular *[Dardanelles]*. I expect you are
wondering how I got here, also why Con. *[convalescent]* Camp. I will
try and tell you briefly what happened since our leaving Egypt. We left
Alexandria 13th August and landed at the new landing at Sulva Bay on
the 18th under shell fire. Not a very nice kick off. Our first engagement
was on the 21st when we took part in the big fight for Hill 70 and 971.
I expect you read about it in the papers, for I see the Daily Sketch had
a page full of it. They spoke of us as the *Irresistable Yeomanry*; very
glowing words of our charge also. It was a very stiff go and we were
fighting from 3pm the 21st until dark on the 22nd and never stopped
advancing and retiring the whole time. We had the Hill on the night
of the 21st but could not hold it, because no support was sent up, so
the Yeomanry (those of us who were left) had to retire at night after
charging and capturing three lines of Turkish trenches. Our Brigade
(Berkshire, Buckinghamshire and Dorset Yeomanry) was ordered to do
the charging for the Division and I think we did fairly well from what the
General said in his report. Of course we suffered pretty heavy. After five
days on the Peninsular we did not have an Officer left in our regiment,
and only barely half the men. I have seen a few of our Officers in the
casualty list, but no men. I was very pleased to get the *GRW Magazine*
while resting in dugouts on Chocolate Hill. I hope no more of the Audit
boys have fallen since the last I saw. I suppose you are still pretty slack
in the office. I find I've run away from the tale, but here in the Y.M.C.A.
tent it is so crowded and the piano on the go, it is rather difficult to write.
After resting from the big fight three days we went into the trenches for
spells of five days, on one case seven days. After five weeks I caught
dysentery and had to come away. I was put on a hospital ship and
brought to St. Patrick's Hospital, Malta. During those five weeks I was
pretty lucky. The only close bullet was one through my right sleeve and
grazing my arm. We all have some very narrow shaves from shrapnel. I

had the sandbags of my dugout knocked down one day, but fortunately I was down to get water. Probably, if I had been inside I would have caught it properly. I expect to be here about a fortnight to three weeks before I go back. I am hoping the boys will be across before that, and the Turkish army cut in two.

I suppose the office still looks more empty than it ever did. How is Mr Jackson getting on in France? I see his regiment has been in action. I have often wondered how he would get on in trench warfare. I suppose McConnel is still going strong. Will not stop for more now as I shall lose the mail…Hope you are still enjoying the best of health and still dodging the bombs…

E.J. Cowles.

W.A. Hastings, 4th October 1915, Northumberland War Hospital, Newcastle.

Dear Effie,

You were doubtless surprised to get a postcard from up here, don't know why they sent us such a long way north, it is alright but I think London would have suited me better, could have seen my pals sometimes. I am not allowed to get out of bed yet, tried the other night and fell down in a fit serves me right for disobeying orders. I have the piece of shell which fractured my skull and shall look after it for a souvenir. The doctors say I was very lucky not to have been put right out. It was a heavy piece (British) would not have been wounded by anything less. We were in an advanced post sticking beyond our front line called the 'Duck's Bill' and naturally pretty close to the German trenches. In fact they surrounded us… *[Lines censored]*

I hear from Bedford that the company has been told to prepare for the Dardanelles. I don't know where he is though, have heard nothing from him. We are having a concert with our ward this afternoon and we have plenty of visitors in every afternoon, some very fair women taking them generally, and very decent too, treat everybody alike. Remember me kindly to Mrs Lewis. I shall make a more determined attempt to see you if I get a sick leave which is most probable. Well, have no more news at present. How about taking up a post in your department when this lot is over, it would suit me to have headquarters in London for a time, mustn't count chickens though. Goodbye Old boy,

Regards,
Billy

A. Smith, 6th October 1915, France.

Dear Mr Kirk,

Many thanks for your interesting letter of Sept. 30th which I was very glad to receive. *[Lines censored]*

I have heard of the Zeppelin raids on London from various sources. It no doubt scared Londoners. I have not received the Great Western magazine for October yet so I was surprised to hear of Mr Goldsack's retirement and Mr Crossley's death.

When your letter came, Stewart of the Statistical department was stationed here and I showed your letter to him so that he might get as much office news as I. I saw him going on to the platform one day and ran after him and had a few words with him. He was just going down the line by train for one night and then was returning to here. Next day he turned up and then remained here for about four days and we had a jolly time together. It was so nice to meet someone who had something common with you in civil life, upon which we could talk. He had met in his travels Messrs Maggs and Woodhams. The former is a Sgt. Major (I believe he said) and the latter a Lt. Corporal.

Since my last letter to you I have been promoted. I am now a Corporal. The promotion dates from August 4th. I have two South Eastern and Chatham Railway clerks here with me at present and we get on very well together.

We have been having damp weather lately and there is plenty of mud about. I have nothing more to say this time so I must conclude. I am hoping to get some leave shortly. I shall try and see you when I come, with best wishes and kindest regards.

I am, yours very sincerely,
Arthur.

P.S. Do you hear anything from Pond?

G. Williams, 7th October 1915.

Dear Mr Hunt,

Thanks for the cigarettes and magazine, all very much appreciated and I want to confess something. I am terribly short of cigarettes just now. Don't know how to get on.

… Lord, how I wish I could get up to London. Some of our chaps have leave but this advance seems to have put a stop to it. That's the only reason I am sorry for the long awaited advance. God knows it was really time we did do something if only to relieve the pressure on Eastern front. We are in this part of the line and are still sitting tight worse luck. I wish they would get a move on here as well. It has cost us a good many casualties, but I think the Germans, what with the bombardment they got and the counter attacks they delivered must have lost many more than us.

I have got an interesting souvenir. It is part of the framework of a German aeroplane, the fourth which our airmen have recently brought down in this neighbourhood. The machine gun in one of our planes had killed the German pilot and the machine getting out of control exploded, or at least the engine did, and the whole aircraft crashed to earth. God, it was an awful mess. Both the pilot and observer were killed, the former being bashed out recognition, but the latter survived the fall but died shortly afterwards. Our airmen seem to be the masters of the Germans now, although the taubes seem to be the faster machines, our men seem to have much spirit and initiative.

About a fortnight ago I saw a fleet of fourteen of our planes cross over our lines on a raiding expedition. They were in close formation, and the Germans sent up a rain of shells without doing any damage. The raid was very successful, I believe, two transport trains full of German reinforcements being wrecked, a large station destroyed.

Well that's about all from me, let me hear from you soon...Best regards to all the section,

Yours very sincerely,
Gilbert Williams

H.W. Martin, 3rd November 1915, Marseilles, France

Dear Bertie,

I thought perhaps you would like a line to let you know that I am still in the land of the living. I have been all over France since I have been here on a train escort taking supplies to the troops at the front. This is a nice city *[Marseilles]*, with kind regards to Sidney Hodges, Mr Levett,

Harry

M.P. Pond, 9th October 1915, France.

Dear Dada,

Many thanks for the Slough paper and magazines. Was very sorry to see that Jefferies and How have lost their lives. I heard from Arthur this morning and he tells me that Fred Blane has died of wounds in the Dardanelles. I expect you remember him in the 'Windsor Operatic Society'. *[Line censored]*...

Harold White (Ginger) who lived with Arthur has joined the Royal Artillery Garrison and is now at Plymouth. Arthur has sold the motorbike. Petrol is too expensive he says. Since I wrote last I have been moved to a little village about 2½ miles out of the town I was in then. It is a dead and alive hole with only a few houses and two cafes, only one of which is open. The other has had all the windows blown out.

We expect to move further on still in a day or two. We have changed our truck for a much larger one and have made ourselves very comfortable. It is about 30 feet long, so we have divided it off (with our ground sheets for curtains) at one end to make a bedroom, and the rest of the truck we have fitted up with desks and cupboards. I spent the other evening making a table out of bacon boxes etc. At present we are living very well indeed, with bacon and kidneys for breakfast, steaks and vegetables for dinner, jam and honey etc. for tea and bread and cheese and pickles for supper. Not bad for 'active service'. The Post Office cook still does all our cooking. There are four of us on the staff here now. One attached to each of the three divisions, and one learning the work who will probably leave soon to take charge of a division. There have been plenty of aeroplanes over here lately. A German came over the other evening and our people shelled it for about half an hour. I don't know whether it was brought down or not. I had a nice long letter from Mr Hunt yesterday. He sent me photo of the 'Roll of Honour' and told me all the latest Audit office news. Well, I don't think I have much more to tell you at present so will conclude with love to all,
Yours, affectionately,
Mont.

H.W. Martin, 14th October 1915, France.

Dear Mr Leeks

I thought that perhaps you would like to receive a line from me to know that I am still in the land of the living. I am keeping well up to now. We are just on the move again I don't know where. I suppose you are still jogging along quietly in the same old groove. One thing we get plenty of variety, it is by no means dull I can tell you. We got plenty of training before going abroad. I was about five month around Aldershot, we had plenty of drill and some firing practice. I am altered altogether. I weigh about twelve stone now. I don't think you would know me hardly. I don't think you thought much of me as I did not come to see you before going away, but I only got four days leave which I spent with the wife at Brighton. I just caught sight of Jackson there, he was on the Black Rock Railway, he has written me often. I suppose you have seen him. Well old chap, I think I have said all for the present. Give my regards to all. Hoping you are all well...

I remain yours truly,

Harry

J.G. Symons, postcard undated, Ypres. This shows the Merghelynck's Museum before the bombardment and after.

J.G. Symons, 19th October 1915, Belgium.

Dear Bert,

Many thanks for your letter received a few days ago, also for the good old Woodbines which I got today. While I think of it in your letter you refer to a report published in the 6th monthly Magazine for August '15, will you send me a copy, as I have not seen it.

Well, we have had about the biggest gruelling we could wish for. The Huns bombarded us in the trenches for over two hours with Jack Johnson* shells, shrapnel, whizz bangs* (terrible things) and trench mortars, blew the parapets to blazes and nearly blew the whole lot of us up. The General Officer Commanding has complimented us on our behaviour. We are now resting at a place called Vlamertinghe, just south of Ypres and a couple miles North of Poperinghe [Poperinge] in Belgium. We deserve a rest for we have spent thirty-nine days in dugouts and the trenches (except three days) and needless to tell you we are very crummy, which tends to spoil the rest we are having. I never thought I was going to another phase of them after South Africa. I was in Poperinghe (where I met Jackson a few weeks ago)…

The beauty of it out here is we can stand a pal a drink, and also have one with him. I suppose shall have to wait for my increase, being an absentee from the office, anyway they can add it on to my salary as soon as they like for I shall then be able to pay more income tax. I enclose a few postcards. They are showing in each card before and after, or during and after the bombardment of Ypres, so you can guess what the place looks like. Well Bert in conclusion I must tell you that one of our Sergeants who is on leave, posted this in London for me, that's why I am able to give you a few details. Kind regards to all friends in the Audit,

Your sincere friend,
Jack Symons.

H. Giles, 17th May 1915, Churn Camp, Oxford, England.

Dear Mr Jones

Just a line to let you know that I'm still alive and am moving to King's Lynn on Wednesday next. Will write you later. How do you like the photo? Best regards to the office. From,

H. Giles

C.D. Mayo, 22nd October 1915, Courtrai, Belgium.

[This was typed and circulated with the newsletter]

Dear Father,

I do hope you and mother have not been worrying much about me as I am getting on all right. My wound is well now and the broken bone is my only trouble– the two ends took the wrong turning first time so a couple of days ago they put them on the right road again. I ought not to be left with a short leg as there is about 40lb weight on the end of it, in fact I should not be surprised if it finishes off ahead of the other. One good thing is I get very little pain except when I am moved.

Did you get my postcard? I haven't had an answer yet but expect letters take a long while. I believe I asked you to send me some fruit but as things take such a long while to get here I am afraid it would be bad, besides they take French money here, and as I drew £5 from the Field Cashier only a few days before I was wounded I am quite well off and the orderly will buy fruit for me in the town.

I expect you are surprised to get a letter when I said on the post card that I should only be allowed to write once from this hospital, but a fresh order has come out and one letter a month is allowed.

Well, I have written quite enough about myself I think. I am longing to get a letter from you and mother, it seems ages since I heard from you. Have you taken a house in Uxbridge yet or are you waiting until Auntie and Uncle move there. I do hope you are getting a little more used to the

90

lonely house. Please remember me to everybody and give my love to all relations next time you write and tell them I should like to hear from them if they would write although I shan't be able to answer their letters. Have you heard how Frank is getting on, I meant to write him but put it off too long.

I expect my kit has been sent home, hasn't it? I am afraid your field glasses are lost as I left my equipment in the wood when I was hit. I am awfully sorry if they are but perhaps one of the men picked them up. I arrived here with only one boot and only one puttee, so will you send me a pair of puttees and a tie out of my kit. I shall be supplied with boots when I leave here, which won't be for a while I expect. One thing I shall be very glad to get will be some books.

We are very well treated here, and the Belgian sisters from the convent are very good and often bring us grapes or apples.

I didn't get a very long run for my money, did I? It is rotten being out of the show, not that I wanted the war to last long, far from it, but while it was on I liked to have a finger in the pie, but it is no good grumbling and the best thing to do is to hope it will soon be over so that I can soon be home with you both again. Please give my kind regards to Kate. Very best, love to you both. Cheer up and don't worry about me.

Your loving son, (2nd Lieutenant Mayo) Charlie.

P.S. I hope you can read this, it is awkward writing lying down.

M.P. Pond, 26th October 1915, France.

Dear Mr Hunt,

Very many thanks for your most interesting letter and the photo of the 'Roll of Honour' which I was very pleased to receive. The latter looks to be a fine piece of work. Please excuse my not writing before, but since receiving your letter we have all moved forward again and have consequently been busy getting settled at our new railhead.

Fortunately, when the whole railhead staff move together we usually take our own wagons with us, so have been spared the trouble of fitting up a new home. We have now lived in the same wagon for about five or six weeks and have made ourselves pretty comfortable. The place we are stationed in now is only quite a small village and very quiet. The chief trouble here is getting water. There is only one well near us, so we have to take it in turns to get a pail full. The weather is fairly good on the whole, but rather cold in the mornings. There is not much going on here at present except the usual visit of hostile aeroplanes. We were watching some being bombarded yesterday. I am pleased to say that I am still feeling very fit and well and am engaged on the same old job, so have no very special news for you. Glad to hear that [censored words]… have been promoted to chief mouse catcher. Also glad to hear that Frosty and the rest of the Agreements boys are alright. So, Shipley and Cronin have got married and gone to the Dardanelles. Well, good luck to them. Things seem to be pretty warm there by what I can hear. Did you know that Arthur Watton has also become engaged just recently? I have not heard from any of the Audit boys I left at the base, so your news of Brackenbury and Gray was quite fresh to me. Have you heard from Cautley at all? Very many thanks for your offer of cigarettes or chocolate. I am sure it is very kind of you and some chocolates or anything of that sort would be very acceptable. Well, I am afraid that I have no other news for you at present. I have applied for leave and hope to get it very soon now. Kindest regards to all.

Yours sincerely, M.P. Pond.

J.G. Symons, 29th October 1915, Belgium.

Dear Bert,

I received your letter of the 22nd instant and many thanks for same. Referring to George Kemball's menu, well, all I can say is, he is very lucky and I should like to drop across his kitchen…

We get plenty of food where we are, but not such variety and the extras I have, apart from army rations, are sent out to me regularly every week by the wife. And when I receive the parcel your humble has his 'at home' day. We are still out of the trenches and at present have no idea of when we return. We had well over a month the last time, so they are giving us a well-earned rest. Unfortunately the weather is very bad and we are up to our knees in mud. We had a route march yesterday and returned to our hut smothered to the top of our putties, boots and socks wet through and no earthly chance of drying them. Personally, I have 'struck oil' for the morning I was inoculated and have been given forty eight hours rest, and intend to do that in the hut with a waterproof sheet underneath and blanket and great coat over me, and that will give the other things a chance to get dry. I enclose a sketch of the last dugout I was living in and it's not exaggerated, absolutely true as the other Audit chaps will be able to verify when we all return home. It is nothing unusual by the light of a candle to see a worm here and there wriggle out of a hole at the side, other insects too numerous to mention by their Latin name also keep us company, but the very ones we detest above all others we have to take with us, you know the ones I mean [lice]. Well I must now conclude. Give my kind regards to all in the Audit.

Yours very sincerely, Jack Symons

G. Williams, 29th October 1915, France.

Dear Mr Hunt

Thanks very much for the cigarettes. They soon went I can assure you. Out here on this game, cigarettes seem to melt away. I am now in the Maxim gun team... Am having a much better time now, than when I was with the Company. The Machine Gun Section in the different battalions relieves each other in the trenches during daylight while the rest of the battalion must wait for darkness. Also we have less sentry duty to do...

We get most of the excitement if there is any knocking about. We are now in the trenches, and as it has been raining for the last two or three days you can guess things are in a hell of a mess.

It is also devilish cold here just now, and the mud and stuff clinging to one's boots makes one's feet ready to drop off. I can now understand why frostbite was so rampant among the troops last winter. Hope I don't get a dose of it.

I am afraid I am not up to giving you the Scottish tongue in writing, but you wait till I get leave in the dim and shadowy future, I'll talk it to you. Also, as I am mentioning things Scotch, I tell you I am just about longing for an extra-large *Black and White [Scotch whisky]*. We are getting little drips of rum here now and again. Just about enough to drown a fly.

Please send me some more cigarettes. Have not any left now. Best regards to yourself, the section and the rest of the folk.

Yours sincerely, Gilbert Williams

P.S. Excuse dirty paper. Not much left.

R.C.S. Frost, 3rd November 1915, France.

Dear Mr Hunt,

I was very pleased to hear again from you especially as it is a long time since I have heard from the office… as I often wondered how different friends were getting on there.

I have not received a copy of the Roll of Honour or report, and should like to have them very much. Please thank Standew for sending on the magazines, the November issue I received last night, also a note enclosed by him… He tells me you wrote on the 7th September but I am sorry to say I did not receive your letter.

I met George Kemball about two months ago in a village, shortly after we came to this part of the front but have not seen him since as we are billeted in different villages when out of the trenches. *[Lines censored]*

I am glad to be able to say I have been keeping well since I last wrote, and we are still garrisoning trenches for periods of ten days, and ten days rest.

Several months ago, when we relieved the French of these trenches it was noticed how quiet the 'atmosphere' was, and it seemed quite in keeping with the beautiful hilly scenery. Since the British occupation however, things here have livened up considerably, and it has been found necessary to greatly strengthen the trenches, and make dugouts much deeper and safer, because of the various kinds of souvenirs sent over from the enemy.

Their latest was the aerial mine, of which no doubt you have read. It is exactly like an oil drum to look at, with wood ends, and explodes with a terrific report. I don't think it can be fired from a gun, as it comes tumbling across in such an awkward manner.

I don't think we manufacture these articles at Woolwich as we can afford decent shells! We are not troubled very much by German artillery, but they make up for that with trench mortars and rifle grenades.

As a signaller I escape some of the hardships of trench life, especially now the winter has arrived, and much prefer duties which keep one under shelter to those of exposure at the parapet! Of course we have exciting times, when any wires are cut by trench mortars etc. and which need to be repaired at once wherever the break is.

Just lately I am having a lot of experience at making and fitting fireplaces in dugouts. We generally use biscuit tins to hold the fire and rummage among old houses in the village nearby for pieces of piping to take the smoke out, usually through the entrance as it is impossible to cut a hole through the roof on account of the sheet of iron. Fuel for burning is generally a problem but a small supply of coke is allowed and we add to it all kinds of wood etc. When sitting up at night it is surprising what good time we keep when waking up the next fellow to carry on, if there is no fire, but if a good fire is on, we get quite generous, and don't mind allowing the next man an extra hour or so to sleep!

We have had several days of rain this week, which doesn't tend to improve life in the trenches, or out. On our journey to billets last

95

Saturday night, we took a road through a wood constructed by the Royal Engineers. It wasn't quite finished, and in places was ankle deep in water, so our march was more of a paddle. Parts of this wood, which is in a valley had been purposely flooded, so the road had to be laid on faggots and will be a piece of work when finished.

We are fortunate in having dry billets, with beds raised above the floor and a small fire. Sheep skin coats have been issued to us, and are very warm. There is a fellow here now imitating a monkey and holding out a small cup to an audience seated on the beds, while another chap is playing an accordion! All we need now are top boots* to paddle through the trenches! There is plenty of water about but very little to drink or wash in. It is a fine place for people who are good at finding excuses for not washing! But there are very good hot water baths here, only it isn't any good having a bath unless one really needs it, on account of the colour of the water!!

We do very well though, for food and clothing both of which are good, and well supplied, and considering the many distant places it is sent from, it speaks well of the splendid way our Navy is doing 'its bit'.

Well I will close this epistle now, and hope it will reach you safely and that your welcome letters will find me also.

With kind regards to Standew and all the 'gallant trio' who are keeping the section going, Messers Taylor, Woodhams and yourself,

Sincerely yours, 'Frosty'

H.W. Cronin, 3rd October 1915, France.

Dear Mr Welsh,

We were only out here a matter of a few hours before we went into the trenches; we were there for eight days and then came on to what is called a Rest Camp. I suppose it is called that to distinguish it from the trenches because the men are at work all day road and trench making and it comes under both rifle and artillery fire. We got here at 7 o'clock yesterday morning and were shelled at 9 o'clock.

In the trenches it was fairly bad, they are so narrow and smelly and one is being potted at and shelled all the time. A turn of eight days was really quite long enough because it is strenuous work and even when you do turn in for a rest you have to be ready to turn out at once on an alarm.

The country is really quite pretty and just like the hills and valleys of South Wales, but there are no brooks or rivers. It rains hard for a month each year usually about this time and then there is no more until the next rainy season. But although it is so gloriously sunny something is wrong with the place and it really isn't as healthy as it looks. I think the flies have something to do with it as well as the heat and the still unburied dead bodies about. There are millions and millions of flies here and they are all over everything. Put a cup of tea down without a cover and it is immediately covered with dead ones, they are all round your mouth and directly you open it to speak or to eat in they pop. It is a game. We have all got nets of course, we should have been worried, no medicine by now if we hadn't.

We get plenty of bully beef and army biscuits, but bread and fresh meat is still a luxury and it is not possible to buy anything. It must have been a 'No Man's Land' because there are no houses or buildings of any kind to be seen and except the flies, the only living things are green canaries and lizards.

We live in dugouts built up the reverse sides of the hills. They are just holes really, but all the same they can be made very comfortable with a bit of digging and a few waterproof sheets. They are not shell proof by any means and the one I slept in during my first night here was knocked in completely by a shell pitching right into it. Fortunately I was not at home at the time. We have another now and I must try and get a photo of it and let you see what it is like. I must send you one of our Mess dugout* too.

Everything here is named after the Regiment responsible for the making or taking. For instance the road we made from our trenches to this camp is called 'New Bedford Rd' and the ridge we took and now occupy is called on the army maps, Bedford Ridge. I have just been filling in and colouring my map and find it is one of the most, if not the most, advanced line of the lot. Standing on that ridge it is possible to see what a lot of country we have taken and now hold, but there is nothing to get wildly excited about. Each position is strengthened as much as possible before another attempt is made to push on and the whole thing is just steady progress. Something might happen suddenly, I only hope it does.

We have had some very big ships out here and they have been bombarding the forts heavily now for some few days, and there are cruisers, monitors etc. standing in the bay helping the land batteries to shell the trenches. You see a flash and then wait a long time before hearing the boom and the shriek of the shell passing over our heads, almost together, then look round quickly and see the burst of the shell in or over the trenches sometimes before hearing the explosion. The first we know of shells aimed at us is the bang of the explosion, and it is too late to get out of the way. Three officers were laid flat on their backs the other day without any hurt except to their dignity and farther on six men were buried without one being injured. It isn't always like that though.

There is quite good bathing here when we can find time to go. As the beach is in full view of the enemy, and comes under their shell fire, it would not appeal to the nervous. We never keep closer together than ten yards when we are undressing and swimming in hopes that the Turk will not consider one man worth the price of a shell. We have had some casualties through the men keeping too close together, but after washing out of a teacup for a week or more it is worth a bit of risk to get rid of some of the trench dust and smell and feel and look clean again. And really is the best bathing I've ever had. The water is warm and clear.

All the hospital work is done on board a ship that stands in the bay. If the cases are serious or lengthy they are transferred to one of the hospital ships that calls daily and then go to either one of the bases or back to England...

H. W. Cronin, Lieutenant.

FOUR

JANUARY 1916

'We do not indulge in such luxuries as a band, but have to contend with the enemy's music, which on two evenings of last week was distinctly heard from across the other side of no man's land.'

RICHARD CHARLES STANLEY FROST

Frost's letter is one of the many collected together as part of this edition of the Audit newsletter. This was by far the largest volume of letters collated by the office, largely because it covers the second Christmas the authors had spent at war. Season's greetings were exchanged and printed Christmas cards, which had been designed specifically for soldiers to send back from the trenches, were posted to Paddington.

The parcels which the office sent to the soldiers had started to arrive. Buoyed by their receipt and the sentiments associated with the time of year, more soldiers than usual made contact. The office deduced that morale had been boosted by the receipt of goods from home:

We have received numerous letters and Season's Greetings from those in Khaki, and they also acknowledge the Cards and Parcels forwarded by those who still remain with "the pen", the kindly thoughts extended to our colleagues on His Majesty's Service during the festive season appears to have been much appreciated.

In contrast to most of the soldiers in this chapter, Jack Symons' morale seemed to deteriorate. He was subjected to shell fire, incessant rain and mud, which, by his account, did not let up. By early December, he was transferred from France to a military hospital in Taplow, England with 'trench feet' and:

A representative visited him there and he appears very comfortable, the latest news reports him progressing favourably but slowly and that it will be another month before he will be out of bed...'

Although he did not write to the office during this period, news of Charlie Mayo had reached his colleagues from his parents who seemed to have passed his letters to the office. According to the newsletter:

'Lieut. Mayo has recovered sufficiently to be discharged from the German Hospital in Belgium, although only to be able to get about by the aid of crutches. Unfortunately, being a prisoner of war, he has been taken to Germany, where, no doubt, he will be well looked after;'

News of the death of George Shipley, who had written to the office in Chapter Two with news of his marriage does not seem to have reached soldiers abroad, but it was announced here:

We deeply regret to record the death of our respected Colleague, George W.Shipley, who died early in December through the effects of Dysentery. George was a well-known sportsman and had seen Service in the Territorials prior to the War, for which he held the Long Service Medal; he also served in the South African Campaign with the St.John's Ambulance at Delfontein. He was at the time of his death, Company Sergeant Major in the 2/10th Middlesex Regiment.

Archibald Kirk had now joined up and by November was training at Longmoor. We learn from his letter that he was given a couple of days off to prepare,

'My wife tells me everything is in order with the office and I should also like to say that we were both personally grateful to you for the time allowed to me from the office the day or two before I left home.'

Leonard Sharpe wrote from France with a sense of wonder as he described parts of France as suitable for a holiday which most likely he would not have seen had it not been for the war. He also conveyed a strong sensibility that he was an active participant in historical events:

'...since I came out our Battalion have taken part in the battles of Aubers Ridge, Indian Village, Festubert, Givenchy and Loos. In fact there's been none of importance at which we have not taken part in...'

In November Nick Boyce wrote about two photographs which arguably encapsulate this entire collection of letters and can be seen on the cover of this book:

> 'Many thanks for the photographs received. We all think they are good and on Saturday the six of us had out photo taken here in a similar position – in khaki. The two pictures together should make a lasting memento.'

They show six Audit office staff, A.E. Kirk, N. Boyce, S.B. Hodges, E. Bright, D.J. Robertson and M.A. Russell, before they joined (in office attire standing on a railway platform), and after they joined (in khaki standing in front of some stables). The photo was posted from Longmoor camp so probably taken there.

J.G. Symons, 3rd November 1915, France.

Dear Sir,

Just a few lines I promised you on my postcard a short time ago. Since our arrival in this country it has been one long stretch of work. We are either in the trenches, dugouts or in reserve. While in the trenches we are fighting men, but when we go to the dugouts reserve we are more like Royal Engineers, doing all kinds of odd jobs, carrying trench boards, sandbags, building parapets, cleaning out ditches and a hundred other things, far different from sitting down at my cosy desk at the office: We have had some very stiff fighting with the Huns while in the trenches and it makes me wonder he's alive now. Our last do with them was as bad as anyone could wish for. The Germans got what is commonly called out here, the 'wind up' and they simply rained fire on us, and above our trenches was like a sheet of flame from the explosions of the shells, great shells smashing in the parapets, whizz bangs which give you no warning and trench mortars. The latter being terrible, but fortunately they give you time to run right or left as you can see them coming. The weather here at the present time is awful, raining day and night and the result is we are rarely dry. Our last official turn of the trenches was 38 days.

We expect to move up any minute now and the prospects are not very rosy, but we are being served out with gum boots, which reach up to the knees, and fur coats, so we shall have to make ourselves as comfortable as we can under the circumstances. I must now conclude, give my kind regards to all...

J.G. Symons

W.C. Davis, 3rd November 1915, France.

Dear Ernie,

Today being the first day that I have had an hour to myself I thought I would use the time in writing a few letters, for at the moment it is raining cats and dogs, and I have just popped into a little room in this town that the Wesleyan *[Methodist]* chaplain has taken for the use of the 'Tommies'. I have been back from the trenches for about two weeks now and am on duty at the hospital where part of our unit has been all along. It is about three miles behind the line so you see we can get up very quick when wanted but of late things on our front have been quiet except for bombardment which seems to be never ending on either side. I have a sound job just now for every morning I take out the men who are fit for duty, and return them to their units wherever they may be and you can guess what sort of a job that is when yesterday out of 21 men there were 13 different units. Luck of course plays a great part in the game for sometimes I really cannot find out where they are for they shift about so...

In the hospital itself we find plenty to do in ordinary times but when an attack is on 'plenty much' at those times half of us are rushed up the line which of course throws more on those left behind... I think that is about all I dare tell you for now or Mr Censor will be on my back, for he is very stern in our district.

We are not overworked just now, being near the winter months, have never yet run across anyone that I know but may do one day... I think that is about all this time. Trusting you are well.

Yours, Will

G.W. Hibley, 8th November 1915, Gallipoli, Turkey.

[This correspondent's signature is indiscernible and research has not enabled us to identify him, however his name appears to be 'Hibley'.]

Dear Nic (Boyce),

Thanks very much for your interesting letter… I wondered when I would hear from someone at the office. Also many thanks for your good wishes and congratulations on my marriage which I have conveyed to my wife. I am sure she will thank you all very much.

Well to tell you a little about our experiences, we started off mysteriously one Sunday from Devonport on the captured German liner *Derflinger*, not a bad boat. The Warrant Officers had 2nd class quarters it was all right. Food was very fair. Submarine pickets* every night for one of the four companies, lights out… at seven or half past. Stole by Gibraltar at night in a fog expecting it to be torpedoed. We did reach Malta in due course after skirting north African coast, spent a day there, went ashore, had a few drinks which we needed being very hot and then on to Alexandria for three days, ashore every night, not a bad place, of course the lower men didn't go, except for a route march on the Saturday. Our movements were kept very secret and we couldn't find out what was to be done with our division, we then pushed to Port Said and had a day there. All of a sudden, we received orders to sail and soon found we were off to Gallipoli as we were passing through the Aegean sea, which is as you know full of pretty islands. Some hours before reaching Lemnos, the naval guns could be heard booming and we ran into the magnificent harbour there full of shipping and life. After a day there, we pushed on to Imbros 4½ miles from Sulva Bay during the afternoon they treated us to a naval shelling of Achi Baba, which is really the other side of the peninsula, but they shoot over the hills and mountains here. It was a fine sight and many of our chaps went sick at once. At night (Sunday 9/8/15) our good ship made for Anafarta Bay where a new landing had been effected two days before. 900 rounds, four days' rations each, as much as a man is expected to carry and they dumped us over the side in lighters *[a type of flat-bottomed barge]* at 7am, a short journey through the boom defences and we were ashore waiting for something to turn up.

Bivouacked on the beach and were put on unloading lighters till about 10 when the Turks spotted us and started shelling, two men killed and four wounded to start with and we lost a few more, wounded during the day although naturally we took what cover we could. I had one or two near me whilst getting a timber out of the hold of a lighter but managed to dodge them all right. At night my company received orders to take picks and shovels up into the firing line which was about five miles away half way up Chocolate Hill... Well Nic the 10th were soon in the thick of it as we advanced across the salt lake in extended order.

Rifle fire now we had to dodge and many of our chaps got hit rather seriously I have since found out. I was glad of a rest at the foot of the hill but had to push on again and deliver the goods, after feeling about in the dark for some time our guide led us in single file up behind the firing line, where we laid down, bullets were whistling round but we managed to escape them... The enemy were yelling for all they were worth and I was glad when our captain ordered us down again to the beach. This took us some hours and when we reached the place, the other three had gone up to reinforce the firing line, so up we went again the next day about 6pm, nearly all things are done here in the dark as we are in view all the time. We again advanced across the take from Lala Baba, my heels were nearly raw through new boots and I eventually had to rest for a fortnight later on. Well on our right was a hill burning furiously with many a chap caught in the flames and so perishing (not our regiment).

We finished on rather a feathered bed and did not find the other Company 'til next day, it was a night, we were all parched with the heat, and no water. Dried up and had to dig ourselves in, it's no light job this hiding being... like an ostrich, 'til you make a hole large enough to get into and make yourself head cover.

We found our other three Companies had copped out; two captains killed and many men killed and wounded, so we were rather lucky in going back to the beach the first night. The enemy snipers were very busy for the next week, and our firing line was changed very frequently to link up with other troops on our flanks. The Turks weren't very good shots and they would have hit more than they did, several of our men were bombed over and after a week of bullets, flies and thirst and heat another regiment relieved us and we were sent down to rest viz. purifying water and unloading stores from lighters for 12 hours a day in four hour night shifts. On this job the men got properly worn out and being always under shell and shrapnel fire about a dozen or twenty a day, they went to pieces and after three weeks we were sent to some rest trenches where we dug roads and trenches all night. What a game, spent bullets through one's clothes and helmets. After a short time here we were sent up again and found the fire trenches all properly made and fitted out it was a pleasure to be in them. We have had various experiences since then but I will leave it to another letter as time is short with me. I have lived in all sorts of dugouts and shall be glad to get under a roof again I can tell you. The wind is bitterly cold lately and our dugouts now are situated at the top of a hill like Beachy Head... Please remember me to all friends at the office... Hoping to see you before long. I remain

Yours sincerely
G.W. Hibley

N. Boyce, 9th November 1915, Longmoor Camp, England.

Dear Lack,

Many thanks for the photographs received. We all think they are good and on Saturday the six of us had out photo taken here in a similar position – in khaki. The two pictures together should make a lasting memento.

We have had little spare time since we have been training here. Having been through company drill mixed with route marches, physical drill, semaphore, knot tying and frog, long jumping etc. Some of our men were able to go to town on Saturday... but I myself with a few others have been under orders for overseas service now waiting to proceed, so popping up town seems out of the question for us. We are numbered in alphabetical order, and in the order we are sent out. We are now fully equipped. I enclose ... postage for the photographs. If you are printing any more you might save me one as I am afraid I have spoilt mine, it got bent in my overcoat pocket on Saturday. Please remember me to all at the office....

N. Boyce

E.W. Jackson, 8th November 1915, France.

Dear Taylor,

Thanks for letter of 28th giving latest office news, also for magazine, both of which I found most interesting. I fear again I can give nothing in the least interesting in return as we have not moved and except for the usual daily exchange of shells there is nothing to record. You see unless we either attack or are attacked ('go over the top' as they say), a day is regarded as a quiet one. All our news, we get from the previous day's papers, which have not been very encouraging of late, thanks to those two bastards, the kings of Bulgaria and Greece. Still on this Front we are sure we can hold the Germans. Perhaps our plan is still to starve them out, though one does not know if the paper reports of high prices of food in Germany are true or not. Prices seem pretty high in England also. It is quite good so many of our people at the office having enlisted, however if half the number had been in the Territorial Force ready warned when war began, I think it would have been more useful. From what I have heard if we had had say 60,000 more men here this time last year, we could have pushed the enemy almost out of Belgium and France... I expect the 110 'patriotic' ones have committed suicide from an official point of view and if they ever get back to Paddington will take the back seats, any job worth having being filled up in their absence. Also the problem of the female clerks is bound to be serious.

... The difference in *[GWR]* Stocks and Bonds interest won't affect me much, as you know; I think the increase was to stop too much being transferred to war loans etc? Yes, your remarks about being on half your income are very much to the point, the idea is about as sensible as the 'no treaty' order... Well it being 4.30 and tea time, and also because my ideas are run dry, I will stop writing and with kindest regards to you and all old friends.

I remain...

E.W. Jackson

W.J.E. Martin, 10th November 1915, France.

Dear Mr Davies,

At last I am writing you a few lines, to let you know I have not got shot yet, and am in the best of health. I will start at the beginning and give you a record of my experiences, as far as I am able. To kick off we marched some forty odd miles from one billet to another till we finally reached Vermelles. We were in reserve to some other division who made the first attack on Loos and Hill 70. I can't give dates as I have forgotten them. We waited till dark and then made our way to the old firing line, staying there about seven hours. In the early morning we advanced to some captured German trenches. I may mention that the whole field and trenches were strewn with dead, both British and German. The trench I occupied had a dead German laying in it and every time we passed up or down the tunnel we had to jump on the poor devil. He had about 50 wounds, and was a leg deficient. I collared a button off his overcoat as a souvenir and have sent it home.

We stayed in the trench till 3 o'clock in the afternoon, and then advanced to take up a position on the left of Hill 70. The enemy's artillery seemed to get wind that we were coming up for they shelled us mighty heavily: causing us to have a few casualties. We had to cross the open ground for about 100 yards, but I got across there safely, and occupied an advanced trench. We stayed there till they ceased shelling, and then formed up on the open ground again for a charge. Suddenly we got the order 'charge', and off we went. The Germans opened fire with machine guns and rapid rifle fire when they spotted us, and we got the order 'lay down'. Then the devils got the range and dropped shells right amongst us, so we were obliged to retire about 50 yards, and lay behind a parapet of a communication trench. The time was about 7pm and we stayed there till 1am not daring to move an inch. The bullets were humming all round me and I could hear several drops in the ground within a few inches, expecting to stop one every second. To make it happy it poured with rain all night and we were up to our necks in mud. Anyway we got the ground we wanted and dug ourselves in with our entrenching tools in case of a counter attack which we were expecting every minute.

The Germans gave us a warm time of it in the trench. They shelled us every day and night. This field again was crowded with dead and wounded. Two wounded crawled into my part of the trench, one a Northumberland fusilier, who was wounded at 11 o'clock Sunday morning: it was 3.30 Wednesday afternoon when we rescued him. He was a very brave little chap. The other was a Scots Guardsman; he had a fractured thigh. We were relieved on Wednesday evening at dusk and went into a reserve trench, staying there for a day and a night. Early Friday morning we went into billets for two days. You ought to have seen us coming down the road, up to our necks in white mud, rifles rusting, and some of the boys walking along asleep. One chap on my platoon lost his rifle on the march, so that will tell you how some of us were. Never shall I forget that march. The battalion was reorganised and the casualty list made out. We lost about 300 killed wounded and missing. After a couple of day's rest, we were for the trenches again, and set off at 10.30 Sunday morning.

For two days we remained in reserve trenches and then went forward to the firing line. Our company occupied a trench of which half was ours, and half the Germans. They were actually in the same trench, only a barricade dividing us. Our platoon was nearest to the barricade. They did not interfere with us while we occupied it, beyond sending over a few shells. We stayed there two days. The snipers were very active though and got four of my mates in the head, one died instantly, the other died a day or two later. Two of them were with me at Caterham. At dusk on the second day we were relieved by No.2 Company. The following afternoon they shelled us awful. They were preparing for an attack. The devils attacked No.2 with hand grenades and bombs, and very nearly got the trench. Our artillery opened fire on them, and through my periscope I could see whole bodies and limbs blown 30 yards in the air. It was awful, and we were practically helpless. The Coldstream Guards came to our assistance however and we soon had our trench back again. We lost a lot of men here including several sergeants and our machine gun officer. He was a splendid officer too, and well liked. The following night we were relieved and went into some ruined houses in Vermelles. While here I helped carry the gas up to the trenches from which the big gas attack was made a short time ago, but I wasn't in the attack. A day or so after this we went into billets again and stayed there for nearly a week. It was Thursday afternoon when we were for it again. This time we occupied the third support line, going down the communication trench which led to this trench. The Germans shelled us very heavily, and it was just like a furnace. The trench I and four of my mates occupied contained four dead and four wounded. These poor chaps caught it an hour before we relieved them. It was a near thing for us, wasn't it? The wounded were taken away by their own stretcher bearers and we buried the dead, before it got too light.

The following day a shell burst on our company headquarters, burying six, including two officers: they were rescued and taken to hospital. We only had one officer left now, so Major Montgomery, our second in command, took charge of our company. A few days after this we had to dig a communication trench to the firing line. Already our other companies had lost several men in digging this trench, owning to German snipers. Our company lost about 20. Our Major went to the assistance of one of our chaps, and he caught one right in the left eye, dying instantly. We were all very sorry to lose him, he was the finest officer we have, and well liked too…

This completes my experience up to now. Roll on <u>duration</u> of war, and England, I used to think it pretty bad out here, but I did not know it was like this, and by appearances, I shall spend my 20th birthday and Christmas out in this awful country. I haven't a very high opinion of France, it is a lot different to England…

I have never had to see a doctor since I have been in the army. Yesterday I was asked to take the stripes, but I am not having any; you are better off as a private out here. Please remember me to all enquirers…

With best wishes…
W.J.E. Martin

J.G. Symons, 10th November 1915, France.

Dear Bert,

Just a few lines to let you know I am alright, hoping you are the same… At the present time we are in dugouts. The weather is simply awful, raining day after day and especially night after night…To tell you the truth, while writing this letter I am wet through to the skin and not a dry thing for a change. We have got our winter fur coats and gum boots, but the latter cause more curses than you can imagine, for instance last night I was sent off to select dugouts for our platoon… It was pitch dark, no light allowed and in a strange place, well honestly I fell over at least 20 times got smothered in mud from head to feet and on the top of that wet though for it rained in torrents. On a round of inspection this morning to see if all were 'comfortable' I was 'blended' up hill and down dale, 'Sergeant this' and 'Sergeant that'.

How can you expect men to live in this, and then to put a dampener on the lot, was the language from the occupiers who unfortunately were in a residence that fell in during the night. They took shelter under a tree from 2am after looking for me for half an hour or so, but they could

not find me, for the only thing that would shift me, after settling down…
would be a 'Jack Johnson' and then I would have no option.

While in the trenches last week we were up to our knees in water
and got our gum boots half full. The line is a bit quiet lately and only
now and again do we get a shelling, but one gets used to it. That… is like
sitting at Paddington and hearing the engines screech.

After our stretch this time I shall be looking forward for a short
leave for I have been here nearly three months now and we stand a
good chance. Well I must now conclude…

Yours sincerely
Jack Symons

P.S. Every other home down near the rest camp is an *Estaminet* [small
French café] where they sell what they call 'beer', and as much as I like a
drop of good beer I have given the stuff out here 'best' for is awful muc.

E.H. Brackenbury, 15th November 1915, Le Havre, France.

Dear Mr Biggs,

… I am at present in that branch of the establishment known as the
Records office… The six from the Audit office, Paddington, have
mostly been split up now… I received a parcel from the GWR the
other week containing: 1 Tommy's cooker, 1 tin of sardines, 1 tin of
cocoa and another which I had to divide between an erstwhile relief
signalman at Portishead and myself, 1 waterproof wallet and 1 khaki
handkerchief.

A letter of thanks has since been sent with the signatures of
all the GWR men here appended, each man having received a
similar parcel.

Things are pretty quiet here now, since as everybody knows the
operations on this front have been practically at a standstill for months
now, but I expect that when they do get a move on it will alter the
present state very considerably. Have nothing more to add now. Kindest

regards to everybody especially the Railway Clearing House section, if that now exists.

E.H. Brackenbury.

A. Smith, 15th November 1915, France.

Dear Sir,

I am back again at my old spot 'somewhere in France' and am quite settled down again. I had a very enjoyable leave. We had a very good journey back. The sea was calm and the night bright with moonlight and fair. All lights were out on board and no smoking was allowed so being in the sea just moonlight was rather nice and the scene was beautiful. A destroyer accompanied us across. On arrival at Boulogne we found trains waiting in readiness to convey us up country. After some minutes I found my train and the right portion for my part so I got into a compartment with seven others, fortunately no more joined us so we were not over crowded. No lights were allowed in the trains and being third class no cushions were on the seats so one had to get as comfortable as possible and try and get some sleep because it was now about midnight. I managed to get a little sleep but after four or five hours of travelling like this I had to change. At the junction where I changed we had six hours to wait. It was between 3 or 4am when we got to the junction. After getting some coffee I turned down on one of the waiting room seats and finished my night's sleep. I eventually arrived here at midday on Saturday... I found a good dinner of fried steak and onions being prepared which was not at all unwelcome.

The weather has commenced to be very cold but we have got a stove in our truck now and we have purchased an acetylene lamp. At present we are keeping the cold out pretty well...

We have a dog in with us now. He came round once or twice and appeared to belong to nobody, and one of the sappers took a liking to him so now he treats this as his home. He is said to have been brought down from the German trenches but I cannot say what truth there is in the statement. If true he is a good souvenir. With kindest regards to all.

Yours obediently
A. Smith

G. Williams, 16th November 1915, France.

Dear Mr Hunt,

Please accept yourself and convey to the other gentlemen my best thanks for the State Express cigarettes. They are fine. Oh what a picnic it is in the trenches just now. We have been in the trenches 10 days up to now, and except for the last two days it has been raining almost steadily. The result is mud, mud and yet more mud, knee deep in places. But luckily we have long top boots from trench wear, so that the mud does not worry as much, except that is making our feet as cold as ice... We have been issued with fur jackets so we can keep our bodies warm.

Just now the whole countryside is covered with snow and moving objects are distinguishable a long distance off. For instance this morning when I was on duty with the gun I could see the Germans walking down a road away behind their lines. I had several bursts at them with the gun but they were out of range. Made me damned mad I can tell you seeing the blighters and then not being able to lay them out.

You can't realise the power one seems to possess when handling a Maxim. Personally I feel as if I could lay out the whole German army. We fire about a couple of thousand rounds every night into Fritz's trenches just to keep them quiet. They (the Germans) have been trying to find the gun, both with their Maxims and with shells, but up to now, they've not succeed. Kind regards to everybody.

Yours very sincerely,
Gilbert Williams

F.E. Lewis, 22nd November 1915, Norfolk, England.

My Dear Bertie,

Just a few lines as promised. I suppose since I left, a good many more have joined up owing to the pressure from Lord Derby*. If any are left who are contemplating joining, strongly advise them to go to an infantry regiment. They will find it easier...

So many men have gone from this lot as drafts that the regiment is full of recruits which of course makes things all the harder for everyone concerned. We are quartered two miles from a small place called Aylsham where there is a decent Y.M.C.A. It is very rarely I go there though, haven't the inclination to do much in the evening, and sometimes impossible to get there as this week I am one of a picquet* who are liable to be called at any time during the night fully armed. I find the life very hard. You see Bertie I am over 40 and not particularly robust, in fact I am the sort of man that should have gone to the Army Pay Corps. Just now I am in the cart, both heels raw, rotten cold and nearly sliced the top of a finger off this morning so you can guess how cheerful I am in the rain.

The training we are getting is excellent from a soldiering point of view as we have many Non-Commissioned Officers from the cavalry and a good number of officers. So unless they keep drawing from the regiment it should be pretty good in about three months' time.

Had a thick day on Saturday; we all got wet through in the morning. Came in, changed into slacks and went to stables. I didn't change boots as I wanted a dry pair in reserve. Half way through stables was called on with 400 others to go to north Walsham booking in 80 horses from the Montgomery Yeomanry who are going abroad as Infantry. Well off we marched to the Aylsham station and on the way got quite sodden to the skin and boots half full of water, felt pretty rotten in train on way to north Walsham. Reached there and took over, took about an hour and all the time hail was terrific. Well to end it short we reached camp about 6.00. I occasionally jumped up but it was so cold for my feet and the horse's back was like a razor (bare backed we were). Was glad to struggle along on foot. One kid fainted ¼ mile from camp and I felt pretty dire especially as our promised hot meal consisted of a piece of cold meat left from a stew. We couldn't trot along as so many recruits were with us who could not ride let alone ride bare back… As we had breakfast at 7.30 that morning and nothing again until we got in I wonder at only one boy going down *[fainting]* as it was a cruel day… Still there you are we are on active service and mustn't grumble as we shall get pretty bad times away on the other side… Kind regards to all in the office…

Best of luck from
F.E. Lewis.

S.H. Dunton, 24th November 1915, France.

My Dear Billy (Dawson),

Very pleased to see you old chap (if I could). My word we are moving about since we left Salisbury Plain last Wednesday. Went to Folkestone, on to Boulogne and stayed in a so called 'rest camp' for a day. We arrived there about 4.00am, after a very calm crossing the same night as the *Anglia* struck a mine.

Sleeping under canvas in this weather is about a joke and how I did think of our office outings but it's no bloomin' outing now I can assure you… After a journey of about six hours (the poor men travelling 44 in a cattle truck) we arrived at a place called Theinnes. We marched about 2½ miles and then the fun commenced when another officer and myself were sent off with 20 men to make ourselves understood and get the men billeted in a small barn and ourselves in the two roomed farmhouse.

Not being able to make anyone hear, we took possession of the barn and put our men in and then my pal broke a small window and climbed into the house. We lit a stove of our own and made some *café au lait* and went to bed. We discovered afterwards that the *Madame* who usually lived there was staying with her sister at a café during the war…

I've just heard that we are moving another five miles nearer the firing line tomorrow. We shall then be within 10 miles, but we have heard the booming of the guns since our arrival at the first village. At present I and two pals are billeted at a broken down old *Estaminet* and can get cheap wine any time of night. Anyway we manage to get plenty of fun out of things in general and are all merry and bright. It is certainly a fine experience being out here and one does not seem to mind roughing it a bit when they think of the hardships that our poor chaps had to put up with the whole of last winter.

Well old chap I shall be pleased to hear from any of the boys at the office, but expect by the time I next get a chance to write I shall be well 'into it'. Goodbye for the present. Love to all.

Your sincere pal

Sal

D.J. Robertson, 24th November 1915, Longmoor Camp, England.

Dear Mr Wood,

Just a few lines to tell you we are all in the thick of drills now, and it is very hard; poor Bright and myself having had to jib *[jump to it]* when the order came to double *[brisk marching]* as that was a bit too much for us, but although they may bend us, I do not think they will break us. We were told to put on our oldest things and nearly all of us got our feet wet and then had to sleep on the bare boards all night but I am pleased to say we all came through the ordeal quite well... Trusting you are enjoying good health and with best wishes to you from us all.

D.J. Robertson

R.C.S. Frost, 24th November 1915, France.

Dear Mr Hunt

Many thanks for your welcome letter of the 20th inst. enclosing a photo of the office Roll of Honour. Judging by the splendid reproduction it must be a very fine piece of work.

I also take this opportunity of thanking... kind friends of the Agreements dept. for their good wishes and the cigarettes... I have a faint idea I sent a card on receipt of the cigarettes, but in case I did not I hope you will accept my apologies for omitting to do so before this.

I was interested in the sketch of the office, and it must seem strange to see so many vacant spaces. I... hope myself to have the pleasure of seeing you very soon.

I am glad to say I am keeping well and we are still spending our time taking '10 day excursions' to the trenches, in fact it is getting almost as monotonous as using a season ticket, as we have for months been occupying trenches in the same district.

In trench warfare there is not a great deal of excitement in a signaller's life, except when the communication is broken by wires being cut by shells or bullets, and have to be repaired immediately. The recent rain has played havoc with the trenches we were in last, and a large number of men have been busy daily for weeks, rebuilding parapets, fixing gratings for walking on, and pumping water. All this work going on interfered with the wires, and it was nothing unusual to see men hauling themselves along the trenches in four feet of mud by the aid of telephone wires.

I expect you have tried your hand at electric bell fixing! But perhaps, not under such circumstances as I had to last week. It was decided to fix a bell push in the heads of three saps*, connected to a bell fixed in the fire trench, in place of a wire which when pulled jingled a small sardine tin in a large one!

These saps are really small and narrow trenches running at right angles to the firing line under the barbed wire towards the German trenches, and at the head of each, at night a sentry is placed to give warning and listen.

In place of the above 'antique arrangement', I had to go with our Sergeant and the Brigade Sergeant Signal Officer, and fix the more modern arrangement. Fortunately, it was a thick misty day, and so we were not seen by the enemy, and except for dirty clothes and a scratched nose on the barbed wire we duly returned to headquarters safely. The bell is put inside a petrol tin with the front opened, but I am doubtful if it will stand the weather long.

We have had it cold and wet lately, but we get about the trenches fairly well and keep well too, by the aid of long trench boots, sheepskin coats and anti-frostbite grease for our feet.

However we get some consolation from the fact that the Germans are paddling about the trenches too, according to reports from our patrols. We do not indulge in such luxuries as a band, but have to contend with the enemy's music, which on two evenings of last week was distinctly heard from across the other side of no man's land… Trusting you are well.

Sincerely yours,
Frosty

M.A. Russell, 24th November 1915, Longmoor Camp, England.

My Dear Bertie,

I expect you have given me up not writing to you before, possibly you thought I was journeying east as quickly as possible and would write you from Salonika, not so my dear friend. They, the authorities that be, are hard at work making me, and also my colleagues, 'some soldier'. I have now been a fortnight here on Friday. It seems more like a dream than real life, things move so quickly.

The Friday we joined up was very wet; we have had nothing like it since, I am glad to say. We met… at 11 o'clock and marched to the central recruiting office, a band leading the way, raining in torrents all the time, no umbrellas up... Here we were sworn in and received a day's pay and rations allowance amounting 4 shillings and 11 pence and were told to parade at 3 o'clock at the Horse Guard's Parade.

So Nic Boyce and I had another chance to have a good *au revoir* to dear old London for the last time, as we then thought, prior to proceeding overseas as per the letter of instructions... After seeing the Lord Mayor's show and drinking success to the venture, little knowing that we should do so again on the following Friday... To the parade ground at 3 o'clock was our next move; a warrant was handed to one of our colleagues for the 69 fellows present: our number should have been 72, but three had failed through some cause or other. So with a band playing, off we marched to Waterloo Station to catch the 4 o'clock train.

The journey down was very good until Bentley *[Hampshire]* was reached; here we changed and waited over an hour in a siding before we moved on to Bordon. It rained all the way from Bordon to Longmoor. There runs a military railway, the title which is W.I.M.R. I will leave it to you to solve; send me your answer in your letter. *[The answer is Woolmer Instructional Military Railway.]* This line runs into Longmoor camp.

The camp is pleasantly situated in pine woods and the soil is sandy. It is therefore quite a health resort, and from the change that has been wrought already on my colleagues, I can thoroughly recommend it. We arrived practically wet through, and not one fellow was laid up with cold after it. The camp is lit with electric light. Of course the night we arrived the rain was coming down in torrents and streams of water were running all over the place. Huts stood here in rows and there in rows, all seemed alike and mud: well, enough said.

We marched to the depot office and here we had to sort ourselves out into A–B–C order to be recorded. We stood outside in the rain during this operation. Soldiers do not mind the wet. A supper had been kindly arranged for us by the Quarter Master; possibly you know who he is. Then the blankets were served out, four each, and some fellows marched away to a place called Apple Pie Hut. These are new huts about quarter hour's walk from the depot. I fortunately, together with all the Audit boys and about 20 others, went to the recreation room and tried the floor. We all rolled ourselves in the blankets and laid down, but sleep would not come to me on so strange a bed as the mat round the billiard table.

Next day we drew part of our kit and moved up to Apple Pie Hut, which we put in a comfortable state. Wet day Friday, working Saturday, also dressed in our old togs for the job, Sunday we presented a fine spectacle; we had not received our khaki.

Monday we commenced in earnest, one party went for drill and another for clothes, then, on Tuesday, those who had not received clothes paraded for clothes and the others for drill. Then we paraded at the tailor's shop to see if things fit. Tuesday following we were inoculated, something like five millions of germs are inoculated by means of a hypodermic syringe. Tomorrow we have another dose, this time about ten million. The first dose gives you a slight touch of enteric fever *[typhoid]*. You are supposed to have 48 hours' rest after this: we did by cleaning the hut…

We are now in full working order. Many things have had to be done before this was attained. Sunday last after church parade I spent the day tailoring, sewing all the buttons on again and marking my socks etc.

To give you some idea of what we do, I will give the day's timetable: Up at 6 o'clock, fold blankets, mattress and stow bed board. Blanket, mattress and boards have to be correctly folded and stowed in correct order. Wash and shave. The wash house is an open thing about 20 yards from the hut, and the water cold. Parade at 7.15 for marching, including doubling *[brisk marching]* for anything up to half a mile. Breakfast at 8am. Parade again at 8.45 for inspection; here the buttons have to shine. Then physical drill, semaphore signalling, ceremonial drill for an hour, then slight break. Squad drill and now company drill, break… Dinner at 1 o'clock. Parade at 2pm and drill till 4.30. Tea at 5 o'clock. Then go easy until 8.30pm when you have to get ready for tomorrow. Lights out at 10 o'clock.

We had a small route march the other morning about six miles it was not far, but the boots! Today after physical drill we had the rest of the morning doing company drill. Pretty thick it was too; we were kept going all the time.

There is one thing in the army here which is an innovation: two half days a week, Wednesday afternoon and Saturday afternoon we mess in our hut, one table down the centre. It is very comfortable and the food is plentiful and the very best. There is nothing to grumble about and we are a cheerful company.

I am very glad I joined the R.T.E*, it is quite a tip-top corps. We are much better done by than many other corps. With regards to my kit; quite a first rate lot. We have received our full equipment; valise, haversack, cartridge pouches, etc. etc. All these things have to be kept just so in the hut.

On parade one morning the Captain asked for those who could speak French to step out. Seven men stood out, including young Tricky, son of L.A. Trick of Swansea, a nice little chap he was. They were told to draw their equipment as next morning at 10.30 they went together with some other R.T.E.s who had been here nine weeks to Salonika via Marseilles. So we lost seven of our colleagues. I am in no hurry to go; the training, such as leapfrog and long jump in the physical drill suits down to the ground.

I must now close. I have been talking about myself all the time and the light is poor and I don't expect you will be able to read all the scribble… In due course, I will write all those I have promised, but with the little time to spare that I have had, this letter must take precedence.

M.A. Russell. (Too late for today's post, go tomorrow.)

A.E. Kirk, 24th November 1915, Longmoor Camp, England.

Dear Mr Wood,

…I have been quite surprised at myself since coming here, as we have had anything but a soft time either in weather or in the amount of physical exercise required of us. But provided you can stand the life it is in every way likely to make you healthy and strong. We rise soon after six and have an early parade which usually includes a double *[brisk march]*… That part of the business was rather a strain at first but comes easier with every day. After breakfast we parade in puttees etc. ready for inspection by officer (usually the captain). Then comes a morning drill partly physical and partly squad drill with a break of 20 minutes about 11 o'clock. Dinner is about 12.45 and we are always ready for our meals.

I think we all eat twice as much now as we did at home. In the afternoon we sometimes have an instruction on signalling and yesterday afternoon was spent in learning how to put together and put on overseas equipment. There are quite a number of GW men in this party and several are in the same hut as… myself. No one knows how long we may remain here and in probability we shall go out in small drafts at a time. Our Captain seems very considerate and if he is on parade does not expect too much of us. My wife tells me everything is in order with the office and I should also like to say that we were both personally grateful to you for the time allowed to me from the office the day or two before I left home.

I find more to write to than time to write here, as considerable time has to be spent cleaning our brass and otherwise making ourselves presentable soldiers. I must ask you to excuse pencil as pen and ink are rare things in camp and those supplied at the Soldiers and Sailors Club (where I am writing this) are always commandeered by an advance party.

I trust you are in good health and should like to be remembered to others we have left behind.

Yours respectfully,

Archibald E. Kirk

P.S.…Mr Pocock of the same railway is in the same squad as myself and at physical drill this morning he and I had to jump one another's backs at leapfrog….

A.E. Kirk, 29th November 1915, Longmoor Camp, England.

Dear Mr Bateman,

I have had a good deal of writing to do since coming here, but have not
forgotten those who I have not so far written to. We had a very rough
start off with weather but it has been pretty dry and we find the life here
pretty healthy. Our party numbered about 70 and we live in two huts.
Our day starts about 6am when we rise, wash, shave etc. and clear beds,
packing them up in barrack room style. We parade outside huts at 7.15
when we have half an hour's march before breakfast. Next parade is at
9 and the morning is spent in various drills, physical first then squad
and company. We had a short route march one morning and are due for
another tomorrow and are to have a field day with the R.E. troops here
later this week.

We have spent best part of today learning semaphore signalling.
I had a slight knowledge of this and got on with it pretty well. It is
interesting work. We were able to do this in the huts being wet, but
when we get flags we shall practice in the open. I have kept remarkably
well and really enjoy the life although it isn't by any means a soft time.
Our sergeant is an old soldier of some 20 years' service and can put us
through it when he likes. Our Major and Captain seem very decent.

I managed to get a pass for late leave last Saturday and had six
hours with my wife and little ones. It was a great pleasure and seemed
strange being in civilian life again. We are just arranging a scratch
football team, Wednesday afternoon being allowed for sports, and I am
going to play again after a lapse of 12 years. There must be some five or
six thousand troops here, R.E. Troops and Cavalry. Besides the Railway
Engineers there are Inland Water Transport Engineers, sometimes
called here 'Kitchener's Navy'. We get Saturday and Wednesday
afternoon and of course Sunday after church parade. Six men of our
party were sent overseas after only a week here, being selected
owing to their having knowledge of French. They were bound for
Salonika. Some more have been told to be ready to proceed overseas

at short notice. They work in alphabetical order and have so far got the beginning of the D's. I might come in the next batch after these go. The fellows are all pretty decent and that makes the life pleasanter. I hope there may be an opportunity of coming to Slough before I go out, but it is of course very doubtful. No one quite knows in the army what the next day will bring forth and they don't tell you too much. We live very well and mostly have pretty hearty appetites. I hope Mrs Bateman, yourself and children are all well. With kind regards to all and friends at office.

Yours very sincerely,
Archibald E. Kirk

F.T. Turner, 30th November 1915, Wallington, England.

Dear Mr Hunt,

Just a line to let you know I am somewhere in England. I spent a week under canvas at Tadworth, but owing to the snow and mud I am now in a billet. I suppose things are quiet in Agreements now and the Railway Transport men have gone. The army life agrees with me and I am not sorry I joined. One thing, there are no bells to ring when I happen to be missing. Well I am not much good at telling the tale.

Yours truly,
F.T. Turner

M.A. Russell, December 1915, Longmoor Camp, England.

My Dear Bertie (Hunt)

Pleased to receive your very interesting letter, it arrived yesterday afternoon just in time to let Nic read it. He, together with 11 others, are now in France. It rained in torrents on their arrival here, and it did the same on their departure. I am very sorry to lose such as a pal as Nic. We put our cots together each night to keep one another warm. As a matter of fact we have been asked 'are you two brothers?' I think Nic also did not care for the parting, but we must be self-reliant in the army and also like the Centurion...

We have a marine job on tomorrow. We are going back to the depot which is 20 minutes' walk from here. All around us are Inland Water Transport (R.E.) men. This was a special enlistment of 1,000 men to work the shipping on the canals of the continent. They are recruited from all sorts of shipping circles from barges to others of Atlantic liners and a rough lot they are.

At the depot there are the regulars attached to the Depot then come the R.T.E.s, despised by those outside but envied by the Royal Engineers as a soft job and good pay. Then there are the R.O.D*. They are dressed in blue uniforms and are the Railway Operators, the men who work on the track and the trains.

Of course beside the Royal Engineers at Longmoor, there is cavalry and it is the depot of the 19th Hussars, and territorial yeomanry troops are also here. I hope to run home to see my parents tomorrow afternoon and shall have a big day, as we breakfast at 6 o'clock and move after. All to be finished by parade at 9 o'clock. Up to town by the 1.20pm and back by the 10.35pm, reaching home here again somewhere about 2 o'clock Sunday.

Kindly remember me to all those that are left, I am sorry you felt lonely, but you should have the ladies in to fill up the blank spaces besides helping to keep you all warm, it would add to the beauty of such a fine room. The censor has gone now so I could write about what runs through my head, but the paper won't allow it.

With kind regards, I remain yours sincerely,
Mark Russell

D.J. Robertson, 2nd December 1915, Longmoor Camp, England.

Dear Fred (Woodhams),

Just a few lines to let you know that we are getting it in the neck properly as they are putting us through all sorts of drills etc. This morning we had a 12 mile route march and then this afternoon learnt all about bombs of different patterns and how to use them. We also learnt semaphore and what with knotting and flashing, our time is fully occupied. I am just going to see Bright off to France as they are sending us off in alphabetical order so I do not think we shall be long here. It is very dreary here as when it rains it looks like a swamp but the countryside is exceedingly pretty. Please excuse more now for the above reason, so with kind regards to Bertie, Billy and yourself,

Joe

J.G. Symons, 5th December 1915, Wimereux, France.

Dear Bert (Hunt)

I received your letter of a week ago and many thanks for same. I am a patient in the above hospital, with trench feet. From what one of the sisters told me, I am leaving by the next hospital ship for England that will be either Monday or Tuesday. I will let you know as soon as I arrive. Of course it's impossible for me to walk. Well I hope to see you before long.

Yours sincerely,
Jack Symons

L.W. Sharpe, 10th December 1915, France.

Dear Joseph (Naldrett),

Just a line to thank you for the parcel I received from the old firm a few days ago. You will, I know, do the necessary for me, by thanking all who subscribed towards the contents, which I am enjoying very much. It is very good of you all to think of us out here and I can speak for most chaps out here and say that nothing do we enjoy more than a decent English fag and some good old Blighty chocolate. So that if you are sending to all the same as I have received, you cannot do better. Am very pleased with the enclosed Xmas card, it's a reminder that we are not forgotten.

Well Natty, I don't know that I have much news, only to say that after six months of almost constant trench work and attacks we are at last having our first decent rest during that time. I don't know for how long we shall be at rest, but we are training in open warfare. This does not affect me as I'm still an officer's servant so do not have to parade. Whether they intend packing us off to another frontier shortly, where there is no trench warfare, I don't know, but it looks somewhat like it at present. We have had a rough time of it and since I came out our battalion have taken part in the battles of Aubers Ridge, Indian Village, Festubert, Givenchy and Loos. In fact there's been none of importance at which we have not taken part in, as before I joined the battalion, they were up at the great Battle of Ypres (at the commencement of the war) and also took part in the Neuve Chapelle affair and the only one we appear to have missed was Hill 60 *[South East of Ypres]* in which our 1st Battalion took part.

I have written Billy Dawson so perhaps you will see the letter. In case not however, I will tell you we are at a new part of our line, some hundred miles further south of our last district. We have only recently taken over this part from the French and are not too far from the Champagne district, where the French have done such good work lately as you will have read. Jack old boy, the scenery here is lovely I bet it would just suit you for a holiday. There are ranges of hills some miles in length, with villages spread here and there in the valleys. We are some three miles from the firing line, and out of sound of our guns (for the first time since I have been out here) so that we have forgotten almost there is a war on.

The worst of it all is that it is that I am some two and a half miles away from the battalion at present with my officer at a farm house and with the brigade bomb throwers. The nearest house is in the village where the battalion are so that it is rather a dead sort of show. I went over to the battalion last evening and came across the hills back. Got lost on the way and arrived back here at 9.15, after about two and half hours roaming about, during which it rained nearly all the time. Shall probably be going over there again tonight, but shall keep to the road this time.

Well Jack, there are no signs of leave yet for me, but of course I shall look in the Coal Hole *[pub]* <u>when</u> I do come home. I sent you a card sometime before to thank you for the tobacco you sent. Did you receive it? And don't forget you have not yet told me anything about your holiday, where you went etc.

I think this is all this time so will close, trusting you are still as well as ever and that you will thank all for the parcel. Best wishes and a happy Xmas to all.

Yours sincerely,
L.W.S. (Sharpe)

E.W. Jackson, 10th December 1915, France.

Dear Taylor,

At last I have a few minutes to send a line in reply to yours of 29th November. Thanks very much for it, also for mag*! I see from your plan that the office is not overcrowded. I agree with you that the system of trying to force our people to enlist by threatening not to give any help to those members who waited to be called on cannot be called voluntary.

Of course the railways now being government controlled, they are trying to bounce the chaps, like they have done, I am told, in the Post Office. I think any man who really does not feel called on to enlist should sit tight and take no notice of the threats and hints to wait till Parliament legislates to make service compulsory. I think at any rate the Audit have contributed their share of men...

We have been back a few miles recently for nearly three weeks out of the danger zone, 'resting' they call it, really about four hours a day training, but of course the men got their night's rest undisturbed by shells bursting or 'stand to'. It seemed strange to be out of sound of gun fire. It was no rest for the Quarter Masters' department as far as we had to refit the companies with clothing etc. In the middle of it, our Quarter Master went away sick to England; I am doing his job again so being Quarter Master and Quarter Master Sergeant as well, keeps me pretty busy.

A vacancy for Quarter Master recently occurred in a King's Battalion near us and our company was asked to recommend some Non-Commissioned Officer for the job. He paid me the compliment of saying I was just the man but specifically asked me not to press him to nominate me, as he did not want to lose me in case of the Quarter Master not getting well as quickly as we hoped. It only makes about nine pennies a day difference whether you are Quarter Master or Quarter Master Sergeant, but that is nothing to me of course... *[censored]*.

You should see the mud on the fields about here, mud well over the ankles, ordinary boots are useless, gum boots they only wear off the roads.

The papers have been very irregular lately and I have not seen one for two days. The recent centre of interest is Greece and Serbia. Also the retirement in Mesopotamia was disappointing. I do not think you can expect anything on this side during the winter, the country being almost impassable for mud.

One of our regimental artists has designed an alleged humorous Christmas card, I do not think much of it, but will send one to the office when they are issued.

I had a field card from young Williams this week and a letter
from Gilson; the latter is Acting Sergeant, he is, as you know, I think
permanently on duty at the rest camp at Boulogne. Our Quarter Master's
illness has stopped any chance of leave for me at present otherwise
I shall have got over for eight days about the New Year. I would
certainly have looked you up one evening when you were 'bobbing'.
Compris 'bobbing'?

I suppose you are having the money draws and raffles for turkeys,
wine, cigars etc. as usual and I hope your luck has not forsaken you.
Have you had the announcements of the Christmas holidays yet
when members of the staff who desire it may be absent on one of two
mornings? Of course being a family man, you won't want to be going
away. A lovely time for stocks and shares is it not?...

Well I must not write any more or you will think me frivolous, so will
wish you all a Merry Xmas, and remain

Yours sincerely,
E.W. Jackson

J.G. Symons, 14th December 1915, in hospital in Taplow, England.

Dear Bert,

At last I have arrived in England. Left Boulogne Sunday and travelled
via Southampton to Taplow. My right foot is still very bad and they
told me at Boulogne that I might have to have my big toe amputated.
Anyway I hope not. If they do start any of that business I hope they will
cut off some of the right side of the foot, for they would do me a favour
by ridding me of a beautiful corn that has troubled me for a good many
years. I hope you will endeavour to make a call on me one day. The first
two or three visiting days my people, and there are a good number in
the family, will monopolise them. Try and get next Tuesday afternoon
off and call down. You must let me know for I shall have to get a pass for
you. The visiting hours are 1 to 4pm. Now don't forget.

Well Bert my last four days in the trenches were about the most terrible days I have ever experienced. No cock and bull story, but I have had the pleasant (I say so now) sensation of having a shell strike the ground six yards behind me and hurled me a good four yards and I landed in a trench full of water!

Out of the party of four others beside myself, two of them got badly wounded and one of the others kept me company he being landed in the same trench. This is no exaggeration but perfectly true. It seemed to have stunned me for they tell me that by the time we got to our support trenches I fell down about 20 times.

We got into a dugout and I went off to sleep and the next day when I woke I was covered from head to feet in mud. I will be able to tell you more when you call.

Jack Symons

E.W. Bratchell, 18th December 1915, France.

Dear Burgy,

Was very pleased to get your letter and to know that all my old friends were still keeping fit and well. Thanks very much for the news... We had some prospects of further travelling the globe a short while back, our division being ordered to leave France for 'destination unknown'. Unfortunately, or fortunately, don't know which, the 'tin pots' decided to leave us servicemen behind and rather against the grain we had to part company with our good pals of the past nine months. Not the least being the blackest Ghurkas 'Gharwals' etc. It will probably take us a few weeks to settle down with the new people we are attached to although they are all London Territorials. Our first job on joining them was to clean our buttons. We found they were out for a month's 'rest', the division I mean, not the buttons. And in consequence a very shiny appearance had to be maintained. Sounds silly to be cleaning buttons, equipment, buckles, boots etc. on active service doesn't it? That's what we thought so anyway, quite sufficient to keep ourselves clean.

Several people have tried without much success to convince us that these little treats are all necessary to make good scrappers. Well I managed to scrape through the month without running foul of the 'cads' more than usual; we had some decent footie games finishing up by being whacked 6-1 in the Brigade Company. We are now once more within striking distance of the mud and water, this time myself and three pals have struck rather lucky being attached to another regiment for the purpose of looking after a redoubt *[defence outpost]*. Being on our own and having a dry cellar for living in we have made ourselves comfortable and may be able to make merry at Christmas in royal style ten days hence… I hope you will all have a decent time this holiday. Must close now.

Wishing you a Merry Christmas and Happy New Year, from yours, E.W.B.

W.A. McConnell, 17th December 1915, Royal Free hospital, England.

Dear Mr Rogers

Please accept yourself and convey to other gentlemen on the Agreements section, my thanks for the Christmas greetings, which I received this morning.

I have not been able to come and see you lately as I do not get any time off during the week. However I make up for that during the weekend as I do not do very much on Saturday afternoon or Sunday. I generally put in a couple of hours on Sunday morning and then shut up the shop. Of course if we get a big convoy in on Saturday, I don't get away at all but things are very quiet now and the only sick or wounded which we are receiving are from the Dardanelles. The *Maurentania* landed 2,500 at the beginning of this week, and we had a good few of them, all dysentery and frostbite cases.

Of course you know I am in the office here now. It happened this way. The clerk in charge is a civilian and he was suddenly taken ill one

Saturday morning, and the Secretary sent for me, and just told me to go in the office and take up Mr Spencer's work. When you consider that I had absolutely no knowledge of army forms or routine, you can guess what a time I had. I was working all day and all night too, just fancy me working overtime and for nothing too. Well anyway I stuck to it, and although I was left alone for two months I got through all right and for my trouble got two stripes which was recognition for my work. I am thankful to say the clerk has now returned to duty, so between the two of us we manage very well.

Although I am in the office the work is not nearly so tedious as at Paddington. It is altogether different and to break monotony I go off to a theatre or concert about once a week with the wounded Tommies. Well I must close now and get on with some work so wishing you all a Merry Christmas.

W.A. McConnell

E.H.C. Stewart, 18th December 1915, Belgium.

Dear Mr Slater,

I have a few minutes to myself, so thought I would seize the opportunity to write you a few lines to let you know how I am faring.

After five months' work on lines communications the battalion moved to a small village named Blendecques, here we entered into hard training to prepare ourselves for the fray. Three weeks later we again moved, this time to a village just on the Belgium frontier, still working hard, about a fortnight was spent here, when we had a hard march to Poperinghe [Poperinge] and a few days' rest then off to these trenches, which are in the Ypres district. The trenches here are in a very bad condition, mud and water up to the knee, and over in parts. The General who addressed us before we moved off informed us we were being sent to a quiet part of the line, personally I think he has made a slight mistake, for all day, at intermittent intervals, we are bombarded by the Huns. Their favourite projectile is apparently small shrapnel, which we have affectionately nick named whizz bangs: they are very high velocity shells of small dimension. Yesterday we had no less than 30 over in twenty minutes, two which exploded right on our parapet, however no one was hurt, as we had all gone into our 'funk' holes *[a Tommy term for a dugout]* out of the way.

How are things going on in the Stats *[department]*, I expect you are very busy and rather short of hands or have they employed a large amount of female labour?

I suppose Paddington station escaped when the Zeppelin raids were in fashion, they seem to be lying low lately. I wonder if they are saving it up as to make one grand attack (from their point of view) on London, sort of now or never style. Are there any more casualties to report from the ranks of the Audit office corps now on active service? Trusting you are in the best of health.

I remain, yours sincerely,

E.H. Cecil Stewart

R. Gilson, 20th December 1915, France.

Mr G. Welsh,

Dear Sir,

Many thanks for kind wishes which I beg to reciprocate. I feel almost ashamed to communicate after having been so silent for so long, but am sure you will forgive any apparent rudeness and must excuse myself for pleading lack of time. After many exciting adventures on the front line, through which I have come without a scratch, I have been transferred to the above camp for duty and classified as permanent base owing to eye trouble. I hope that before long I may be paying you a visit at the office.

Please accept all good wishes for Xmas with a much brighter New Year and kindly convey same to the staff. And believe me, yours truly,

Richard Gilson, Lieutenant Sergeant

F.G. Woodhams, 20th December 1915, Belgium.

Dear Mr Clarke,

I am writing to thank you and the other fellows of the office for the parcel which I have just received.

As I expect you know our regiment is now scattered all over the place... I am at a little place in Belgium about 12 miles from the line. They are even now bombarding the next village up and have been *[illegible]* for the last 48 hours, shells bursting about every 10 minutes. It's lucky for us they haven't got the range of the place as there are large stores of ammunition, and one shell properly placed would blow the whole station sky high. The chief thing we have to fear here though are German aeroplanes and just lately they have come over a number of times. Yesterday morning I witnessed a fight between a French and German aeroplane, both fitted with machine guns. Unfortunately the Frenchman came off second best, his machine being damaged and he himself badly wounded, nevertheless he managed to keep control but in landing turned a complete somersault owing to the rough ground. This caused quite a lot of excitement in this small place and crowds flocked to see the airplane, parts of which were swamped in blood.

It is rather monotonous in this job, but I much prefer it to the trenches and honestly... we don't mind if we are kept in it 'til the end of the year.

We are making preparations for Christmas and doing our best to make it as good as possible at any rate, I think we shall have a much better time this year than we did last when as you know we were in the trenches.

...Wishing you all a very happy Christmas. Yours sincerely,
F.G. Woodhams

E.W. Jackson, 20th December 1915, France.

Dear Hunt,

Many thanks for the cigarettes and Christmas card received last night. It is very good of you all to think of us out here, particularly as we are so slow at finishing the war, thereby causing much inconvenience to the publicans and others who are still in the country... I hope to see you in a few weeks' time... Am fearfully busy just now, and have no news. Wishing you all the best possible time at Xmas.

I remain yours sincerely,
E.W. Jackson

D.J. Robertson, 20th December 1915, Longmoor Camp, England.

Dear Bertie *[Hunt]*

I have to thank you very much for the Xmas card, which I will treasure, and as I have no place to keep it down here I have sent it to my wife to take care of. I have tried in what spare time I have to obtain our regimental card that I might send one to you, but I cannot get one for love or money, so I trust you will take the will for the deed. Kirk and Russell went overseas last Thursday, and they asked me to tell you that it may be some time before they can write to you, but they will do so as early as possible, wishing a Merry Xmas and a prosperous New Year to all in the Audit, I am yours sincerely,

David J. Robertson

W.C. Davis, 20th December 1915, France.

Dear Mr Rendall

Thanks for the card from yourself and staff of the Passengers. I am sure that it is the wish of us all out here that before another Xmas arrives the present war will be over and things settled down again.

As you are aware from the papers there has not been a great deal doing on our Front since September 25th other than small powered attacks but I can assure you that these can cost the country a good many lives and the wounds are something awful to look at, but after the first time in the trenches and the first shock one sets about the work to be done unconcerned with the conditions prevailing.

I have not had the pleasure of meeting anyone from Paddington out here yet, but still live in hope of coming across someone one day, for a chat about railways which I am sure would do me good. I expect there have been a good number of the men in the Audit enlist under Lord Derby's scheme…

Wishing all my friends in the Audit good luck for Xmas and the New Year, trusting there will be a corner left for me *apres la guerre [after the war]*.

I remain yours faithfully,
W.C. Davis

R.W.S. Court, 21st December 1915, Parkhall Camp, England.

Dear Mr Welsh,

Many thanks for your kind wishes for the season. They are heartily reciprocated in every sense and I am wondering when the time will come, if ever, when I shall again sit in the Audit in civilian clothes.

We are all confined to camp over Xmas owing to a rather serious outbreak of measles. Rather hard luck but has to be borne with a soldier's fortitude. Trusting that you are personally in perfect health, and your staff also.

I am yours truly,
R.W.S. Court

G. Williams, 21st December 1915, France.

Dear Mr Hunt,

My best thanks for you... for the Xmas gift. The cigarettes are much appreciated. We are in the trenches just now and as it has been raining pretty well continuously the last two or three weeks, you can perhaps realise the state of them. Literally over the knees in mud in parts. Very messy all over. Don't know whether we shall be in for Xmas or not.

The German trenches opposite are 150 yards away, and the other morning we were shouting across to one another. I think Fritz is getting fed up. The conditions are enough to make anyone sick of the whole business.

Had a letter from Jackson the other day enclosing a plan of the office.... How bare the place must look. Well, here's to a Merry Xmas and prosperous New Year to yourself and the other gentlemen of the office.

Yours very sincerely,
Gilbert Williams

R.C.S. Frost, 26th December 1915, France.

Dear Mr Hunt,

Just a few lines to thank you... for your kindness in thinking of me again, and sending the compliments of the season, and the useful present of cigarettes.

Xmas here has not been quite uneventful, although it has been quiet, and of course no truce was allowed. This battalion spent it in billets as we have been relieved by Kitchener's army on this front and in a few days are going on a two days trek back for a few weeks' rest.

About 10 o'clock on Friday night the divisional brass band paid us a visit and played carols and other pieces outside the billet and on Xmas evening we signallers had a splendid feed in our billet and for a few hours we forgot all about the struggle which is going on about four miles away, and I have an idea a few extra thirsty members were unconscious of the war until the following morning! However it was an enjoyable evening and thanks to kind friends at home and the generous response to newspaper appeals for Xmas gifts for the troops, and a kind French lady who cooked several fowls, our improvised table of doors and pieces of wood almost collapsed under the weight. We had a route march the following morning, but everyone was able to see it through, and I think the hours spent in the fresh air did all concerned much good!

This afternoon we had a visit from the brigade pipe band consisting of 16 pipers and 13 drums and really it was good pipe music but I still prefer to hear a fine military band like the Guards have, perhaps I have heard too much pipe music! Although of course the Scotchmen don't agree with my views.

I had a change a short time ago by visiting the Highland Field Hospital and staying for a week as I slightly sprained my back in the trenches. It was a treat to ride in motor ambulances, sleep in a bed, and be waited on hand and foot and I really enjoyed the rest. When they sent me to the convalescent camp however I was pleased to stay on night only, as it reminded me too much of Howbury camp, Bedford, where we were staying 12 months ago, so I reported myself fit for duty and returned to the battalion.

I am glad to say I am quite well again, and hope this will find you well too. With best wishes for the New Year to you, and all other friends in the Agreements dept.

Sincerely yours, R.C.S. Frost

A.E. Kirk, 27th December 1915, France.

Dear Mr Hunt,

You have possibly heard that I am across the water being ordered out the day following my return to camp after my Xmas leave and what with the upset of getting packed up and having been kept hard at work since we got here, I have not found time to acknowledge the handsome Christmas card which you sent on behalf of yourself and the office.

I should like to say I was very pleased to receive such a kind remembrance and wish you one and all a happy and brighter New Year. I have kept in excellent health.

Our journey to this place… took us from breakfast time Saturday morning (18th December) until Monday (20th December) 3pm to accomplish, the last 16 hours being spent in a covered goods wagon on the French railway.

We were sent here especially to help cope with the Xmas rush of parcels to the troops and a pretty tough job it was, our usual finishing time being after nine or ten at night. However now it is over we are having a little more leisure and Xmas Day, yesterday and today (Monday) have been half days only. How different to an Audit Xmas holiday, but soldiers always come up to scratch… There are quite a large number of GW men here altogether and Lt. Veltom (also GW) is the officer immediately over us.

I hope all are well with you, please remember me to all friends, yours very sincerely,
Archibald E. Kirk

M.A. Russell, 28th December 1915, Le Havre, France.

My Dear Bertie,

Greetings to you and all the friends in the Audit office kindly accept my sincere wish that you may all have a happy and prosperous Christmas.

I have been here now about a week, and like my surroundings very well. Sapper Kirk, myself and eight others came out together. I have met and am working with Sapper Boyce, S.A. Brown and Bright and many of my Longmoor chums. Kennett who used to be on the S.W. Railway is a corporal in our crew and Ferdi (the Sergeant of the Line) is also an old hand here. Sapper Brackenbury who is on the depot staff, called upon me on Sunday afternoon but I was not at home in my hut. May see him later on. I must say I have been very lucky since arriving. There's plenty to do, but to come to the seaside for Xmas well it was beyond my hopes.

We spent Xmas day in proper style. Knocked off at midday, dinner at 1 o'clock. Good old English roast beef (a la Argentine) potatoes and Brussels sprouts, sausages and mash. Christmas puddings, prunes and custard, cheese and as much Exportation in bottles (French beer) as you wanted. We did good services to the dinner I can assure you after bread and jam and jam and bread, cheese and bully beef, bully beef and cheese and so on, it was a change.

The afternoon I spent in town and we had a smoking concert in the evening.

It took me from a Saturday morning to Monday afternoon to get here; one journey lasted about 17 hours in a closed truck. Whatever you may think it was much better than travelling in a compartment; there were about 30 of us all going different ways, I mean those beside our party.

It was a sleeping car and dining car combined, we stretched out and slept as much as the jolting of the truck would allow, on our kit, and dined on bully beef, bread, jam and cheese carried in a sack. I would not have missed the experience I can assure you, by travelling first class when I was up at the office. I did not think I should be away so soon I went back from leave on Thursday night and was told Friday evening 6.30 to parade, 7.45 marching orders overseas. I am very pleased I am out at work.

This town is a really fine place and later on I will send you a few pictures for your collection. Kindly remember me to Mr Wheeler, Mr Wood, Mr Taylor and the rest.

141

Nick *[Boyce]* wishes me to convey to you by my letter his compliments and trusts that you all may have a happy and prosperous New Year. We both received the cards and return thanks,

With kind regards, I remain yours very sincerely, Mark. A. Russell

P.S. With kind regards to J. Higgs.

T.H. Watts, 23rd November 1915, Dardanelles, Turkey.

Dear Arthur *[Bateman]*

I really must make this effort to write to you and let you know how I am progressing. Well so far as a little internal trouble I'm keeping fairly fit now that the cold weather has started, and on my present job I can doctor myself, I am prepared to stick this campaign until further orders.

We are now in our winter quarters and a very nice place it is. Right on the edge of the cliffs, with a beautiful sea below, it reminds me very much of Cornwall. Then just across is the island of Imbros, and the sunlight on those mountains is sometimes marvellous. On a quiet, warm day, with the birds singing, one wonders if there is a war on, but the blooming shells soon drive that idea away. It's jolly cold now though, but we have been served out with nice thick underclothes, and waterproofs, and top boots and except for always living in the ground, our comforts have been looked after as far as possible. Our food is as good as anyone could want, also I'm now used to a lot that before I'd turn my nose up at, and so long as the ships can land the goods I don't think we shall be so badly off.

Mind it does blow, and the sea gets awfully rough and then no ships can come near us. We have the sea on three sides and the Turks on the fourth, so we are truly between the devil and the deep sea. The Turks still find some ammunition from somewhere whether our guns and the warships knock the very dickens out of them. It's very exciting to watch a battle especially now it's on our side the guns are not like at Antwerp where we were the ones potted. Now I am too sleepy to continue and as the firing has quieted down I'm going to sleep and continue tomorrow.

5/12/15. I've not had a chance to finish this letter before, so here goes. We've had snow and rain and thunder and such lightening, and Lord it has been cold, everything frozen and even the water in my water bottle. But today has been beautifully mild and calm, almost like summer again. I have just received a packet of letters from my wife, written at different times since May, so am still in hopes that there may be some more back dates knocking around the world for me. We had three men killed last night in a little spasm, and today our guns and the Turks have been flinging dirt at each other. We used to duck once upon a time, as the shells came over, but now everyone seems curious to see what sort of a burst it will be and how much dust is knocked up, and heaps have cameras taking photos.

Enclosed is a bit of heather which grows in great profusion all over the peninsular. And the troops use in the trenches to boil their dixies on. And now about the office. Do you know but, it's quite an effort to remember the routine now...

I suppose Mr Millow is still with you and is there any chance of H.R.H. Goff joining say as a S.C. *[probably Senior Clerk]*? There is now a singing in the air and bang just as I write they've dropped one over to us. Sometimes a shell bursts, and when we are working at something we don't even know it's come along. It's funny what you can get used. But to get back to the office. I expect you have heaps of ladies there now, lord I haven't seen a woman since April. What do they look like? I expect they scent out the office, and how careful you all must be not to swear. We often laugh here at the thought that if ever we do return to civil life again, we'll be digging a little hole in the garden to live in and stirring up our tea with a bit of stick or our finger and just spit on the floor when smoking and if a little tickling in our shirt, just hopping it off in the street.

I am out of paper *[he is writing this on an envelope]*, but it don't matter. How are the lambs going? Here's one that's doing a little doing a little bleat far from home. I'd like to come you know, and have a rub at a bed and a roof, also a drop of beer perchance. Living in a hole for seven months now and the blue sky above gets a bit monotonous at times especially when the dirt will persist in falling on your face when you are trying to sleep and when it rains you're up to your knees in no time, and that's always at night. We had rum served out tonight and do you know, I can't bear the stuff, just pause and think by the wayside, I can't drink rum, in fact I hate it. How we do change by time. Now how is everyone down the club? Remember me to Emmie and Mrs Fellows and May. I understand that Mr Welsh and Mr Davies have been awfully kind to my wife, and I reckon its jolly good of them. This war seems to have found me so many kind friends, I don't know what I'll do to repay them all if I live through this…

What has become of Beaumont and Jackson, and is my pal Jimmy Edwards still alive,… Bert I'd like to send you a Turkish shell but the post office won't accept them for transit, anyhow perhaps I'll bring home a nose fuse for a paper weight. Do you know back in the summer I had a shell drop just off the seat of my trousers and it did not explode. Kaw! It was a bit of luck, I didn't stop to pick him up though, in case he changed his mind later. Well now I've tried to remember everyone, but do you give heartiest good wishes to the office for a Merry Xmas and a victorious New Year and trusting you'll all be safe from Zeppelins.

Yours very sincerely, T. Harold Watts

J.G. Symons, 29th December 1915, Canadian Red Cross hospital, Taplow, England.

Dear Bert *[Mr Hunt]*

Just a line hoping you enjoyed the Xmas. We kept up Xmas day on the Friday as I can assure you there was plenty of fun, but Xmas day was very quiet, for the majority of those able to get about were invited out to dinner etc. There were only six of us left in the ward, bed patients so I passed the time away reading. My foot is going on fine, except the big toe and they don't appear to make much difference to it. They pulled out the toe nail and then tried to get a good grip of the skin to pull it off but it is still very hard, so tomorrow they are going to try very hot water with something in it I believe and if they manage alright, I daresay I shall be out of here in another month.

I have had nearly five weeks now on my back and I can assure you it's not in my line. I have heard some fine work was done across the water by the 13th County of London Battalion when they lost so heavily and that they were the admiration of the Regulars. No doubt it will please Freddy to hear this as his two boys were in it.

Will you let me know when you are coming down again and if E. is coming with you? I will get a pass and send it on to you.

I must now conclude, kind regards to all, yours sincerely,
Jack Symons

A. Smith, 30th December 1915, France.

Dear Mr Davies

Just a line or two to let you know that I am still in the land of the living.

About a month ago we removed our quarters to this spot which is nearer the line of fire. We have still got our old truck, I am pleased to say, so regardless of outward surroundings we still have our same home. This village is not so nice and convenient, for many things, as our last spot, but I am quite settled down here and am not anxious to move again in a hurry. Close by we have an Expeditionary Force canteen, which we have fairly well patronised by buying fruit, nuts etc. there this yuletide. I believe a Y.M.C.A. is going to be opened here too, so that will be another attraction.

Six of us spent Christmas day together in this truck and on the whole we had a jolly time. We were not free from work on Christmas day but the work was not extra hard. For Xmas dinner we had two roasted stuffed chickens, roast potatoes, lime juice and Perrier water, Xmas pudding, nuts and last of all a bowl of champagne. Of course, we had to buy these extra things, but that was of our own free will as a good dinner would have been prepared for us in any case. The Xmas pudding we had… was the gift of one of the daily papers. Our officer, the R.T.O* gave us cigarettes and bought, or helped to buy, a pig and some beer for consumption on the railhead. We six in our turn contributed and presented him with two boxes of Marcella cigars with which he seemed to be pleased. Temperance was our motto through Xmas and so things ended happily.

The weather here lately has been generally wet and many fields adjacent to the river, are under water. We have plenty of good clothes and, up to the present, have been able to keep dry and warm.

I have heard through Mr Kirk that about half a dozen more Audit men have joined the R.T.E. He was at Longmoor when I heard last. Then again, I suppose, many more will be called up for service under Lord Derby's scheme. I have heard that Messers Dent, Anglesy and Goodall have been rejected, so there will still be a few left to keep the flag flying at the office...

I think I have told you all for the present so I will conclude with my kindest regards and best wishes to all in the Parcels Department.

I am yours very respectfully,
Arthur Smith

FIVE

MARCH 1916

'All the fellows seem a jolly lot and to hear them talk of things that happen at the front, well, you would think they had come back from a football match'
SIDNEY HODGES

As intimated in Hodges' words, this appeared to be a fairly peaceful period for at least some of our letter writers. There were no fatalities amongst the Audit soldiers, although there was some further news concerning George Shipley, who had died in early December 1915:

> In our notes in January issue we referred to the death of our colleague, George W.Shipley, we have since received news that his remains have been laid to rest in Alexandria.

Many writers for this newsletter were preoccupied with their domestic arrangements, namely where they were sleeping or if rations were up to scratch. However, as usual there were marked differences in their fortunes. M.A. Russell wrote of his disappointment when, upon arriving by boat at a 'quaint' city he found that they weren't allowed out for a day's sightseeing. He felt lucky at having found himself in a safe office job, secured for him by another GWR man. By contrast Freddy Woodhams

> The last time I wrote I think I told you we had lost our comfortable job on railheads. We have been shifted from G.H.Q. and are at the most God-forsaken hole there can possibly be in France. We had a rotten journey raining all the time. Reveille was at 4 a.m. and we eventually left the station about 10 a.m. The accommodation consisted of the old cattle trucks,and rations of bully and biscuits, it was a very cold and uncomfortable journey.

The letters in this chapter were predominantly sent from those at training camps in Bordon and Longmoor. F.J. Serjent wrote several times conveying a sense of the uncertainty that the soldiers lived with when awaiting deployment:

'We are still in the dark as to what our fate will be, whether we go out shortly or not.' Clearly fed up, he adds *'I trust shall be able to get leave (which is very hard) before departing. If I don't get it I shall abscond.'*

We also hear from Jack Symons, at hospital in Taplow.

Sometimes letters seem to have been written primarily as a way to make connections with old work colleagues. Arthur Smith wrote from France: *'Although there is very little to say, I think that it is about time I wrote to the office again.'* There's more evidence to show that the soldiers were aware of the letter collections being assembled and shared amongst those who remained at Paddington. The fact it's safe to assume that this had became a motivation for writing in itself. Sidney Hodges opened his letter with *'don't put this in the book as I have not time to write properly.'*

The newsletter continued to be a place to report news of colleagues who had not written, but had visited the office:

'We congratulate our old sport Sgt. Billy Hastings on his promotion to this rank, his colleagues will be pleased to hear of his recovery to health after such a prolonged stay in Hospital through wounds. On his calling at the office recently, he looked remarkably well and we learnt that he would shortly have to report himself at Ripon for service once again with the colours.'

T.H. Watts, extract of a Christmas card sent from the Dardanelles, Turkey.

Extract of a Dardanelles-themed Christmas card which celebrates the achievements of the Royal Naval Division from Harold Watts.

'An interesting Christmas greeting to Mr Price and staff appears herein, from Leading Seaman Harold Watts... We have just heard that our old friend lost most of his kit on the evacuation of the Dardanelles and the transfer to Salonika...probably he will have many amusing episodes to relate.'

F.J. Serjent, Deepcut Camp, England.

Excuse scribble

Dear Mr Smith,

... 'I am now in the army as you will see by my address, learning to be a soldier. I asked for a transfer to the R.F.A. and after waiting a decent time, I was shot off down here at a very short notice. I might tell you that by the events that are taking place down here, the division I am in, namely the 16th, expect to move overseas very shortly, and I trust shall be able to get leave (which is very hard) before departing. If I don't get it I shall abscond.

Our daily programme is generally up at 5.30. Parade at six for riding instruction, on real live nags. At eight we go to breakfast. You get hold of as many pieces of bread as you require. Then a lump of butter is smacked on, and you are left to do the spreading yourself. Our tea we get in basins which are filled from huge pails. Gun drill generally takes place until dinner time, of course we get plenty of meat and potatoes cooked in their skins, but although not very decent you seem somehow able to eat anything.

Of course we have guards, stable picquets and town picquets. We have at present about 54 deserters from our brigade, and the guard room is full. One managed to escape the other day, but he has managed to slip being caught…

I should like to know whether I can have half a ton of coal for my mother and the price. I daresay if mother forwarded the cash you would see it through for me, trusting I shall not be troubling you too much.

I remain your sincere friend.

F.J. Serjent, Bordon Camp, England.

Dear Mr Smith,

…You will see our brigade has shifted from Deepcut, which took place last Saturday, in most awful weather… This place is a dustheap compared with Deepcut. The last brigade left the camp rather suddenly and were unable to put things straight before departure. The only dinner we get is stew, and the breakfasts and tea are wicked, still it is all in the game, perhaps the worst is to come… I suppose you have more girls than you want, so please export a few like Rigger and Miss Spear *[Audit staff]* down here.

Since being in the crowd, I have not yet managed to get a crime against me, and no promotion, still there is time.

I should much like to pay a visit to the old office, but when we get leave it is usually midday Sat. till Sunday midnight... Hoping you and all the boys are quite well.

With kind regards,

J. Serjent.

F.J. Serjent, Bordon Camp, England.

Dear Mr Smith,

...I am extremely sorry to hear your son has been so bad, and I trust he will have a speedy recovery to the best of health. I suppose Lord Derby's scheme has made a great many of the younger men at Paddington go up and enrol their names.

I can imagine Paddington offices in the midst of Christmas raffles, draws etc. at the present time. There is very little excitement down here, as only 10% of our brigade have been allowed passes for Christmas. This means that the remaining 90% will take French leave*, and our cooks, who are a lively lot, are also arranging to go, so I can see what's left of us down here will be cooking our own dinners. We are still in the dark as to what our fate will be, whether we go out shortly or not...

Trusting you will spend a jolly good Christmas.

With best wishes. From Serjent

C.D. Mayo, 19th November 1915, in hospital in Flanders.

My Dear Mother,

I was awfully glad to get your letter last Friday, it only took 11 days to get here. You must have been worried all that time not having heard from me; 'wounded and missing' is such a beastly, unsatisfactory verdict. You didn't say how you both were, but I hope you are alright.

I got up for the first time Monday and get along pretty well now on my crutches, the only thing the matter with my leg now is stiffness, the muscles above my knee are quite hard but are getting slowly better. The day after I wrote my last letter I had some more weight put on, so there was a 50lb weight on my foot and another 30lb slung over the top of the bed to pull the top part of my leg into place. The result was worth it as my right leg is now very little shorter than the left, so little in fact that I don't think I shall ever notice it. ...

Very best love to you both.

Your loving son
Charlie (Mayo).

...I hope there is some tobacco in the parcel, the Belgian stuff is filthy; it smells like tobacco and that is all.

J.G. Symons, 8th January 1916, in hospital in Taplow, England.

Dear Bert,

They amputated my big toe yesterday, so I can say goodbye to my little military career, but I may be of some use for the National Reserve, if only to attend the Sergeant's Mess and annual dinner to put me in mind of old times. Well it had to come off so it's no good of me getting downhearted. It will not do me out of my walk across Kensington Gardens on Saturdays, when I return to Paddington, for I hear they can supply an artificial one.

My tongue was very bad after the operation, and on asking the doctor the cause, he said 'that the ether rolled the tongue up and forced it to the back of the mouth and they had to pull it out'... For the first few minutes after gaining my senses, it put me in mind of old times, for once or twice I grabbed the side of the bed, as if it was going round and round. Well Bert, I will write again shortly. Give my kind regards to all

Yours sincerely,
Jack Symons

M.P. Pond, 17th January 1916, France.

Dear Mr Hunt,

…Thank you for the very pretty card I received at Christmas from the section…We shifted into a new wagon last week. They are doing away with all the wagons at railheads by degrees, so we shall probably go into huts sooner or later. We spent a fairly enjoyable time at Christmas, under the circumstances. We received a good many gifts of plum puddings etc. and 14 of us had a dinner together on Christmas day. Several of us also had a private dinner at one of the cafés the following Monday evening with a concert afterwards… I have bought a fiddle and had it sent out, so we manage to have some musical evenings sometimes. We had some nice weather here during December and I did quite a lot of motoring, visiting the various dumps behind the firing line where the supplies are taken for the troops in the trenches… There is very little doing round this way except the usual air raids. We had 13 over yesterday, but they were driven off.

Wishing you all a very happy new year…
M.P. Pond

H.W. Cronin, 18th January 1916, Egypt.

Dear Mr Welsh,

A lot has happened since I last wrote to you and we have moved, and moved, and moved again, and still we are moving. There is nothing at all to say about the actual coming off. We were told to pack up, and having done so, were marched off and soon afterwards were making up a four for Bridge in quite a comfortable cabin and enjoying the unwanted luxury of electric light.

The only thing that struck one in coming away was that nothing had altered and it might easily have been the night I landed. The same old beach apparently full up with boxes of bully beef, tinned milk and jam, the same old destroyer, with its search light playing on the shore, keeping up its systematic bombardment and the same old swish of bullets around and dropping into the water. No sooner was Christmas here than we were packing up again, to come on here. A large town a few miles on the interior, it is a filthy rotten smelly hole and we always carried loaded revolvers and walked about in batches and were never out after dark. Probably the people are not ill disposed to us but some of them looked pretty villainous and it was better to be on the safe side...

We have had quite a good time and the regular hours and regular meals have backed everyone up well and now we are all as fit as ever– apparently.

Thanks very much for the Xmas card it was a bit late but then all our Xmas letters and parcels were on account of the way we have been moving about; we lost a good mail, too, on the *Persia [S.S.* Persia, *which was torpedoed and sunk in December 1915].* I am enclosing a few photos that might be of interest to you. I have some more snaps coming later on and will let you have some if they turn out to be any good...

Yours sincerely,
H.W. Cronin

F.G. Woodhams, 16th February 1916, France.

[These are typed extracts of a letter that Freddy had written to his family.]
The last time I wrote I think I told you we had lost our comfortable job on railheads. We have been shifted from General Headquarters and are at the most godforsaken hole there can possibly be in France. We had a rotten journey raining all the time. Reveille was at 4am and we eventually left the station about 10am. The accommodation consisted of the old cattle trucks, and rations of bully and biscuits. It was a very cold and uncomfortable journey.

We arrived at our destination about 4.30pm and after standing in the rain for 2½ hours with full pack on, we set out on a ten mile march. It's the worst march I've ever done. The majority of us at the finish were absolutely knocked up and were only too glad to crawl into the billets before going to bed, which was about 12pm. They gave us a mug of tea (the first we had since six in the morning) and best of all a ration of rum.

The up to date soldier kit to carry about from place to place consists of 150 rounds of ammunition, inside the pack; overcoat, fur coat, two pairs socks, one pants, one shirt, ground sheet, iron rations*. Outside pack; Mackintosh and mess tin, in haversack; cleaning kit, hold all, 24lbs rations, soap and towel, and on top of that extras such as handkerchiefs, plate, mug, tobacco, etc, two smoke helmets* in a satchel slung over the shoulder, a respirator in the left flap of a tunic and field dressing on the right, and of course the rifle, in all it's no light weight on a long march, it takes all one's strength and staying power to keep going.

We are billeted in a barn and have a sea of mud to get through. We have no boards, so sleep on the ground, fires are not allowed in the billet and at night time it's devilish cold.

In the village there is a little general shop (now nearly sold out), one pub where they sell something they charge 2½ d for and call beer, there are no shops of any description and of course no amusements.

Rations are not so good now (today's dinner, Sunday, bully beef, stew and two potatoes between 35 men. We have a loaf and a bit (small loaf) and two tins of jam between seven men, the short bread issue being augmented by the world famous army biscuits.

Our captain is a perfect gentleman and about the most popular man in the regiment, the junior captain (an absolute sport) and the platoon officers are all very decent sort of fellows. We appear to be much better off in this respect than before, and certainly think that D. Co. has got as good a selection of officers as any other company in the battalion. One of our fellows ran across a number of Audit R.E.s and they enquired after Maggs and myself.

Freddy or
what's left of him after
some very stiff marching.

A.H. Lambert, 20th January 1916, France.

Dear Mr Welsh,

I hope these few lines will find you quite well. Pleased to say I am
keeping quite fit in spite of active service conditions. My departure from
Farnborough was so hurried that I had no time to get either home or to
the office, but perhaps it's as well, as this is certainly more interesting
out here than staying in England all the time... We motored to a billet
(farmhouse) where I spent ten days sleeping in the hayloft with such
huge rats scampering about. We washed in the duck pond before it was
light; we turned out at 6am, and finished about 5pm, with plenty of real
hard work.

Things are much better now that we have arrived at headquarters
and on clerical work now... I am already looking forward to a few days
leave possibly at the end of six months or so.

I am sure you will excuse the apparent abruptness of this letter Mr
Welsh, but our description is of course very much limited...Mr Webb
will look after my life assurance if you will kindly let him know when and
how to pay in the premium. We look out for news of home so eagerly out
here and should be so glad to receive a letter from you when convenient
to write...

Yours sincerely,
A.H. Lambert

A. Smith, 25th January 1916, France.

Dear Sir,

Although there is very little to say, I think that it is about time I wrote to
the office again...

We got here at the end of November. We are nearer the firing
line here. This is a small village and not at all attractive. Still, we have
brought our same old truck with us which is quite a comfortable abode

and we are very used to it. There is an Expeditionary Force canteen here
where we can get all necessary things and a Y.M.C.A. has just
been opened. In the latter place there is a piano which is an attraction to
the troops...

I hear about half a dozen from the Audit are out here on this job. I
have managed to ascertain where they are but have not been fortunate
enough to meet any of them yet...

We spent a good Xmas under the circumstances and made a
point of having a good dinner on Xmas day, including chicken and
champagne in our menu. And this, in spite of the Premier's exhortations
in favour of economy. However, it doesn't happen every day. With
kindest regards and best wishes to all for 1916.

I am, yours very faithfully,
A. Smith

S.B. Hodges, 'Saturday 1916', France.

Don't put this in the book as I have not time to write properly.
Dear Hunt,

...We have been under canvas and been going out with the R.E. field
works party, cannot say how long it is going to last, as we are expecting
to be sent away every day. All the other fellows are back from the
trenches and they bring plenty of livestock [lice] with them, in fact we
are just as bad now, but after a time you take no notice of that... I must
say it's a jolly fine life and all the fellows seem a jolly lot and to hear
them talk of things that happen at the front, well, you would think they
had come back from a football match. Must now conclude in haste.

Yours sincerely,
S.B. Hodges

M.A. Russell, 21st January 1916, France.

Mostly private
My Dear Bertie,

Pleased to receive your welcome letter giving detailed account of proceedings at the office. Since writing you last, I have moved; it came rather suddenly one evening after tea we went on parade at 6pm and would have knocked off at 9.30pm, but instead of commencing work I and Nick, and also Kirk together with a few others were told off for marching orders and parade at 7.30 and proceed that night to G.H.Q.

We had been hard at it from 7.30am and to go at once was short notice, anyway I was pleased to get a move on, I can assure I had already had enough of what I was doing. To revert to my story, we journeyed that night and detrained at a quaint old town some distance inland early next morning; town I think is hardly correct, it would be called a city.

Here we anticipated seeing the sights because we were to stay all day and go on in the evening. There are some beautiful things to see so I am told and we were anxious to do the place properly. The day however was spent in the boatyard not allowed out; great was my disappointment. I sent you a postcard, I do know whether you got it so you will know of what I am writing.

In the evening we were pleased to get a move on, we entrained for G.H.Q. reaching our destination about 11.30 next day. This town is quite a pleasant old fashioned place, we spent the afternoon and evening in it and quite enjoyed ourselves. I am in an office now somewhat like a Divisional Support Office, and I consider myself very lucky, and I hope I stay. Four of us arrived here, the three others went outdoors and I remained in.

Upon my entering the office first time he recognised me, and as one of the four had to stay in the office I believe he worked the oracle after my interview with staff sergeant.

There are only three chaps; the staff, the corporal, the sapper (that's me). I fight with the typewriters mostly.

Anyway I consider myself very lucky in getting in here, I do not know how long I stay, but I hope for duration, but nothing is sure in the army. We have a very comfortable billet and the food is excellent. This place is a fair sized mansion and fairly comfortable. The officers are gentlemen and treat you very well.

Our office hours are from about 9am until 10pm. You have time off during the day or the evening, sometimes a motor spin is thrown in to brighten things up.

This town has figured a good deal in the news of war and the result of shell fire can be seen all around. You are well within the sound and roar of the guns…I am working in the office of the A.D.R.T.* and get our letters pretty quickly…

Have you heard from Peacock lately? When you write, please let me know, of course I do not expect you to write for some time knowing what a busy man you are and to what an extent your correspondence has grown…

It is rather remarkable that I should serve under Corporal Walford, I knew him some eight years ago but of late years have not run up against him because I believe he moved away from Ealing. I am sending this via home so it will be posted in Ealing, thus saving a green envelope. With kind regards,

I remain, yours very sincerely
M.A. Russell

P.S. I promised you some photo postcards. A recent order prohibits them so I must save them up for you.

J.G. Symons, undated, in hospital in Taplow, England.

Bert, received pass all right... I hope you are keeping A1. My foot is going in grand and hope to be quite well in a weeks' time. Yours, Jack

Symons used this postcard to send a note to the Audit office.

R.C.S. Frost, 2nd February 1916, rest billets in France.

Dear Standew,

Just a few lines to thank you for sending out the magazines so regularly. I can assure you they are of great interest to me (this is not an unsolicited testimonial for the editor!) since being in France, as it helps to keep one in touch with 'the line', which of course was not necessary before!

We need plenty of exercise to keep warm, as the billet is well ventilated and no hot water pipes are fitted yet! We dare not try experiments with such things as braziers on account of the keen eye and tongue of the 'old wife' (the owner of the barn) who during our occupation is very watchful over her 'valuable' property. The Government should really only pay for hiring the place during the

Private F.E. Secrett R.A.M.C.
sent a letter from his base in
Blackpool, along with this
photograph: 'Am enclosing a
photo of myself. It is, I have
been told, not a good one,
but there it is.'
29th April 1917.

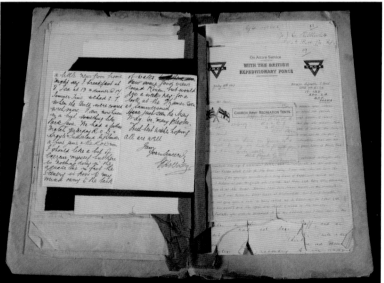

One of the Audit office newsletters, which were put together
by GWR staff in Paddington.

A postcard sent by A.E. Morris to the Audit office.

Postcard titled Limonade Seller sent by Private H.G. Langford with the Berkshire Yeomanry, 12th May 1915, Cairo. On the other side was his message to the Audit office.

Two photographs of J.G. Symons sent from Belhus Park Camp, England, 30th June 1915. Of the photographs he wrote: 'You will see by it how they like to get at the innocents, anyway it's all in the fun of camp life during spare time.'

Symons recovering from trench foot. The caption read: 'Sergeant J.G. Symons with the King's Royal Regiment (with crutches). Taken at the Duchess of Connaught's Red Cross Hospital, Taplow.'

Field card from J.G. Symons, 27th September 1915. The Audit office had added the note 'Since the last big fight.'

This photograph was sent from F.T. Turner, 13th July, 1916 to Mr Porter who enlisted later. Turner was training with the Royal Flying Corps in Winchester.
The photograph shows his hut named L20, which soldiers nicknamed Hell 20.

Photograph sent by Private Giles from Churn Camp, Oxford, England, 17th May 1915, along with a promise to write to the Audit office.

Photograph of R.C.S. Frost. The caption read: Private Frost, Argyll and Sutherland Highlanders now serving in Flanders, October 1915 Audit newsletter.

Signed photograph of George Shipley, 10th Middlesex Regiment. Shipley had written on the back: 'Sat 17.7.15. Off at midnight to the Mediterranean. Raining like cats and dogs. Kind regards to all. George.'

One of the huts. On the reverse of this post card the following note was written: 'This is one of the huts we were in down at Warminster when I was with the 2nd Batt, the huts here at Winchester are much better.'

Postcard from S. Hodges to Mr Hunt, 30th December 1915, Longmoor Camp England, describing his Christmas at camp.

Wishing you a Happy Christmas
and may we all meet in the
New Year.

Christmas, 1915.

*Reverse of a regimental Christmas card for 1st Queen's Westminster Rifles
sent by E.W. Jackson to Mr Hunt, December 1915.*

*Regimental Christmas postcard sent from W.J.E. Martin to the office,
21st December 1915, France.*

Photograph of F.J. Serjent on the right, with unnamed soldier on the left. The reverse of the photograph read: F.J. Serjent, 67 Delafield Road, Charlton.

Photograph of W.P. Mansbridge (Royal Flying Corps) sent to Mr G. Burgoyne.
This appeared in the Audit newsletter for May 1916.

A signed photograph of Gilbert Williams, 1/6th Seaforth Highlanders 'now serving in Flanders' according to the Audit office.

Photograph of George Kemball, Passengers Department, 1/6 Seaforth Highlanders included in the newsletter for August 1916. On the reverse Kemball had signed and dated the photograph 'Saturday July 3rd, 1915.'

The caption read: 'Captain Cronin, 5th Bedfords, taken on the steps of the Officer's mess, 15.1.16)'. *This caption was provided by the Audit office for the March 1916 newsletter and the reverse was signed by H.W. Cronin.*

Soldiers from the Royal Flying Corps which included 'Cpl. Morris (Agreements Department), Top Row, 5th from the Left and G. Paice (Coal Department, Top Row, 2nd from Right)'. On the reverse of the photograph, Paice had written '25.3.1917, kindest regards, Gerry Paice.'

Photograph of Sergeant H. Beaumont. On the reverse was written:
'May 1915, Kuldana, India.'

Photograph of Corporal W.C. Davis, Royal Army Medical Corps.
His surname had been spelt incorrectly in the Audit office caption.

Card with cartoon from W.C. Davis entitled A few days' rest in billets, January
1917. *The card was sent to Mr E.H. Serjent in the Passengers department.*

Photograph of M.A. Russell, Royal Engineers Railway Troop,
January 1916 Audit newsletter.

Photograph of F.H. Ferdinand, Railway Transport Section,
from the August 1915 edition of the newsletter.

Alfred. E. Evans, Officer in charge of the St John's Ambulance Brigade, no. 37 GWR London Division, included in the March 1917 newsletter.

J.R.H. Higgs, Royal Engineers Railway Troop which appeared in the November 1916 edition of the newsletter.

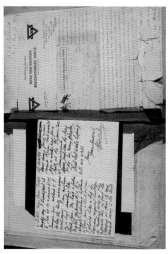

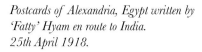

Postcards of Alexandria, Egypt written by
'Fatty' Hyam en route to India.
25th April 1918.

daytime, as the rats have supreme control at night and don't forget to let us know they object to our intrusion.

Although this life tends to harden our hearts against cruel scenes, we were disgusted the other morning to see the 'old wife' slowly putting a rat to death by putting hot water on it in a trap, a drop at a time! I fancy she imagined the Kaiser was in her hands in place of the other specimen of vermin.

There are a good number of French soldiers working on the roads here, men who are past fighting, and similar to the men in our labour battalions...

Well it is tea time now, so I must bring this to a close...

Sincerely yours
S. Frost

J.R.H. Higgs, 4th February 1916, Longmoor Camp, England.

My Dear Taffy,

As you will observe I have arrived at this most beautiful spot and am now 'some' soldier. I'll endeavour to give you a rough account of my experiences since Wednesday last...

I was eventually taken over to the doctor for the wretched medical exam. I was shown into a beastly cold and dark room and told to strip and then go into the next room where the doctor was, however I did not relish walking about in my birthday costume along corridors and left my socks pants and trousers in and walked in. He looked a bit surprised and told me to back and take 'em off and put on a dressing gown which I should find hanging up behind the door, also a pair of felt slippers which I found on the table. No doubt scores of fellows had worn the gown, still I had to put up with that. In I walked again and after going over me thoroughly he pronounced me very fit indeed...

After this I was told to get back and dress and proceed to the jolly old Sergeant again and get my papers sealed, signed and delivered. Wednesday morning we caught the 11.05 to Bordon and then a train to Longmoor camp where we arrived at about 2.30 and a more bleak spot I should imagine it would be difficult to find... We were told to report again at 9pm for the purpose of receiving four blankets and a straw mattress, and pillow. We did so and were sent off to Hut 33. It was some hut too. One of the new ones and a rotten one at that. Nasty cold place and no fire for the night. However Watton and I contrived to keep warm by placing both beds together and making one. Not a very great success though, for we felt very cold about 4am. I might tell you lights were switched off at ten but having a rather lively crowd we did not get to sleep until about 11.30- telling jokes etc, much to the annoyance of one or two 'sobersides'. We understood we had to parade at 7.15 for physical drill but nothing came of it and after breakfast (which we all tucked into pretty well), paraded at the Quarter Master's stores to receive gear etc...

Yesterday evening we were placed with a corporal in charge of the hut and of course things quietened down much that night...

Regards to all

J.R.H.H.

E.W. Jackson, 5th February 1916, France.

Dear Taylor,

Many thanks for your letter of 19th, also for magazine received this morning. I have read all your office news with much interest, and am always ready for more. Things don't seem very bright anywhere, do they? What a scandal it is that nothing can be done to stop these Zeppelins wandering where they like over England. I have no news to write. We have been in the same place since June, and the winter is the quiet time... I am grateful to be able to say I am still quite fit. I had a letter from Symons at Cleveden last week, saying he had to have an operation, he did not stick it out here long, did he? Well it is all a matter of luck.

Are not stocks and shares rotten? With that and the price of living so enormous, the poor middle class is almost finished, I fear.

Still they struggle on though. I quite agree with your remark about the Irish and the compulsion bill. Still I don't think they will ever really get home rule, do you? 'Wait and see' however is better than prophecy...

Well goodbye, hoping to see you all before very long.

I remain, yours sincerely, E.W. Jackson

F.R. Morris, 13th Feb 1916, France.

Dear Mr Taylor,

No doubt you have thought I have forgotten you and the old section I used to be so familiar with, but it is not so, and that thought can now be dismissed to use an army term.

I myself am pleased to say am quite well and keeping very fit, and I also have a fancy I am filling out somewhat, which reminds of a song, 'they will never believe me when they see me', which we sing when we are doing certain work here. Anyhow my enclosed photo is the best the camera man here can do for me, and I hope you will like it. I hope the other boys from our section are doing well, and keeping fit...

Well, we will now start right from the very time I left the office (some leaving do that). Joined up at Farnborough December 29th and arrived in France on January 3rd. Then I was moved about in cattle trucks, carriages etc. for about four whole days, and finally settled down where I am now. This place is not up to much, very dirty, and the stinks are terrible, but you get used to it in time.

The streets are made of big stones, and never washed down, and there are pumps down each street for the French public to draw their water from, of course it is not fit for drinking until boiled, and all the refuse from the houses seem to be put in the streets and left there, which does not improve the atmosphere.

The postman here before he goes to a house, blows a small horn, and dogs are used to pull milk carts round the streets, and some are very fine specimens of dogs, of course dogs are not taxed here only cats, and I have seen very few of them about up till the present.

Everything is very dear here, and an English-made article costs nearly four times as much as if bought in London.

When I first arrived here I was put on fatigue work for some time, and it did tell on me at first I can tell you, but I soon got used to it, of course clearing mud away and digging for bricks and then breaking them is hard work at first. Then I was posted as a stores clerk and am doing this work up till the present, I like it very much, it is very interesting.

We are staying at some French barracks here, they are old, I give you my word, they have no lights at all, and we have to provide our own candles for lighting purposes, (and they cost 1d each at present), and when I want to wash I have to run down four flights of stairs out into the open to an old pump and wash from under it, and sometimes the water is a bit nippy.

We get up at 6.30 in the morning, have breakfast at 7.15, and are on parade at 8 o'clock, we then work till 12 o'clock having had an interval at 10 o'clock of ten minutes. Dinner 12.15 and on parade at 1.30, then work till 5 o'clock, then tea and after that we are free till the roll call at 8.30pm and lights out at 9 o'clock, so you will quite understand that I don't get very much time for letter writing. For breakfast, we have bread and jam and tea, for dinner, stew one day, and roast the next, and bread and cheese. For tea, tea, bread and jam and sometimes we get a tin of butter of course the jam is in tins. We have these meals every day, and I don't think they are bad considering we are in the field.

We have our own sports club, and also own concert party (Perriots etc) of which I am secretary, we have some very good talent here, and I am sure that if you know anybody who has any spare songs or music and will send them to me, they will be greatly appreciated by the boys out here, who have to make their own amusements.

We are just forming a band to go with the concert party so you see we don't mean to be dull in our spare time…

Yours sincerely F.R. Morris

J.G. Symons, 28th February 1916, Canadian Red Cross hospital, Taplow, England.

Dear Bert,

I received your letter and am pleased you liked the tie. As regards leaving hospital, I'm afraid it will be quite another month. My foot has not healed up yet, but no doubt it will by next Wednesday… I have had three months now of hospital life and I shall be pleased to get out of it for a couple of days.

I am allowed up every day, but the last three days has been so cold that I do not budge out of bed till 11am and back again at 4.30pm, as my foot gets like a block of ice; these wards are very cold.

I don't know whether I get my discharge from the Army, as I hear they are keeping old crocks with one leg, one eye etc, but I'm not anxious to soldier anymore in England, it's all running parades and physical exercise and I have had my share of that…Give my kind regards to all.

Yours sincerely

Jack

SIX

MAY 1916

'Another year wasted at this awful game playing at moles and water rats.
Am fed up with it'
GILBERT WILLIAMS

Since the March edition of the office newsletter the total number of men who had joined up from the Paddington Audit office was one hundred and twenty five. At that point W.P Mansbridge had been wounded by a shell dropped from a taube whilst trench digging. Acting Sergeant Cowles was still in Malta keeping well but had 'no further news'. Sergeant Jack Symons, after five months treatment at Taplow hospital and later High Wycombe, had been discharged and granted leave.

Practically all of the letters sent to the office that were collated for the May 1916 newsletter came from W.P. Mansbridge, A.E. Kirk, Mark Russell, S.C. Douce, Nick Boyce, R.C.S. Frost or 'Frosty', W.C. Davis, Gilbert Williams, Jack Symons and M.P. Pond. These letters cover the period from January to April.

They explored the routine of training in England, the differences with office life at home and fighting abroad. Some men described their specific duties at the front and what it was like to be 'in a warm shop', like W.C. Davis of the Royal Army Medical Corps working at a casualty clearing hospital. A.E. Kirk modestly pointed out that

'of course I have none of the thrilling stories which a man of the fighting line can
tell but there is a good deal of everyone's experience who crosses on Active Service
which are interesting'.

Other writers like Gilbert Williams, expressed weariness with the war and an absolute desire for it to be over as seen by the quotation at the start of this chapter. Nick Boyce could not see an end to the conflict either and also wrote about the problem of censorship when he declared:

> 'I am afraid I am unable to tell you what I should like to in regard to the war as they are very strict in these parts so will not commit myself, but I cannot see the end in sight.'

All of the 'Audit fellows' retained a tremendous desire to keep in touch with Paddington. It must have been a welcome release as well as a chance to catch up on office gossip. Mark Russell also appreciated the increased volume of correspondence for men like Bertie Hunt who wrote back to those away

> 'I understand that your correspondence is very large nowadays, never mind you are doing your bit.'

This month, E.H. Brackenbury commented on Lord Derby's scheme for recruitment also known as the 'group system'.

> 'I suppose that since the Group System* was invented the office has presented a more deserted appearance than ever.'

This was a common topic of concern for other letter writers, including F.J. Serjent in the previous newsletter, who had pointed out that a great many of the younger men at Paddington had gone to register their names. But for E.W. Jackson it seemed that extending his service in the army was paramount; he wrote to Mr Hunt that

> 'I could have left the army yesterday and come home my time having expired, but I could not see myself in civil life these days, so I signed on again, like a fool, most people would say, but I could never let the regiment go anywhere without me.'

Sadly it was confirmed to those at home that J.C. Phillips of the London Regiment (Kensington) who had been reported missing in May 1915, had officially been reported by the War Office as having lost his life on 10th or 11th May 1915. Phillips had been in the same regiment as Sergeant E.C. Chamberlain who had died on the 9th May 1915.

S.C. Douce, January 1916, Fovant Camp, Wiltshire.

Dear Mr. Riches

The worst has happened. The W.O. has sent us down to this place which is miles from nowhere. The camp however is made up of hundreds of huts is according to the 'old uns' at the game the finest they have ever been in, certainly everything is alright but the place is so muddy and my time is split up. One half getting frightfully dirty and the other getting myself clean again. However it's all in the game and can't be helped. There are twenty to a hut. The beds are three long boards on two trestles about eight or nine inches off the floor, a straw mattress and a straw pillow, and four blankets. Not a bit what I have been used to. However I am now quite comfortable in it and sleep like a top. Marvellous how you think we settle down to it. Don't you think? We rise at 6.30am. Breakfast (porridge and bacon) at 7.30. Parade at 8.20. Drill till 10.30. Then half an hour's rest. Then more drill up to 12.30. Dinner at 1 o'clock (meat and two vegetables and sweets). Parade again at 2.20. Then more drill which brings us up to 4pm. We are then dismissed for the day. Tea at 5pm (bread, butter and jam). After which we can do what we like until 9.15. By this time we have to be in our huts for the final day's roll call and at 10pm. All lights have to be out. That's what my day consists of at present. It may not seem much, and really it isn't, but I am half the day cleaning up. The grub is alright but there is not quite enough of it at present. I think however this will be right as soon as they have made all necessary arrangements. For the time being the Non-Commissioned Officers seem to be a little overworked. This is the same every day, varied on two mornings a week with a long route march in the morning. Of course we only have half a day on Saturday and only a Church parade on Sunday. So altogether things are not so bad. The only thing is I can't get away for weekends, as it would take up most of the time to travel to London and back. I shall try however and run up to town in a few weeks' time if possible.

Kind regards to all... Yours, S.C.D.

M.A. Russell, 5th February 1916, France.

My Dear Mr Wood,

Just a line to let you know I am still A1. And that I am back again in office life. The office I am in is somewhat like the D.S.O. *[Divisional Superintendent's Office]* at home. It is the Assistant Director of Railway Transports Office'.

From England I was despatched to one of the large ports and worked on the M.F.O*. staff, here I met Nick Boyce and several others who preceded me. Lieut. Veltom is the officer in charge of the M.F.O there I also found Ferdinand and other G.W. fellows who came out early in 1915, including Brackenbury who is attached to depot office here.

The work was very heavy and I can assure you I was not sorry when on parade one evening was told that I had to report at Company Headquarters and proceed there that night with several more fellows, including Nick Boyce and Kirk.

The office in military life is somewhat different to civil but one can soon fall into line. The office in a chateau we should call it a mansion, somewhat dilapidated now on the outskirts of the town.

Here are both of the offices and billets, our sleeping accommodation being in the bedrooms upstairs. There are no beds of course, I curl up in my blanket and sleep in a corner and my office colleagues in the office in the other two corners. It is not a three cornered room, the door is in the other corner.

My colleagues at the office are a Staff Sergeant and a corporal, the latter is a G.W. fellow from the Chief's Goods Department, whom I had the pleasure of knowing prior to my coming out.

The office hours are from about 8.30 say to 10pm (22.00 hrs time a la France). I get a couple of hours off however, generally in the afternoon and have a walk round. It's not very pleasant in the evening to wander about this town I am in.

There are several amusements including pictures for the entertainment of the troops. Various divisions have concert parties, and the Municipal Theatre and a couple of halls are also taken for the purpose. On Sunday they are used for divine worship. Military bands also come and perform in the afternoon in the open if fine, in the evenings, in the theatre.

The town is a quaint place rather dirty mostly in all places. We are close up to the line a few kilometres away, and souvenirs come over occasionally.

I am parted again from those I came out with, Nick Boyce, Kirk, have gone to the northern railhead Area. I do not know where Hodges has gone, but I believe Joe Robertson is still at Longmoor, fed up with fatigues etc. John Higgs writes me to say he is also coming to join us, I suppose many more will have gone by now under the Derby Scheme...

A.E. Kirk, 9th February 1915, France

[This letter is presented with the May 1916 newsletter, however, its date suggests it could have been misfiled by the Audit office newsletter editor or else it was delayed in the post sent to England and was therefore circulated with the latest crop of letters for the May edition].

Dear Mr Wood,

I have now been out of England nearly two months and felt that you might be interested in hearing of my experiences. Of course I have none of the thrilling stories which a man of the fighting line can tell but there is a good deal of everyone's experience who crosses on active service which are interesting. I did not know when I saw you in December that I was so soon to come out and naturally as everybody's thoughts were on the approaching Christmas, and wondering what sort of time we should spend in Longmoor Camp, we almost wished we might have spent a few more days in England. However in war, it's all part of the game to take what comes and make the best of it. We started on our journey early Saturday morning and arrived in Boulogne at 9pm. There we were accommodated in Soldiers Rest Home, in the basement, the other part all being occupied and we made ourselves pretty comfortable for the night on tables. We were just a small party of ten, nine being G.W. men, Mr. Poebets the L. & N.W.R auditor being the odd man. Russell and myself were the only two of the Audit office party. We had all Sunday morning free and had a pleasant walk along the promenade looking across to Dover cliffs perhaps rather wistfully.

We left Boulogne at 1.30pm and except for a break of about four hours had a continuous train journey until 2.30 Monday afternoon, the second part being in a covered truck together with about twenty men on leave or travelling for various reasons to the base. Your first impressions on being so entertained are not perhaps the happiest, but as the hours pass you get more accustomed to the business and begin to feed, and so make the experience as much a picnic as you can. Bully beef, which perhaps is not nearly as bad as you imagine, bread and jam are your principal items on the menu, sometimes biscuits instead of bread.

As you know, I eventually reached Havre and became one of a crowd engaged on the enormous stacks of Christmas gifts which were still arriving in boatloads daily for the troops. Here I met Sapper Ferdinand, who I believe has since been home on leave, and he had spent all his time there since coming out. I am glad that my stay there was short, although naturally there are social advantages in being in a large city.

I shall always remember how I spent Christmas day 1915. We worked until 12.30, by which time the largest hut, the one I slept in, was made ready for the feast. Everything was very nice and was a great surprise to us, as the feeding arrangements normally were not of the best. We turned out in the afternoon for our first promenade and had an excellent walk along the sea front. Nearly all the city folk were out promenading too.

Before the end of the first week in January a number of us, (the party of ten which I came out with and about four others) including Boyce this time, started on another long journey. We had an enforced halt for a whole day at one place, but had no freedom to leave the railway premises, so couldn't see the place which was an interesting one. Our next halt was at G.H.Q. where we spent one night and from here we were distributed in small parties into the various areas and again parted further on. Boyce is my nearest friend, being only two stations from me. I went on that much further than him to a village station quite close to the Belgian frontier, now an important railhead. Here my work is much more closely connected with the war than that on which I was engaged at the base. There are roughly two branches of the work, R.T.E. and M.F.E, the former being in connection with the transportation of men, materials, supplies etc, while the latter corresponds very much to the parcels department of a railway at home. With my companions I was lent to the latter section at the base but am now working in the former section at this railhead, my address being C/O R.T.O, R 24. I work in an office on the station under a corporal with an officer in charge of the railhead. The corporal and I are billeted together quite close by. One of us has to turn up at the station about 6.30 in the morning for about ¼ of an hour, but work starts properly as at home at 9 o'clock. Naturally, on such work you cannot normally count on being finished at regular hours, but normally we get tea about 5.15 after which we return to the office for about half an hour before 7pm. to clear up any odds and ends, when we are usually finished.

The work is fairly interesting and I find the time passes very quickly. Of course every day is a work day, there are no weekends and you sometimes nearly forget which end of the week you are. I am sufficiently near up to the line to hear the bombardment pretty plainly and from a hill close by, the towers, (or what remains of them) may be seen on a clear day.

We are often able to witness 'scraps' in the air or to see a machine of either side being driven off by anti-aircraft guns. Such then is a little account of my experiences. As I said nothing very exciting but of course all very novel and of more than passing interest, so far as I am concerned. I am pleased to say I continue to enjoy splendid health and in these parts we are well fed. I should have mentioned that on the voyage out after having got right to the entrance of Boulogne harbour, the steering gear of the vessel broke down and we simply had to drift about until a repair could be effected, which fortunately was done in about half an hour. I get the G.W. Magazine sent out from home, so keep in touch with what is going on.

I trust you are in good health with kind remembrance to all friends at Paddington.

I am yours respectfully,
Archibald E. Kirk.

M.A. Russell, 4th February 1916, France.

My Dear Bertie

… I am pleased to say I am still in the same job and getting to understand the run of things. It is very interesting work, as you would imagine. It is a real line here, sometimes we are pushed and carry on till the early hours of the morning. I might say there is no grumbling about tea money, overtime or bonus quotas putting in as much as eighteen hours a day sometimes and it would not do to send deputations to the chief who is also hard at it, in his room; there is a special way of dealing with such in the army.

Of course one never knows how long this may last I may have marching orders to proceed elsewhere any day. Each day is absolutely a day unto itself here. We don't count tomorrow.

I see you have been visited with a blizzard, we also have had a severe touch of winter and at the present moment it is snowing hard outside. The shutters are closed and the work is being carried on by lamplight, this is necessary owing to the glass having recently left the windows in small fragments some souvenirs [shells] having called upon us. When the weather is fine we are fresh air fiends now both day and night except that we close the shutters when snowing or raining. The latter it is often doing.

There are hosts of interesting things I could write you about but these will do later on when I have the pleasure of seeing you. Lieut. Dunton's crowd was hereabouts, but I did not run up against him.

I suppose the Derby* entries have commenced to run now. I met another G.W. fellow the other day, Sergeant Gregory, a Slough fellow. I think George Jones would know him. I have seen this fellow at Paddington but did not know him to speak to.

I had a letter from Longmoor Camp. Must correct information. J. Higgs is in the Railway Transport Engineers with another friend of mine, Watton of Windsor who was in the Finance office...

F.R. Morris, 10th March 1916, France.

Postcard showing barracks

On the reverse of this photograph sent as a postcard Morris wrote:

Dear Mr Taylor

On the other side of this P.C. is a view of the Barracks where I am now stationed. X indicates the door I go in and O where my room is. Glad to say I am well and hope you are. Kind regards to all

Yours sincerely
F.R. Morris

W.C. Davis, 15th March 1916, France.

Dear Charlie *[Serjent]*

How are things going with you now? I expect like the rest of us will be glad when the better weather sets in for there is no doubt about it, it has been rough lately.

Since I last wrote to you we have shifted to another part of the line and it is a warm shop, for both sides must have all guns they can find and it is nothing but one long duel all day and every day but thank goodness it gives over a bit a night so that one can get on with their work. You see of a night the flashes of the guns can be seen so plainly that is why they do not fire a lot then.

Just on our right our people retook some trenches we had lost, oh what a rough time the poor devils had, snow and mud as much as you like and they had to lay in it for two days and grub could not be got to them. I expect there have been a few more from Paddington called up by now, it seems if the authorities mean to have all the men they want and if they can't get them one way they will another, and it certainly looks as if they will be wanted for out here. One cannot see any signs of an early settlement. I see by the papers that the air raids have been busy in England again. I suppose you have not seen anything of them yet, has Rory Moore had any more frights? We have the taubes over our hospital nearly every day or night and I can tell you we got some starts at times. The nearest we have to them since I have been here is just one yard from the main door, at 12.30 it blew in two pairs of double doors and shattered on end of the building to bits but not a great deal of damage to life which after all is the main thing. The arrangements we in work is five or six days up the line and four or five down if you are lucky. Of course at times these arrangements go to pot when there is an attack and we get a warm time and I should like to enlarge on these things but of course you understand I cannot.

Give my kind regards to all and trusting you are well.

Yours Will

A. Smith, 16th March 1916, France.

Dear Sir (Mr Slater)

Thank you very much for your letter of 2nd February, which I was glad to receive. The Stats has twinddled (sic) down! I have not heard of Higgs this side yet so I suppose he is still at Longmoor.

I was very pleased to hear of Stewart again for I had not heard of him since he was here last summer. He told me that he intended getting married when next he went on leave. You have had quite a number of marriages lately. Did Chichester call on you as expected? Is he well?

Since my last letter to you I have moved back to an old spot. Have got three assistants with me here. We no longer live in a railway truck but we are in billets. We are not all billeted together– another fellow and I are together. We have a good place and we have all our meals at the billet, of course, we bring our own rations and Madame prepares the meals. We make our beds on the front room floor. On the whole we are very comfortable. Our food is splendid. We have a wooden hut to work in at the railhead.

Last week we had heavy snow storms, but the last two or three days have been quite like summer. I hope that this better weather will continue.

In this town we have two cinemas, a recreation room and a canteen so we are fairly well off. It is quite a decent place.

I am glad to say that I am getting on nicely and am quite well...

A. Smith...

W.P. Mansbridge, 17th March 1916, France.

Dear Gerald,

No doubt, perhaps you had thought I had forgotten old friends at
Paddington, but such is not the case. We do not have much spare time
for letter writing now. To tell you of all our adventures since we left
England would take too long here to relate but I will save for when I
come home. Perhaps you have heard, we were only at Farnborough four
days, before we were sent over there. By God, old chap we did have a
time of it, the first fortnight. Living on bully beef and biscuits, travelling
day and night and sleeping anywhere and doing long tramps with full
kit on nearly done us in as we had no training. We managed to stick it
through, but I thought poor Percy Smith would have to give in as he was
very queer with toothache. The first six weeks we moved about from
place to place doing all sorts of fatigue work, bar our own. Lambert,
Smith, Collins and myself are now settled down in H— the place where
Mr Laker's son was so long at. Collins and Lambert have been fortunate
enough to get temporary clerical work during the last months.

I was promised one when on the 17th of last month I was wounded
by a bomb from a taube which landed clean through our billet at 12
o'clock at night, when we were all sound asleep. I caught it in the thigh,
but luckily it was only a flesh wound, but I had some awful bruises
from the debris which fell on it. I have been in hospital ever since at
the base, but I am pleased to say I am now nearly well again and in a
convalescent camp three miles from there, overlooking the sea. We are
not allowed to put our address at the heading of a letter ... After I am
discharged from here, I shall be sent up to the base and then up the line
with the 'best of luck' as the Tommies say out here. I am hoping to get
back to H— as I was so happy and with such decent fellows there, but
I don't think it probable. Lambert, Smith and myself, often used to talk
of old times and wondered how things were at Paddington. I daresay
Gerald, there are not many young fellows left in the Audit are there, has
Mr Horsley gone? Do drop me a line when you have time, as I assure

you old boy, it is a real treat to hear Paddington news. I have never felt in better health, army life certainly agrees with me also with Lambert. Billy Button is at headquarters, got a cushy job. I believe I saw him once there, but I have no idea where the other G.W. fellows are. I am afraid I am not very fluent with my French yet, I could have done with your services on several occasions. How are Mr Slater and other members of the Stats. (or is that department disbanded?) Please remember kindly to them. *[Lines censored.]*

Cannot stop to write more now as I am just off to a concert in the Y.M.C.A. hut in the camp here. *[Lines censored]*

Yours very sincerely

Dick Mansbridge

P.S. I am only about 12 miles from where you used to go to, so perhaps you can guess the place I am at, E- - - - - s. *[Etaples].* Do you ever hear anything of the other boys out here?

R.C.S. Frost, 24th March 1916, France.

Dear Mr Hunt.

I was very pleased to hear again from you, and to know the latest regarding the doings of old friends at the office. I am sorry to hear Mr Taylor is not up to the mark, and hope his complaint is not serious, and he will soon be well again.

Fancy Fatty Hyam a married man!! He seems to be doing well out of the war doesn't he?

I have never seen any of the other men you mentioned out here. Hull and Williams I met several times last month when we were all staying in the same town resting, and they were both well. As you remark I have been a bit of a tourist just lately, with lunch included you know! After our rest was over (from end of December to end of February) we marched to another part of the line, and relieved some French troops. They were rather stiff marches, as of course we carried our winter kit, although blankets and waterproof sheets were taken in motors and the last day we were tramping from 11am until 7.30pm with an hour's stop for dinner.

We have been in action since last Saturday week, and so are getting used to the old life again! We miss the hills, woods and water, that were so common at the other part of the front as it is quite flat here consequently the difficulties are greater for getting food, and water, on account of the great length of communication trenches. During the day time the Germans can see such a long way, from their observation balloons, that it is dangerous to be seen in the open nearer than about two miles from the firing line.

Our rations are brought up at night and we cook our bacon (if any) and make tea over coke fires in the trench. Of course everyone lives underground, and I and three other signallers have a small dugout. It is just a small cave in the chalk and several steps leading down to it. There is room for three in the hole and the other one sits on the stairs! Any visitors who call have to sit on the stairs too, and I expect you will say it is best to leave your card!! It is passable when the weather is dry but on wet days the mud gets on the steps, and your kilt mops it up again, and it's about the limit when you have to sit on the stairs! However we manage to jog along and have very little to do, since we are in support this week. Last week we were in the firing line, and had a splendid dug out, sharing it with the company officers. It was handy for the Captain, as when he wanted to speak on the phone he only had to put his hand out of bed to get the receiver. This is a great place for bombers, as the exchange of bombs takes place about three times a day. One of our saps runs very close to a mine crater occupied by the Huns, and both sides try to catch the other napping and raid each other's trenches.

I notice in the papers there is a pretty general feeling that the end is drawing near, and H. Bottomley *[Horatio Bottomley, ex Liberal Party M.P and founder and editor of* John Bull magazine*]* says we are on the last lap, which I hope won't be a long one. I haven't been home yet but hope to get away very soon…

'Frosty'

J.G. Symons, 25th March 1916, High Wycombe, England.

Dear Bert (Hunt)

Things are lively compared here with Taplow. Invitations were sent last week for two concerts and a cinema. We also had a whist drive and the Buckinghamshire Territorial Band in the hospital. This afternoon we were taken in taxis to see a football match. The favourite team made a very poor show, so we are thinking of issuing a challenge to play them. We are having another whist drive Monday evening, invitations out to concerts on Tuesday, Wednesday. I am getting about without crutches now and was able to take part in three games of golf yesterday. I hope to be able to manage a few hour's leave at the end of the week. I hear that our Battalion has had another smash round Ypres district. If ever I am returned to them I'm afraid I shall see all new faces, for they have lost pretty heavy since I left four months ago...

Yours sincerely,
Jack Symons

E.H. Brackenbury, 16th March 1916, France.

Dear Mr Biggs,

Just a few lines to let you know that I am still in the land of the living. I was sorry that I was not able to see you when I was home on leave in January, but since it was my first since enlisting you may imagine I had plenty to do in the few days. And it was not possible for me to make a second call at the office. As a matter of fact I completed something just under 500 miles in the five days.

Messrs Boyce, Bright, Russell and co. whom I met here a week or two before Christmas had departed when I returned from leave and I believe have been distributed up in the railhead area, but perhaps you know more about them than I do.

As regards news generally I dare say you are as well posted up if not better than we are. Sapper F.H. Ferdinand was promoted to 2nd Corporal a few weeks ago.

We have an A.S.C. Railway Labour Section attached to us at present. And 2nd Lieut. Edwards who is in charge of it comes I believe from the General Manager's Office, Paddington. One of the men from the latter is now employed in our office and brings our staff including the officer up to seven...

There was a rumour came down here that Pond had been wounded by a bomb from an aeroplane and that he been sent home to England, but it afterwards turned out to be somebody else.

I suppose that since the Group System was invented the office has presented a more deserted appearance than ever. I understand that there are about a hundred and thirty now from the office altogether. J.F. Warren-King is a Lieutenant and R.T.O. at Etaples. I believe he comes from somewhere near your way. Have nothing else to mention at present...

E.H. Brackenbury

F.R. Morris, 1st April 1916, 'In the field'.

Dear Mr Taylor

Just a line to let you know I am quite well, and have now been in the army three months. Today I have been appointed 1st Class Air Mechanic at the rate of 4/- per day or 28/- a week, and this is the first step to promotion. Kindly remember me to all interested, and will write long letter later,

Yours truly,
F.R. Morris

E.W. Jackson, 1st April 1916, France.

Dear Hunt,

Many thanks for your long letter giving me all the news. Yes I shall be very glad of leave, as one never gets a day's rest in the Quarter Master's department, men having to eat every day, although they only fight occasionally. Still difficulties keep arising, and though I have asked to go on the 15th, I am by no means sure it will come off...

There is really little of interest a man may write without getting into trouble so we say very little, at least I know I do. Of course people joined since the war find something to write home about every time they see a horse or a gun or a motor ambulance, but the old hands take such things as part of the show and think nothing of them. I am sorry to hear of Warner's accident, which I had not heard of before.

[Censored lines]...

I have been out of the firing line for the last few weeks, but expect to be back again the end of April, but we might be rushed up any minute if there was anything by doing...

As you know I am acting Quarter Master and get an extra 1/- *[one shilling]* a day for that screw now 6/- *[six shillings]* a day and all found, not too bad, as there is no expense but drink and bridge of a night (no nothing doing as regards what you are thinking about). Still expect to spend a bit on leave when I get it. *[Censored lines]*

I could have left the army yesterday and come home my time having expired, but I could not see myself in civil life these days, so I signed on again, like a fool, most people would say, but I could never let the regiment go anywhere without me.

Well I must stop now, hoping to see you at the end of the month, if things go favourably. I remain yours sincerely,

E.W. Jackson

M.P. Pond, 5th April 1916, France.

Dear Mr Hunt,

I was very pleased to receive your letter for which many thanks. It took nearly a fortnight to reach me as I have changed about a good deal lately from one division to another and it has followed me around. I am pleased to say I am still keeping very fit and going on in about the same way. I think the last time I wrote we were living in trucks. Well we have now moved into huts about ten feet square, which are very comfortable although not quite as large as the trucks. They are well built and stand about a foot from the ground so keep very dry. We have two of them, one which we use as an office and the other to sleep and live in. We also have a tent which we use for keeping kits etc. in, but we shall probably sleep in it when the weather is a bit warmer.

We have had some lovely weather lately, quite like summer but rather cold at night. We had a great deal of snow last month also plenty of rain and wind, and were over the tops of our boots in mud. We are stationed at a very small village which stands very high (about 600 feet above sea level) you can guess it is a bit breezy at times. It is a one-eyed hole with only two cafes and no shops. We have all our meals cooked at one of the cafes, and we live very well although there is not very much variation in the menu. I have managed to have one or two musical evenings lately. The fiddle I bought appears to be a fairly good one but my fingers are not quite so nimble as they were. I am afraid I shall have to put in a month or two's practice before I get back to where I was before I came out here. Glad to hear you have taken it up again. We shall be able to get a band for our next 'lamb' dinner whenever that will be.

Things do not seem to make much of a move round this way. We get plenty of aeroplanes over and see a good many fights in the air. There have also been a good many shells dropped not very far away from us, but we have managed to dodge them so far although, one of our fellows, who comes from the Midland Railway and who I worked with for some time, has been wounded and sent to base. There is only one G.W. man anywhere near me as far as I know and that is Colcott from Chief Goods Manager's Office but he is some distance away and I hadn't seen much of him. I was surprised to hear that Morris had gone into the R.F.C.* after being rejected for the Infantry. I was also surprised and sorry to hear about Jack Symons. I had heard nothing about it. How did it happen? It must be very quiet at the office now with so many gone. *[Censored line]*. As you say it is quite a change from the old days. I have not yet come across any of those who joined the R.E. Transport lately. Did you know that Arthur Watton has joined?

We had a concert party belonging to one of the divisions stationed round here, staying in the village last week, and they gave us a show two nights running. They had a proper stage with scenery and footlights, everything complete. They were very good indeed. The programme consisted of songs, sentimental and otherwise, also a 'Sketch' and some Charlie Chaplin pictures which were very laughable as usual. Well, I don't think I can tell you much more at present. Please remember me to all at the office.

Yours sincerely,
M.P. Pond

G. Williams, 6th April 1916, France.

Dear Mr Hunt,

Thanks very much for your letter which I received a week or two ago, also for the magazine.

We are in the trenches just now. In fact we seem to spend about three times as much time in as we do out. Also we are in a pretty warm spot, it was about here, towards the end of last summer that the French and German had some of the fiercest fighting of the war. The country around about is a veritable maze of trenches. The fighting at one time was so fierce that there was only time just to bury the dead in the sides of the trenches, and now that the trenches have crumpled one is constantly seeing the bones of men's legs or their boots, or skulls sticking out from the sides of the trenches, pleasant, eh? There will be a pleasant smell here in the summer. I only hope we are not here then. In places we are only about twenty yards away from Fritz and company. Consequently all times the air is pretty thick with bombs, grenades and trench mortars. These last are pretty hellish sort of toys. They have an explosion like about ten earthquakes rolled into one. But even these are not the worst we have to put up with. The trenches being so close together there is of course any amount of mining going on. So one never knows when the particular lump of earth one is standing on is going to take a trip through the solar regions. When a mine does go up, there is some excitement knocking about I can tell you. Suppose for instance we were going to explode one, all the artillery in the neighbourhood is ranged on the spot and directly the mine is exploded, there is hell let loose on the crater. Of course as soon as he gets the range the enemy replies, so that the air is fairly full of everything that kills quickly. One can on these occasions always rely on a good many casualties. Since we have been in this spasm there have been five exploded in this neighbourhood, while others are expected to go up at any time. So much for conditions here.

How is everything in town? Pretty quiet I suppose. I see you've had the zepps *[Zeppelins]* over again? Is it a fact that one dropped in the Thames? *[Lines censored].* That is about all the news, so will close, kindest regards to everybody.

Yours very sincerely,
Gilbert Williams.

N. Boyce, 6th April 1916, France.

Dear George *[Jones]*

In case you might think that I am not in the land of the living. I am dropping you line. Until I had a letter from Mark *[Russell]* the other day I have had little news of the office, this probably due to my own fault in not letting my whereabouts known. However I am now somewhat settled down in a rather nice place with the Cavalry division– and consequently getting quite a good judge of horse flesh! We left the base early in January, and it was at that time that our merry little party got scattered all over the place after reporting to G.H.Q. Poor old Bright got left at Havre and is still there as I had a card from him recently. Mark went South and Kirk and myself North (near the Belgium area). Hodges, I fancy is here, but I know not where Robertson is but I trust they are all keeping well and cottoned on to their jobs all right. I have been very sorry for Bright as he is rather handicapped by his deafness, and as regards Kirk he was very fit when he paid me a visit on one occasion when I was stationed near him, in fact it was the next station. I also saw Jackson as he was passing through on the train one night and had a few minutes chat with him. He doesn't alter much with the exception perhaps of an addition of *avoirdupois [weight]*: he is looking forward to his next leave. A day or two after this I was shifted to this railhead miles away– involving the sleeping of another night in the train…

It's a very pretty place here and I should think in normal time quite a resort. I am assisting the R.T.O. and work with him all day in a truck. I sleep also in the truck and manage to make myself fairly comfortable despite the draughts. As the railhead comes under the R.T.O. you may imagine there is plenty to do for his 'one and only' clerk, and in addition to the transportation work I do such things as the pay books, billeting, clothing etc, so there is very little time to spare. I am generally up at 6.30 and tuck in about 11 and no Saturday afternoon or Sundays off! This by the way is not in the nature of a grumble– on the other hand it seems to make the time go quickly, and the R.T.O. is not at all a bad sort– a 'Liverpool' man by the way and a Territorial Captain.

Mark tells me that John Higgs is at Longmoor. I wonder what of the world he will be despatched to. Should so like to come across him out here, it's quite a treat to meet someone you know. Jackson also tells me that 'they are all joining the Flying Corps', is this so? Any news of 'Sonny'? I trust he is alright probably he has been home or else is on leave. My word, what a reunion!

Beyond that, things are moving somewhat rapidly out here I am afraid I am unable to tell what I should like to in regard to the war as they are very strict in these parts so will not commit myself, but I cannot see the end in sight yet. Possibly you at home know more of the general news than we do here, although sometimes I see the Telegraph only a day late. The French people here are very nice and quite above the average and the youngsters in particular are quite smart in picking up our 'lingo'. What about the taxation of railway fares? Of course this means a revision and consequently more work for you at home. No doubt will suit *[censored]* all right. I haven't had time to read the budget through but quite agree with the taxation of amusements especially cinemas. Then there's the income taxation but I shan't trouble about these things until I get back. I have been out here over four months so am qualifying for some leave gradually. My experiences here have been most varied and on that account I do not regret having come out here–at the same time Roll on the finish!

Kindly remember me to all in the office –I trust all are well– also the wife and George 'Junior' with kind regards…

Nick

J.G. Symons, 11th April 1916, High Wycombe, England.

Dear Bert,

Just a line to let you know I am getting on very well indeed. Last Sunday I went by motor to the Canadian Hospital, Taplow and there joined about another dozen cars and the lot went to Windsor. We had half hour to stroll about and then off to Burnham Beaches and had tea. Tea finished we continued the run back to Taplow and were allowed to visit the old wards. I only knew three in K1 ward, the others having been discharged or sent to other hospitals. We had a nonstop run from Taplow to High Wycombe arriving back at 7pm. It was a most enjoyable day.

I will know definitely Thursday whether I am being discharged next week as fit. I do not feel any pain except when I attempt to walk quick.

The party who does the massage told me last evening that she would report favourably, and it's on that report that the doctor will decide. If everything is satisfactory I would be discharged in Thursday week.

Went to a concert last night at the Town Hall, having a whist drive this evening and very likely another motor run tomorrow.

It was amusing last Sunday, when out in the motor and nearing Wycombe, we put on some decent cigars and sat well back and all at least fifty T.A's *[Territorial Army]* gave us the salute. Of course we were travelling at a very good pace and they did not recognise that we were an ordinary tommy attachment.

Well I must now conclude,

I remain, yours sincerely
Jack Symons

F.T. Turner, 12th April 1916, Warminster, England. [630,631]

Dear Jim *[Mr Porter]*

Just a few lines to let you know I have not gone yet but might be going in a month or two if we are lucky. Have just been on week-end leave (first leave since Xmas) and over stayed it, had to go before our Colonel and got off with four day's pay stopped. I managed to get in the final of our middleweight boxing competition and got 2nd prize. Have just been on a bombing course and had to throw live bombs. The weather is fair now, which makes army life grand. I suppose things are much the same in the Audit. Hoping to have a line from you when you have time...

M.A. Russell, 6th April 1916, France.

My dear Bertie *[Hunt]*

I have been so long in replying to your letter that possibly you may think I have forgotten you. No I have not forgotten, but keep putting it off from day to day.

Your last letter was so full of interesting news of the office that I forwarded it to Nick Boyce, I hope you don't mind. Nick has moved back and being somewhat lonely was greatly cheered by receiving it, at least so he told me in reply.

Well how are things going in the Audit, still making the most of it, no doubt you have had some changes now the Derby boys are getting into swing.

I have little to say, things go on very much the same daily, sometimes harder than others, but I turn up smiling every time as it is the only thing one can do under the circumstances. No not downhearted, oh no!

By the bye I must tell you that although we may be away from home we still have the amusements and entertainments for those who are off duty to go to. There are a couple of cinemas besides a concert party in the municipal theatre. This town possesses a very fine theatre belonging to the municipality and here Tommy's Concert Troop give performances nightly. We are also visited by military bands. Then there is boxing, some very good displays are given especially when Divisional Finals are competed for. As the boxing generally takes place in the afternoon, I pay it a visit. I have only been to about three entertainments as we are busy then in the evening.

Then we sometimes have a trip around the area with the colonel in the car, this is enjoyable, it takes the best part of the morning and we run up against several chums who came out with us...

When you write I understand that your correspondence is very large nowadays, never mind, you are doing your bit. I shall be glad to hear from Harold Watts and George Peacock, of the later especially. I wrote him by have not had a reply.

With kind regards, yours very sincerely,
Mark Russell

G. Williams, 25th April 1916, France.

Dear Mr Hunt,

Thanks awfully for the cigarettes. They were absolutely fine. Arrived just about in time for my birthday which was last Tuesday, the 18th. Another year wasted at this awful game playing at moles and water rats. Am fed up with it.

We are stuck knocking about in the same part of the line. We are going up into the firing line from the reserve today.

I should much prefer you to send out cigarettes as before, and not the money because we cannot always buy them when we want to. Also the cigarettes out here are out of Bond stuff and nothing like as good as those from home. There is really no news.

Kindest regards to everybody,

Yours very sincerely,
Gilbert Williams.
P. S. Saw Frosty the other day. He's looking well also heard from Jackson. Hope to hear from you soon.

Routine of a soldier's life told in a few well known hymns composed by members of Heather Tent, Scotland.

This was included in the newsletter for this month. It is not clear who sent it, but was probably typed out by the office. It provided a wonderful insight into the training schedule and possible thoughts surrounding it!

The Routine of a Soldiers Life told in a few well-known Hymns.

Composed by Members of Heather Tent, Scotland.

5.30 a.m. Reveille	Christians Awake.
6.45 a.m. House Parade.	Art thou weary, art thou languid.
7.0. a.m. Breakfast.	Meekly wait and murmur not.
8.15 a.m. Co's Parade.	When he cometh.
8.45 a.m. Manoeuvres.	Fight the good fight.
11.15 a.m. Swedish Drill.	Here we suffer grief and pain.
1.0. p.m. Dinner.	Come ye thankful people come.
2.15 p.m. Rifle Drill.	Go labour on.
3.15 p.m. Lecture by Officer.	Abide with me.
4.30 p.m. Dismiss.	Praise God from whom all blessings flow.
5.0. p.m. Tea.	What means this eager anxious throng.
6.0. p.m. Free for the night	Oh what will the Harvest be.
6.30 p.m. Out of bounds.	Oh Lord how happy shall we be.
10.0. p.m. Last Post.	All are safely gathered in.
10.15 p.m. Lights out.	Peace Perfect Peace.
10.30 p.m. Inspection of Guards.	Sleep on Beloved.

GOD SAVE THE KING.

SEVEN

AUGUST 1916

'I expect that by now only old stagers are left, to work side by side with nice young ladies'

FREDERICK RONALD MORRIS

Since October 1915 Franco-British forces had been based at Salonika (now called Thessalonika) in Greece to support the Serbs in their fight against Bulgaria. D.J. Robertson and F. Witt wrote from this fortified town where

> *we get a very fine view of Mount Olympus'* but *'at a place like this, one has to be content to stay until terms of 'Peace' are dictated.'*

By contrast, G.F.W. Halls, J.R.H. Higgs and F.R. Morris were situated in France and kept in touch with other GWR men. In their letters home to Paddington they shared their experiences from washing outside in the snow to descriptions of the countryside.

Also in France, A. Smith seemed to enjoy doing things in style as he had access to a marquee with a waiter for his corporal's mess. A.E. Kirk admitted that he was 'quite satisfied with France' and pleased to be his own master noting that

> *'It will certainly seem strange when I return to a life of so many hours regular work day by day, although if I may say so, with all respect, I enjoy my present freedom in being more or less my own 'boss'.*

Perhaps this comment shows that Kirk was anticipating some of the difficulties experienced by men when they returned to the work place after active service.

One innovation from the Paddington Audit office recorded in the GWR magazine for April 1916 had been the introduction of a French class to help workers who came in contact with the influx of French and Belgium refugees who were now using the railways. F. Witt from Salonika wrote

'I have not picked up the lingo yet, but French is chiefly spoken, and I much regret not having studied it more when I had the opportunity at home.'

Meanwhile back in Britain, F.T. Turner wrote about his training with the London Irish Regiment in Winchester. He enclosed a picture of his hut, L20, that the soldiers had nicknamed 'Hell 20'. At this time A.E. Rippington had another operation on his leg at Dinton near Salisbury but had to be discharged from the army and Jack Symons likewise returned to work in Paddington Audit office in August 1916. According to the newsletter notes G. Kemball contracted trench fever and was sent to hospital in France. Quite a few of those on leave had also found time to visit the office including Gilbert Williams, Nick Boyce and Stanley Frost.

Freddie Woodhams, the son of Mr S. Woodhams in the Agreements Department, achieved promotion to Sergeant with 1/13th (County of London) Battalion (Kensington). Quarter Master Sergeant E.W. Jackson was promoted to Quarter Master Lieutenant in July 1916 and also mentioned in dispatches for 'good work in connection with the transport'. Finally, by this stage conscription, that is compulsory military service, had been introduced in March 1916 for all single men aged between 18 and 41. As result the Audit office at saw an increase in the number of female workers, a concern voiced by many including F.R Morris in the opening quotation to this chapter.

G.F.W. Halls, 4th March 1916, France.

Dear Mr Davies,

I thought you would like a line from me to let you know how I am going on. I was rather surprised as you may suppose when on the day following our enlistment we were told that our destination was to be 'somewhere in France'. There are four other fellows from the Audit that came in my draft, Paice, Elmes, Morris (Muggins) and Wheeler and so far we have been fortunate enough to keep together. The other fellows Lambert and Button etc. were in different drafts. On the following Sunday we were off arriving in France the next day. We had it pretty rough going over and nearly everyone was more or less feeding the fishes, although I was lucky enough to escape it myself. We are at present stationed in barracks where we sleep on the floor with a groundsheet and two blankets. It felt a bit rough for the first two or three nights but you can soon get used to it and I think I could sleep practically anywhere now.

Our working hours are much the same as at the office, parading at 8.0am and leaving at 5pm with one and a half hours break for dinner. I find it a bit parky sometimes first thing in the morning and having a wash under a pump especially when there is snow on the ground, and I feel none the worse for it so suppose it not doing me any harm. We are not at loss for amusement so they have some very good concerts held in the town hall every Friday night and there is also the Y.M.C.A. that is always open for anyone to go in and write letters etc. These Y.M.C.A.s are a boon and a blessing for the fellows and here and I think the 3d subscriptions we used to have round the office sometimes for the upkeep of them is 3d well spent. There is also a very fine cathedral in the town that has not lost its traces of 1870 as it still has a large bullet embedded in it... I think this is all I have to say for the present, so will close. Wishing to be kindly remembered to Mr Welsh and all the General Staff.

I remain yours sincerely
G. Halls

D.J. Robertson, 21st April 1916, Salonika, Greece.

Dear Mr Wood,

Just a few lines to let you know I arrived safely after visiting several
places which I am not allowed to mention. This place is quite oriental
as the fronts of the houses are for the most part looked after and kept
in repair, while the backs are allowed to go, and it gives one a shock
to see a fine building in the front, and then to go to the back and see
it all neglected and ready to fall down. It is very hot here during the
day and the swarms of flies and mosquitoes keep one very busy and
I dread to think what it will be like in the summer. It seems strange
to see oxen drawing carts and donkeys with packs on, but it is a very
common sight here. I sometimes have to go to the big steamers in a
small pinnace *[ship's boat]* and when it is rough it requires some nerve
to walk along the sides of barges that are pitching and tossing and
then climb up the ship's side by a rope ladder, but it comes easier in
time. It is very mountainous here, and we get a very fine view of Mount
Olympus and the snow-capped peaks. I had to go by motor up country
the other day and I had to grip the side of the car as the roads are awful
and sometimes there is only just room for the car to travel and a sheer
drop on the other side. The labourers at the docks are Greeks and when
they are taken on in the mornings it is a regular Babel 'till the Military
Policeman uses his *persuader [truncheon]* right and left and that calms
them somewhat. I have not met Mr Cox's son yet but should I do so I
will make myself known to him. I have had to revert to sapper again as
there are not sufficient men of our staff for us to remain N.C.O.s but if
it is brought up to strength I am promised them again. The first person
I saw here was Gray of the Statistical Department, and we are working
together. Trusting that you are quite well and with kindest regards to
Messrs Cox, Slater, Rogers and Hunt.

Am yours obediently,
D.J. Robertson

F.R. Morris, 7th May 1916, France.

At last I have found time to write a few lines to you in the hope of finding
you well, of course one out here in this dead and alive hole does not
know how one's health is at our office of the Great Western Railway,
where I expect that by now, only old stagers are left to work side by side
with nice young ladies. Well, I am very pleased to say that I am very
fit and well, and that the country lanes and hedges here look a treat
now, and you don't have to go very far to pick cowslips, and the best of
wild flowers.

The land being very flat here enables one to see the country for
miles around, and for some time past the women of France have been
very busy sowing wheat, oats, etc., and now they can see the fruits of it,
for the crops have come up grand lately, owing to plenty of sunshine,
and one storm. The storm has done a lot of good, and washed the roads
down, everywhere was beginning to smell, my word the natives here
keep the insides of their house or huts clean, but as regards outside
the house, the pavement and road is simply a muck-heap, everything
is thrown into the road, and if it was not for the Tommies here cleaning
it up, the place would be alive. We are still at the barracks but expect
to be under canvas in a very short time near to our work, some of our
fellows did start making a field flat, but owing to some hundred and fifty
horses being buried there some months ago, the work was stopped.
Well I should very much like to tell you a lot of interesting news but
you of course know, I cannot. On the 3rd May, I was on guard alt-night
[alternating night duty], guard is about the only thing out here I don't
care for. I took the 1st guard, that is from 5 o' clock till 7.20pm and on
again at 12 o'clock midnight till 2.20am when I finished and tried to
have a quiet nap, but one can't sleep with belt, revolver and pouch
on, including boots etc., you keep these on for 36 hours all told. I saw
a paper out here: Middlesex Times saying Simmons had paid a visit
to Paddington, I am glad he is getting better, and do you know how
Mansbridge is now? Of course I knew where he was out here and all
about it, but have heard nothing lately from where he was. Paice of the

Goods and Audit is in the Orderly Room* here, so he keeps us G.W. fellows in touch with all the news, we are altogether in the barracks, and all in the same squad, and Elmes is working in the next section to mine. Of course I should like to come and see you, but am afraid that I shall not be on leave until next December, and perhaps not then. *[Line censored]*.

Must close now, kind regards to you and all of the Agreements, I remain, yours truly,

F.R. Morris

J.R. H. Higgs, 29th April 1916, Longmoor Camp, England.

Dear Taffy *[Mr Edwards]*

I intended dropping you a line many times but have always put it off. Think my motto must be 'never do today, what you can put off tomorrow'. Rather a bad one isn't it especially as now I'm in the office down here, but of course you know that by now. Am hoping before long now to be able to pay you a visit. I just moved on draft for the Wednesday. Cried off at the last moment as my pals were not included in the list. This was my very first chance since my arrival here, now nearly four months ago. Still, we are not having such a bad time now that the weather is good but we have had to put up with something especially during the first two months, it was simply atrocious.
Cheery oh!

Yours,
J.H.R. Higgs

J.G. Symons, 1st June 1916, Sheerness, England.

Bert, *[Mr Hunt]*

Many thanks for *Great Western Magazine* received this morning. I am still knocking about and every now and again doing a bit in the Company office. I put in two hours work a day, so you see I am busy at times. I must say I don't care for Sheerness, I would much prefer to be at Westcliffe. On a clear day we can see Southend from here. Every day N.C.O. men from the 7th Battalion are reporting, most of them quite fit again for the front. I should think the old 7th Battalion is wiped out. Two of the sergeants of my company out there are here, who left after me, and one is in hospital in Manchester. Leave is hard to get. Give my kind regards to all. Hoping to see you shortly,

Yours, Jack.

A. Smith, 13th June 1916, France.

Dear Sir, *[Mr Slater]*

I have arrived back from leave safely and am now quite settled down to work again. I had a very pleasant journey back. The railway journey this side is rather tedious but before I left London I met a Sergeant whom I knew so we stuck together all the way and the train journey was not so bad. We had plenty to eat and drink with us but about half way we stayed at a station where we could wash and get rations. Biscuits, bully, cheese and tea were given out. The train took just over twelve hours to get us here.

Since my return the Casualty Clearing Station, which is near us, has commenced a Corporal's Mess and they have been kind enough to invite two other corporals and me from the railhead to join them. The Mess is reserved to ourselves in a large marquee and we have a waiter. We actually sit down to meals at a table and it has a white tablecloth on too. We are doing things in style now.

Our weather has been rainy and rather miserable this last week. Will you kindly address letters to me at the 30th Division Railhead for the present.

With kindest regards to all, I remain, yours sincerely,
A. Smith

M.A. Russell, 6th June 1916, France.

My dear Bertie *[Hunt]*

Received your letter this morning. I tell you, I look forward to your budget of information and must thank you for so kindly writing to me.

So Nick called to see you with the report of the doings of the last R.T.E. crowd. I think he is the first to go on leave and very fortunate he is too, he explained how that arises.

He is not in the same area as I am. I am in the A.D.R.T. office and from the present arrangement I shall probably stand a chance in 1918 if we are still here, one of course never knows. Still smiling, oh yes.

There are one of two things I should be glad to know. Harold Watts is near me I believe, would you kindly pay my compliments to our friend Bateman and ask him when writing to Watty to let him know, also would you please let me have Watty's address. Also are Frosty and George Kemball near me? I am not aware of the numbers of the regiments or I should know, perhaps you would give me their addresses when next writing.

I had a visit from Lieut. Gregory of the Royal Field Artillery, a Paddington fellow either in the Engineers or Estate office. I don't know which. He is an Uxbridge fellow. He was here for a course on firing.

So you worked on Bank Holiday, so did we, it was Tuesday morning when we ceased, a late sitting that night. The weeks simply fly by. One hardly realises how quickly the time flies.

We have adopted the Day Light saving scheme here. The clocks have been put forwards an hour, it makes no difference; we do not finish any earlier for that. I suppose you have received some post cards, there are many in the shops. Hardly think they would permit such things. But this is France...

I remain yours sincerely,
M.A. Russell.

J. Davies, 23rd June 1916, France.

Dear Charles *[Mr Baker]*

Just a line to let you know I am getting on fine. I have been in France since Good Friday morning. Well it is not so bad, but of course not so comfortable as the office work. We had the Lord Mayor of London over to see us the other Sunday when we were resting, he made a little speech.

How are all at the office? You might remember me to Mr Woodhams, Mr Jones and Mr Cowan and the boys also the girls. I suppose Mr Redford has retired by now.

We have been in the trenches since the 13th and I expect we shall go out shortly. Our little dugout has just been flooded out, a very heavy thunderstorm, but we have run it out. It is rotten to see how the towns have been shelled to pieces. I don't suppose they will ever be rebuilt.

My brother was home on leave some time ago that is the second time so he has not got off badly. He has been promoted to Sergeant now. He seems to be getting on fine. Have you seen Ernie Smith? How is he getting on, is he still in the A.P.C.*? As I hear a lot have been transferred into line regiments.

Well here's to the time when the war is all over and we are back in the same old place. The trenches where we were are only 25 to 30 yards from the Huns so had to keep a bit low. You might drop me a line to let me know how you are getting on and any news,

Kind regards...

A.E. Kirk, 4th July 1916, France.

Dear Mr Wood,

I fear that there has been rather a long gap since I last wrote but all the same I have been getting on quite well. April and May brought me a change of scene and more variety of experience after which I returned to this, the place of my initiation into Railway Transport work.

But now instead of being junior to a corporal under direct supervision of an officer, I am in charge without a resident officer, the R.T.O. at the next station acting for both places. They have not given me any recognition so far, but recommendation has gone forward and whether I wanted it or not, it is really necessary as a number of men work under direction of the office which I am in charge of. Well, the work is varied and interesting and every person or thing received or despatched at this station either for the British, French or Belgium armies has to come under my personal direction. All ordinary matters I deal with directly, but special events requiring an officer, are covered by the officer coming up from the next station. These special events are often matters of great military importance and frequently involve an all night's work. This I put in quite cheerfully but naturally when you get two days and a night continuous work you feel a little washed out at the end. It will certainly seem strange when I return to a life of so many hours regular work day by day, although if I may say so, with all respect, I enjoy my present freedom in being more or less my own 'boss'. I heard that Boyce had been home on leave. Well that is lucky. He would not have got it where I last saw him in January, as that was in the same area as myself and I know there is not prospect yet for men who came out in December. I believe at the present time it is all in abeyance, which nobody minds if the end is in sight. Whether that is so or not, things are moving in a better way now.

The bombardment up this way was most intense Saturday night. I have heard nothing like it before. Several very loud shocks shook the houses in the village and were we suppose caused by mine explosions. The past week has also been full of interesting aerial scraps. This activity is chiefly in the evening after tea time and is usually on the part of our own airmen, who have to run the gauntlet of a perfect hail of shells. A taube came very near the other evening and our men got in some good shots too, but without apparent effect.

While I have been writing there has been a thunderstorm proceeding and the rolling thunder has been taken up by the guns which seem to be getting to work again. I don't hear a great deal about the Audit men who are scattered about doing their bit, but it may interest you to know that I met Lambert, Percy Smith and Mansbridge some weeks ago, all as you know in the Royal Flying Corps.

It was soon after I had received your last letter and they were interested in reading it I remember. At the time I was fairly close to their quarters but I am out of touch with them here. Has Beaumont written lately? I suppose he is still in India. It must be worse for his wife as regards the chances of his visiting her from there, than in my own case. The days of AM2/ section seem a long way back now. We are now in line with you as regards hours of daylight, which I suppose works quite beneficially for you, giving a long evening's daylight. I heard that Robertson went on a long sea voyage, presumably to Salonika.

I am quite satisfied with France myself. I have now quite a little circle of French acquaintances who make me very welcome. The chief drawback to paying too many friendly calls is the amount of coffee drinking it involves, for you hardly enter a French house before you are invited to drink a dish of coffee. Sometimes it is good, but normally pretty black and strong. Still it shows a true Allied spirit and makes life here very pleasant, or at any rate as pleasant as possible. I maintain quite a clean bill of health and generally speaking most of the men here also. I hope you keep in good health. All the familiar faces are well remembered and it will be a very real pleasure to me when I can see you all again.

Quite recently an officer who had arrived here with an artillery party, got into conversation with me and it turned out to be Lieutenant Veltom of the family so well known at Paddington. I had previously worked under his brother Lt. Veltom of A.M.F.O at Havre. This one asked if I knew Bert Leeks and Boyce was also known to him. It was one of those pleasant little surprises which frequently crop up on this work. I shall have to finish now to catch today's post. With hearty good wishes and sincere regards to yourself and all friends,

Yours sincerely and respectfully, Archibald E. Kirk.

F.T. Turner, 13th July 1916, Morn Hill Camp, Winchester, England.

Dear Jim (Mr Porter)

Just a few lines to let you now things are going. Am having a fairly good time nothing at all to grumble about. I don't think I shall be going to France for a few months yet. I met one of the chaps from the tickets department last week he is in the R.F.C. down here. Some of us were feet under canvas for a fortnight but owing to the wind and rain we were moved back to the huts. When we were under canvas, we used not get up till 8 o'clock, we were supposed to go on parade at 6.15am, but we dodged that. I enclose photo (not dressed for the occasion) outside our hut L20 or Hell 20 as it has been called I am looking forward to seeing some of the office chaps when I am able to get leave. I hope your brother is getting on alright in France. Hoping you are 'in the pink' like myself,

Yours very sincerely,
F. Turner
Please write as soon as poss.

J.R.H. Higgs, 16th July 1916, France

My Dear Taffy,

Am afraid I have been rather a long time in writing you but since my arrival here opportunities have not presented themselves very often.

I arrived back in camp on the 27th June quite safely but of course cursed my luck at having to return so soon. The leave one gets is never long enough. I could really have managed the most of the week. Still I had a jolly good time so perhaps mustn't grumble. After I left you I had an appointment at Praed Street and found my friend already waiting. I was about ten minutes late. We journeyed up West for some grub and afterwards took a taxi to Waterloo and caught the 6.45. When we arrived in camp we learned to our surprise that we were off next evening. Next morning we paraded as usual and were promptly dismissed for a time. I might mention that the whole day was given over for inspection parade etc. The final one was at 9.30pm and we were eventually dispatched by the train from camp station. I really think everyone had obtained permission to be out of bed till then, for when we were marched off at 10 with the band in front nearly everybody came along with us and judging by the send-off we got, I really think they were sorry to see us go. It was by far the best farewell I had seen since I have been at Longmoor. Needless to say it was the topic of much conversation on the way down... We did not come up to town but had a cross country journey travelling all night and arriving at our port of embarkation at 7am after a very uncomfortable journey.

Ten in a compartment with all our gear makes a bit of a crush as you can well imagine. Our boat did not sail till 11.30 so we put the time in at a rest camp situated right on the front. Here we had breakfast. Our journey over was a very stormy one and lots were unwell though all our party and myself kept fit. On arrival we were promptly marched off to our billet for the night and what a billet it was. Beastly, draughty hole with plenty of rats as companions. Some of the beggars were a decent size too.

However, they did not trouble me much as I was too tired to think about them. Next morning we had to make another journey. Caught the 7.22 and after a very wearisome journey arrived at a place about twelve miles back from here. Should not have minded resting there for a few days. However we had to stay the night only. (I might tell you we had to be back in the billet at 9pm). This time we slept a bit more comfortably in a railway carriage as another fellow and myself shared a compartment... Next morning as three of us had to catch the 5.52. I eventually disembarked here about 7am, the others going further on. Originally the distance from the line was not very great, but of course now it is a few miles further. We hear the shells firing quite plainly and some nights the racket is pretty severe. For the first two or three nights after my arrival it was very heavy and last night (just a fortnight since my arrival) old Fritz was going through it pretty much. His nerves must have suffered somewhat. Have seen a good many prisoners, and most of 'em to my mind, look just like a lot of criminals, a whole train load passed through here last night. Expect some more will be coming down either tonight or tomorrow... Old chap, I cannot say how long I may be here but anyway letters will be sent on. I'll write again as to my work etc., but at present time presses. Please give my regards to all I know and thank Claydon for taking these things along home. I'll write him later. Hope you are fit.

Cheerio oh,
Yours, J.R.H.H.

R.C.S. Frost, 18th July 1916, France

Dear Standew,

Many thanks for the magazines which continue to reach me, also for your note enclosed with the last one. I am very pleased to hear of 'Jacko' *[E.W. Jackson]* being mentioned in dispatches. I have seen *[G.]* Williams since his return from leave recently, and am glad to hear there are a few of you left in the office. I suppose you don't know when you will have to go?

You will observe by the notepaper that I am 'back from the front' as you can guess the Y.M.C.A. people are well out of the range of big guns. We left the trenches a fortnight ago, and after a long march reached very nice village, so fresh and bright after the battered bits of places in which we have lived for the past few months. We enjoyed six days of ease and comfort here, bivouacking in an orchard, good spot eh? and then were recalled. Since last Tuesday week we have been very unsettled, and done a good lot of marching, every day in fact we have to be prepared to move away. Last Saturday we travelled more than twenty miles in motor lorries and it was no joy ride! I can assure you, we were so tightly packed, that we could only sit in one position a very short time. The dust was also very unpleasant, and we were covered with it from head to foot, our hair looking quite grey! But a long wash soon restored us to a more juvenile appearance.

Our last spell in the trenches was rather severe, especially the last four days. What with mines, bombardments, raids and a heavy list of casualties, and very little sleep the whole time, we were glad to hand over the sector to new troops, who were fresh, and up to full strength. I was doing duty at our battalion headquarters at the time and although there was plenty to do, it was fairly safe, being some distance back from the firing line.

We are getting fine weather now, and today it has been awfully hot, making us feel thankful that we have not spent it 'on the road'. We only had a short parade at midday, for the presentation of medals to two men who rescued some miners who were overcome with gas in a mine in the trenches a short time ago.

I must close this short letter now, and shall be glad to have a few lines from any old friends in the office. Please remember me to all, who are left with you, particularly Messrs Hunt, Taylor and Woodhams, and I trust you are all keeping well.

With kindest regards

Yours sincerely,

'Frosty'.

T. Cautley, 13th July 1916, Le Havre, France.

Dear J. *[Naldrett]*

How are you getting on at Paddington now? I was on leave about two months ago could not find time to come up, was down at Goring and Streatley. I suppose you are all in the same place, how about McMeeken, has he joined yet? Dunton, I am told has been bad. Saw our old friend 'Humphrey' here one day. Of course saluted him in my best style. I am keeping fit. Manage to get some exercise occasionally. We have a cricket team. I am Vice Captain, so am still keeping up spirit. Hope you are fit and well. *[Line censored]*.

Au revoir
Yours, T. Cautley
You know Brackenbury, he is here with me, (was in the Audit General Department).

F. Witt, 28th May 1916, Salonika, Greece.

Dear G. *[Mr Gerald Burgoyne]*,

I guess you wonder what has become of me after this long silence, but you will see I am a good distance away from the homeland now. I arrived here early in April and since the start have been getting on quite well. You may be interested to know that Gray from your department is also here. It is rather strange that I should rub against him.

The weather is brilliant, cloudless skies day after day, but it is very hot. There are plenty of mosquitoes about. They are very tantalising. A net is practically a necessity for sleeping purposes. I am billeted in a warehouse, it is a very old place, and has stood hundreds of years. I should think, according to its general appearance. I have not picked up the lingo yet, but French is chiefly spoken, and I much regret not having studied it more when I had the opportunity at home. This town is a queer sort of place as compared with some of the French towns we know, and am sure I shall not wish to see it again when once I leave. The cafés are not so gay as the French, but I manage to have fun occasionally. We have got a piano and gramophone to amuse ourselves with. I hope we shall be able to have another trip to Paris, when the war has cleared up, but of course when is a question nobody can answer yet awhile. Shall be very pleased to hear some news of you, and conclude now with all the best.

Yours sincerely,
Frank.

F. Witt, 24th June 1916, Salonika, Greece.

Dear Gerald *[Burgoyne],*

I was very pleased indeed to receive your long and interesting letter this morning. What changeable weather you must be having in England! It is the same pouring heat day after day here. When you get old Bill's address you might let me know, and then I can get in touch occasionally. I suppose he still preserves that unruffled demeanour, which was such a characteristic of his in Paris. Yes, those rambles in Boulogne have not yet faded from my memory. You ask what the beer is like here. As a matter of fact it depends upon where you go, but there are few places where you can get good stuff, and then it is not on a par with the English. The other place we went to in the West that night was the 'Palace Tavern', with the automatic doors remember? Next time you roam in that direction, drop in and have one for me.

I was surprised to hear that Boyce had given you a look up as he enlisted the same day as me, though of course he has scored through being sent to France, whereas being stationed at a place like this, one has to be content to stay until terms of 'peace' are dictated. Some of the boys you saw must have had interesting news to relate Harold Watts has done well. Yes, I knew of Bill Ford's transfer, having heard from him, as have his address. I suppose you know that Robertson is here. I delivered the necessary to Gray. I should be pleased if you would remember me kindly to Jack Naldrett, and give him my address in case he cares to write, I will try and send him a line as soon as possible. There is not much exciting news to relate just now so I will draw to a close, and shall hope to hear from you frequently. Trusting you are keeping O.K.

With Kindest regards,

Frank

EIGHT

NOVEMBER 1916

'…we have anything from an elephant to a cockroach creeping over our blankets at night time, the chameleon is our chief pet and will crawl over one's body just like a tame mouse and the different colours they can change their body to suit the thing they settle on is wonderful.'

Henry Bullen

The November 1916 collection of letters was small, but as usual it reflected the diverse experience of the Audit staff. In the opening quotation Bullen marvelled at the wildlife he encountered near Mount Sinai, where he had recently arrived. 'Old timer' Thomas Cautley declared that he had been soldiering for 17 months and, like most others, saw no sign that the war would end at any time soon. His letter suggested that he had started to worry about job security and money matters:

> *'Have you had a rise recently? Mine was due a year ago last June, no chance of getting it.'*

After an extended period away, Cautley had begun to make himself a life of sorts in France, more 'normal' activities, like swimming had become routine for him.

> *'Well for the past week or so we have had splendid weather, ideal battling weather, and I have not missed going in for a dip, it does one good.'*

In contrast to the relatively routine existence that Cautley was having, Kemball had been in 'pure hell' but wrote elatedly about the experience, mainly, it would seem, because he survived it. There was also a just sense of pride conveyed in his letter because he was able to write about his personal contribution to events which he felt sure his colleagues and family would have heard about in the news:

'..., *good old 51st, no glory, but damned hard and risky work, consolidating the positions gained as the papers say!*'

The lengthy office newsletter had an update on Donald Hambly, who

> Was in training first on the East Coast, then going to Scotland for a short period, where he experienced the pleasures of flying in one of the crew, finally he reported at Dover, eventually crossing to France on Sunday 29.10.16, to take up his duties as 1st Class Warrant Officer, he reports all intensely interesting, and one really feels quite near the real thing.

There was news of the fortunes of Stanley Court, Freddy Woodhams and Syd Douce:

> In Honour of the Fallen.
> We regret to place on record the death of Corporal S.W.C.Court of the 2/16 Queen's Westminsters (late Goods Audit) He was fatally wounded at Arras and buried at the Military Cemetery about 4½ miles from that place at the end of July 1916 (see photo No.5 in this issue)

> F.G.Woodhams, Kensingtons (Goods) was wounded by shrapnel, in the head, taken into Canadian Hospital (France). We since hear of him receiving his discharge therefor as perfectly fit, now being stationed for a while at Havre.

> S.C.Douce has been admitted to Bethnal Green Hospital, being wounded in the ankle, we understand he was 2 days and 3 nights in a crater after receiving his wound, having no food and only a very limited supply of cigarettes. Making his way back under great difficulty, he at last reached our lines, eventually to be shipped to England. Representatives from the Audit have paid him visits at the above Hospital, where he appears merry and bright.

One staff member was discharged for being underage, which of course was not uncommon during the war. His attempt to fight was applauded in the office newsletter, which reflected the widespread patriotism and support for those who enlisted:

'*W.E. de Turberville (Passengers dept.) who was reported in our last issue to have joined the R.F.A. as a driver, was eventually discharged, being under age. No discredit, try again!*'

The newsletter included this newspaper cutting from the Daily Mirror of 9th August 1916. It was short feature saying that letters could be written to Edward Stewart via his home address in London. Under the clipping the Audit office had added the simple caption '*E.H.C. Stewart of London Rifle Brigade (and Stats dept). Missing*' A later issue of the newsletter was to confirm that Stewart had been killed in action on 1st July 1916.

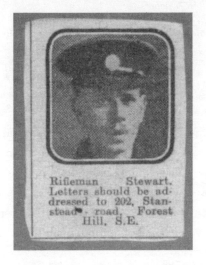

Rifleman Stewart. Letters should be addressed to 202, Stanstead - road Forest Hill, S.E.

E.H.C.Stewart of London Rifle
Brigade (& Stats. Dept).
Missing.

H. Bullen, 24th July 1916, Egypt.

[An employee at the Audit office added the following note at the top:]
Private H. Bullen, late of the Passengers dept, went through 11 months of Dardanelles campaign... Later moved to Malta, then to Egypt and Aden. Now encamped near Mount Sinai.]

Dear Percy [Dalton],

...I am sorry I have been so long replying to your letter, but I have had my hands rather full just lately, so hope you will not mind. As I cannot get at my kit bag at present I shall only be able to write you a short letter because I have nearly run out of paper envelopes, so I shall have to make up for it next time.

Well my dear Percy I am glad to know yourself and all at home are in the best of health and please convey to your father and mother my appreciation of their good wishes sent to me.

I received your previous budget, but it arrived after I sent you the field postcard, my word it must take you a good time to write all those sheets of foolscap, but I delight in reading them, since being out here I find I cannot write an interesting letter. I am afraid my letters must often bore you, I have read your letter carefully and noted all the news about the office and some of our friends who are doing their share overseas, but the chief item you mention is poor old Rippington, it is the first time I have heard about him, poor old chap. I guess he was pleased to see you and I am sure it was an excellent idea of yours to send him some luxuries in the way of food with the proceeds of the money you collected for him at the office…

We are not having such an easy time as one would imagine, the heat is still very intense and the flies very troublesome and we have anything from an elephant to a cockroach creeping over our blankets at night time; the chameleon is our chief pet and will crawl over one's body just like a tame mouse and the different colours they can change their body to suit the thing they settle on is wonderful.

Now I must close Percy as you will see the paper is nearly filled up, so hope you will not mind this time, please remember me to all at home and all inquiring friends…

Private H. Bullen

S.W.C. Court, 6th July 1916, France.

[A note has been added by the office in Paddington: 'Fatally wounded end of July. Buried 4½ miles from Arras.']

Dear P.D. *[Dalton]*

We are fairly comfortable, resting after a stiff march and are awaiting further orders... Nothing very exciting has happened up to the present except the shelling of stray aeroplanes.

We (i.e. my section) were at first billeted in a dirty old barn which had been visited by the Uhlans*. I acted as interpreter and managed to obtain supplies of bread, *vin rouge* etc. for the boys of the section. We are now living in huts, originally used by French troops, who must have been a dirty crowd of fellows, as the place is infested with rats and mice.

How is poor Ducat now? I suppose he will get another pip when he is patched up. I suppose you heard from Dolly that *mon frère [my brother]* Sydney has a staff appointment and will probably come out here as an R.T.O. shortly.

If the war doesn't end shortly I shall seek after a similar change. Today for the first time since our move from Warminster we had an issue of bread. Bully *boeuf* however, is still supplied in great quantities. Will write again shortly.

Stan

T. Cautley, 8th August 1916, France.

Dear Jack *[Naldrett]*,

Thanks for your letter I was pleased to hear all the news about the office and the various fellows. Yes I have been here now 17 months. I can't say though I am an expert linguist; one does not get much opportunity of conversing, but I am improving slowly. I really meant to look you all up when I was home on leave, couldn't manage it somehow, I went down to Goring & Streatley, had a grand time. Do you remember young

Brackenbury? He was here until recently. He has now gone up country.
So I am the only GW man here...

Well for the past week or so we have had splendid weather,
ideal battling weather, and I have not missed going in for a dip, it does
one good.

Well we may eventually see you all out here soon although I hope
before the time comes we shall have peace... Things must be very
different there now, although you don't seem to have many more girls
than when I was there... I have managed to keep pretty fit most of the
winter we played footer and we run a cricket team. So we do fairly well
in the way of exercise still it is not quite like being at home. Havre itself
is not a bad place and the country round is very pretty...

Have you had a rise recently? Mine was due a year ago last June,
no chance of getting it. Some of the railway companies are giving their
fellows rises out here; Great Central for one. Why don't they all follow
suit? Well old chap hope you are keeping fit and well... Kind regards to
yourself and others...

T. Cautley

F.T. Turner, 'Sunday', Morn Hill Camp, England.

Dear Mr Wood,

Just a few lines to let you know I am still at Winchester. I am having a
fairly good time, but like the rest will be glad to get out of the army.
I have only a couple of months till I become of age as I am looking
forward to a change from the monotony here. A large number of men
are getting discharged on medical grounds; most of them have been in
training for over a year. It shows how many are passed into the army as
fit but are really otherwise. Most of them have heart trouble. The training
here is very hurried now. Men are considered trained now in three
months, but from my own experience I think training is much too short.
That is where we younger chaps have the advantage; we get a thorough
training. I find that the men who joined up this last few months are much

better class of men in all ways than those who were joining up at the time that I did. All the ground round the huts here is being cultivated; we look like getting a good crop of vegetables. There is a prize of 30 shillings for the hut with the best garden. Well I have little interesting news, so will close now.

Yours sincerely,
F.T. Turner

A. Smith, 7th August 1916, France.

Dear Sir, *[Mr Slater]*

Thank you very much for your letter of 19th ultimo. Am surprised to hear of so many expected resignations within the next year, especially during war time. I suppose in ordinary peace times we should have been having a holiday today but under the circumstances it is much the best to forego holidays. If you have not already heard, you will be surprised to know that Higgs is stationed at the next station down the line from here. He has been up here three times. He was up here yesterday afternoon. He looks very well indeed and seems to be fairly happy where he is. No doubt one of you will hear from him one of these days. Our weather has been intensely warm during the last fortnight but it has not reduced me to a patch of grease yet. I am still in a wooden hut and have two sappers with me at present.

I have heard today that Pond is somewhere near. I should like to see him, have not seen him since a year last April. I am glad to say that I am quite well. With kindest regards to all.

I am, yours very sincerely,
A. Smith

G. Kemball, 13th August 1916, France.

Extracts from letter dated August 13th 1916

After leaving the hospital came the chase after the battalion! I went by train to *[censored]* and had four hours to wait there thence to *[censored]* once again, the transport were lying just behind *[censored]* and I stayed with them for the two days. I told you I was resting from there I went straight into Hell the battalion were in reserve in *[censored]* from thence we moved up into support just in front of *[censored]* and after two days there, into the front line in High Wood, otherwise *[censored]* – phew! We were up there for just a fortnight, in the three positions I mean, all told, good old 51st, no glory, but damned hard and risky work, consolidating the positions gained as the papers say! It doesn't look much in print, but my God, I'd sooner go over the bags any day, every night we were groping about in no man's land digging advanced trenches and saps ready for the next move and on reconnoitring patrols– crawling about on hands and knees finding out where Fritz had dug himself in. On several occasions we ran into him on the same game, result– an exchange of bombs and oaths and a scuttle for your own lines before they found you with their machine guns. If you could take one of their party back with you, so much the better. We managed it one night and they're just as fed up as we are, say we don't know what it is to be under bombardment! Good luck to the folks at home, who have made it possible for us to 'lay in' the shells. It was a pure hell, but thank God I am through it untouched and now feel very proud to think that the old 51st was concerned in the big push, even though there was not much glory in it. We lost pretty heavily our own platoon officer was severely wounded one night in front with me. We were spotted, and he got a bullet right through his throat, had a rare job to get him back, poor chap.

J.R.H. Higgs, 16th August 1916, France.

My dear Taffy *[Edwards]*,

I was glad to get your letter with all the news. Letters as you can well believe are much appreciated, though the opportunity of replying may not often present itself. As an instance you will observe that I started this a couple of days ago but had to knock off and carry on with a job which came in.

I am quite settled down now to the life and up to the present have had a fair time. The one thing though which has troubled me has been how to exist solely on our army rations. I've managed it but how I've stuck it cannot tell you. For some time now we have been on reduced rations and the fare usually is not very appetising. The way it is served up and where we have it puts one right off. Then there is another thing, only this has affected your humble self only, since my arrival here I've had the enormous sum of *five francs* paid to me so you can quite understand that it he been impossible for me to buy an occasional luxury, much less go on the burst for an evening. However I believe we are going to be paid tomorrow and if I get what I've put in for shall be quite rich for a time.

I've already had a change of scenery. A fortnight ago I was ordered to a place about 20 miles back from here to carry on for a time. Am on the way back to fitness now though, for which I'm very thankful. You ask me what sort of place this is. Well in my opinion the least said about it the better. It is a very dirty hole and the sanitary arrangements leave a lot to be desired. The streets appear to be very seldom swept, result the refuse smells horribly and as for the flies, we are simply eaten alive. We have tried all sorts of things to keep 'em out of the office but no good. The surrounding country is very pretty but of course it does not come up to English scenery. As to amusements there is a picture shown two or three evenings a week which I believe is pretty well patronised. Beyond this, there is nothing, only cafés and canteens. The hours of the former are restricted to two in the morning and six till eight in the evening and everyone is supposed to be in billet or camp by 9pm.

We can get English newspapers a day late so are not badly off for news. The continental edition of the Mail can be obtained about 4pm daily. As for baccy I get a supply every now and again from my sister. We get an issue of cigs, but they are not up to much as a rule. I'm enclosing a photo which you can either keep or put with the rest. I must close as time is getting on. Hoping you are fit and with best regards to all my friends. Believe me,

Yours, J.R.H. Higgs

H. Beaumont, 18th August 1916, Rawalpindi, India.

G.W.R. men with the Colours, on arrival at Multan, India.

Photo from the GWR magazine.

Dear Bertie (Hunt),

Just a few lines to let you know how we are getting on out here, I forgot when I last wrote you last and what news I told you. We marched down from the hills, 9,000 feet up in the Himalaya Mountains last October to Rawalpindi, then shortly afterwards out to camp returning just before Xmas. In February I obtained a furlough and had a fine tour of places of interest, down to Delhi then right across India to Calcutta, had several letters of introduction from brother Freemasons to awfully nice people there and had a most enjoyable time, spent a few days at Agra on the return journey, travelled roughly just over 3,000 miles with several nights in the train. A few days after returning the regiment was placed under orders to march 83 miles to Noushera on the frontier border, where over 10,000 British and native troops were concentrated, a similar number at Peshawar farther down the frontier, in readiness for threatened trouble with the Afghans, whom German intriguers had been amongst. Noushera was a cruel place, nothing but a dust heap at the foot of the mountain. We spent several weeks there, training in mountain warfare, my word, it was chronic, the terrific heat and the awful climbing for miles day after day, with all transport on mules and camels through the rocky mountain passes. At one bivouac we encountered bad water, and about forty of our fellows went down with enteric fever *[typhoid]*. One died, but the others pulled through as they had been inoculated; a wonderful thing inoculation has proved to be in India.

Well in spite of the hard time, we returned to Rawalpindi in fine condition after the Afghan trouble had subsided for the time being, it is always liable to break out at any moment and we are always in readiness to move at any time.

Then we changed to another barracks in Rawalpindi in April, and have been stationed on the plains all the summer. The heat has been intense; one never goes outside after 10am; after tiffin at 1 o'clock the barracks and in fact everywhere is dead to the world until between 5 and 6pm, when sports such as tennis, cricket hockey and swimming at the baths are possible.

Every soldier has a punkah *[fan]* swinging over his bed all night and during the hours off duty during the day. Many men sleep out on the barrack square on their beds at night. During the past few weeks the monsoon has been on, with torrential rain which I would fail to describe. Now the intense heat of the sun is draining the moisture out of the earth with the result that it is like living in the moist fern house at Kew Gardens, only worse, and many men are being bowled over with fever. Ever since arriving at India, getting on for two years ago, I have been as fit as a fiddle and enjoyed exceptional health, until a fortnight ago, when I was suddenly taken ill with sandfly fever, a most painful, lowering form of fever, and was carried to hospital and also found to be suffering from pleurisy. I was in bed several days subsisting on a small quantity of milk with the result that when I was allowed to get up I was too weak to stand. I was discharged after ten days and am getting on quite alright now, and am leaving on next furlough to a hill station in the Himalayas shortly to recuperate. In November we are on the move again, marching about 80 miles to a big camp, for manoeuvres of several weeks, returning again just before Christmas. But marching eighty miles in five days under an Indian sun is very different to cloudy England. Every regiment in India, both regular and territorial, is being heavily reinforced by drafts from England. We have had three drafts one consisting of nearly 300 men, then another of 67, now another of 84, bringing us up to nearly 1,100 men. There are thousands of British troops, mostly Terriers *[members of the Territorial army]* (there are only eight regular infantry regiments left in India) stationed at various frontier places, and all sorts of rumours prevalent about a big expedition moving during the next few months, all possible preparations are being made for it, well, if the Indian govt. make as disastrous a muddle of it when the fighting does come off as they made over the Mesopotamia campaign, then with foes like the ferocious Afghans there will be a terrible price to pay in life, for the country and the terrific heat will be enough without having to fight every inch of the way.

...I can quite picture the changes which must have occurred in the staff of the Audit since I left. Of course you are over the age limit, so have not been called upon. I expect if, and when, I do return safely that life in England will seem very different under the altered conditions. I shall be glad to get home again and only wish I could see a prospect of doing so, with the conclusion of this terrible war. I have had a very enjoyable time in India (apart from soldiering which I always did enjoy, although I think I have had sufficient now) having made the acquaintance of awfully nice residents in 'Pindi, and by virtue of rank, being allowed the privilege of wearing mufti makes it so much more comfortable when going out of barracks than being in a tight uniform in the climate.

I hear regularly from my wife and little one every week. Am glad to say they are well.

Please convey my kind regards to all those left in the office that I know. Trusting you are all fit and well and that we shall meet again before many more months elapse.

With best wishes. Harry Beaumont

E.H. Brackenbury, 19th August 1916, France.

Dear Mr Biggs,

I thought it was about time that I dropped you a few lines to let you know that I am still alive: the fact of the matter is that I had intended doing so some time ago but I had counted on having leave –such an unknown quantity nowadays– and would have paid a visit to the office; afterwards I found that there were other things that persisted in engaging my attention that I am afraid I was thwarted at every step.

Since the last time of writing I, in company with several other fellows, have shifted to a place which is considerably nearer the zone of operations than the last place we were at. The country round about here is very pretty, and there is a river close at hand where some good boating and fishing can be done. Football is sometimes played here, and at the last place at which we were we had quite a presentable cricket team.

I hope you will not wonder whether I am aware that there is a war going on, for I am very well aware of it but at the same time think it quite a good scheme to talk about other things sometimes.

I met H.W. Martin some time ago, and he seemed to be quite jubilant, but whether this was due to the fact that he was not then 'on the line' or not I could not say. All the same I don't think he will be terribly upset when the time arrives for him to get back 'on the line'… No doubt the office by this time presents a more deserted appearance than ever, except I suppose where skirts have superseded trousers…

E.H. Brackenbury

P.S. I hope Mr Levett doesn't have quite 'as many things to try him' as before.

R.C.S. Frost, 23rd August 1916, Devonport, England.

Dear Mr Hunt,

I expect you have heard at the office about me being in England suffering from gas poisoning, and as it is quite a long time since I last wrote to you, no doubt a few lines will be acceptable, to explain matters.

We left the trenches at Vimy Ridge on July 5th, and marching back about 14 miles we eventually reached a village named Ostreville for the purpose of having a divisional rest. The signallers thought an orchard would be very convenient to erect bivouacs in, so when we were busy carrying out this idea an old Frenchman appeared at the scene, and raised objections. However he agreed at last to allow us in at one end of the orchard, thinking, I suppose, that we would wander about his place! We had an enjoyable time here for six days, and then had to return to our old billets near Mount St. Eloi until the whole of the division had retired. We guessed by this move that our 'rest' was over, and the following days were spent in marching, and travelling by motor lorries and train until we arrived at Mericourt Station on July 21st near Albert.

After a delightful swim in the river near the billet we marched off the following night, to take part in the 'big push.' We slept in an open field that night near Fricourt farm, and were rather rudely awakened by a few German shells landing near us.

For five days we were lying in reserve in this district, and occupied our time in watching an army of men at work in the valley, making roads, railways, boring for water and laying down water pipes, also practicing attacks in the old trenches. It was very interesting to see the great amount of artillery, busy practically all day and night, and to read their messages sent by visual signalling [often using lights] from a ridge across the valley.

Our period in reserve being up, we moved to Mametz Wood to lie there in support for five days, before going into the trenches at High Wood. On arrival at the edge of the wood at night, we were welcomed by a big dose of gas shells and shrapnel, which was applied steadily throughout the night by the German artillery. Having to assist in putting our signalling gear into a hole for safety, I was prevented from using my respirator for the first quarter of an hour, as we could not see on account of the darkness and dust made by the ammunition columns rushing along the road, and it was during this time that I must have breathed in enough gas to put me out of action. Afterwards of course respirators were used, when we were settled in holes by the roadside for the night.

I remained with the battalion until I was sent to the casualty clearing station on August 3rd and reached Rouen hospital the next day. I had to wait until the 9th and crossed the channel from Havre to Southampton on the New Zealand ship *Marama*, with about 800 other patients, the day after. It was a splendid boat with every convenience for carrying wounded men, and the sisters and orderlies were colonials.

It was last Friday week when I arrived here, and must say it is very comfortable and quiet. I had to remain in bed until last Saturday, but of course I cannot do any route marching yet! So I have to take life quietly, which is no hardship I can assure you after France. I am on an ordinary diet, and taking medicine.

I hear you have Mr Symons back again, is that so? And is he back in the same old spot? I hope he is pretty fit, although I suppose there must be something wrong with him, to be back again.

I suppose things are as quiet as usual with you. Have you had your holidays yet? This is about your time I believe. I shall be glad of a few lines when you have time, to hear the latest about the office. I hope you are keeping fit, and with kind regards to you all.

Frosty.

P.S. It is a treat to write a letter without the censor's shadow over one!

W.C. Davis, 10th September 1914, France.

Dear Charlie (Serjeant)

Expect you have been wondering what had become of me of late well I am still safe and sound and enjoying a few days' rest in a French town after a rather rough do for we have been in the thick of it of late and the boys of our division have given the Bosh something to go on with for a time. I have had rather hard luck having lost four special chums through gas shells but they are well out of it I can tell you, whether they are at the base or Blighty, for you can take it from me our work out here is no light task. Shall be able to tell you more about it when we spend that hour or two ... Have received the postcard alright for which I am obliged. Give my kind regards to all...

Will (Davis)

S.C. Douce, 2nd October 1916, France.

Dear Sammy (Smith, Fares)

A few lines to thank you for the fags, the news, and to tell you I am fit and well. Glad to hear you are all likewise. When we had a walk over through a place which fell a little while ago, although we were under heavy shell fire after getting through, I was offering anything up to a franc for a cig but couldn't find a taker. So you can see what a scarcity there is in this particular luxury. In fact everything is the same about here, even food and water. This war is a most horrible and terrible affair.

To sum it up in one word it's absolutely *[censored]*. Still we keep on jogging along with the hope it will all end much sooner than some of the critics would have us believe. I am sure none of you would like it a little bit, so you better keep where you are. Well old boy give my kind regards to everybody. Will write more another time. Always pleased to have a letter.

Syd Douce

R.C.S. Frost, 9th October 1916, Dartmouth, England.

Dear Mr Hunt,

I expect you have been wondering what has become of me lately, as I have taken such a long time answering your last letter. Nevertheless I can assure you it was most welcome, particularly all the news regarding old friends at the office.

I am sorry to hear of Court's death. What a lot of familiar faces we shall miss, when we return to civilian life again. Some have passed to the 'great beyond' and others… have passed to happy retirement.

You will observe my address that I have changed my residence in 'sunny south Devon', which has been since last Monday. I had a most pleasant time at Ford House, Devonport and made some good and kind friends, but as I improved in health, I was sent here.

There are 15 of us here, and three sailors, put ashore from ships because of sickness, so you see we are a small party, in fact the hospital only contains 29 beds, in two wards. As a building it is a great improvement on Ford House, and we are the first lot of convalescent soldiers to be sent here, consequently there is just a 'little fuss' made of us, and I hope we shan't get spoilt!

On our arrival the mayor called upon us, and welcomed us on behalf of his fellow citizens, and ever since members of the hospital committee have been to see us, and brought gifts of flowers, book, cigarettes and fruit.

The weather has been none too kind to us so far and yesterday was the only day without rain, and a trip to Totnes by steamer had to be postponed on Friday, but we have that still to look forward to, eh? Four of us here have made a few fishing expeditions with tackle lent to us, also a boat, but our 'hunting ground' is of a limited size on account of our crew. One chap has lost his right leg, another hasn't got full use of his left arm, the third still limps about, and I am not yet able to put much energy into rowing. Some crew eh? We usually go across to Kingswear and sit patiently waiting, close to the landing stage, and have so far caught seven fish of various sizes. Not very encouraging you will think, but it passes the time away, and suits me better than hill climbing. Tonight we are going to hear the 'Welsh maids' a party of singers from Wales, who are giving concerts this week.

I am glad to say I am feeling stronger than I was, but anything like strenuous walking soon upsets me, so I hope to remain here a few weeks…

Sincerely yours,

Frosty

F. Witt, 20th July 1916, Salonika, Greece.

Dear Jack,

… No doubt you have heard of my being stationed at this place, which is now a period of over three months. I am pleased to say I'm getting on quite well and feeling fit, though the place is not considered healthy, and the climate is very trying. It has been intensely hot, but during the last few days it has turned much cooler. The town is an interesting place, but I've seen as much of it as I want, and now look forward for the day when we shall be homeward bound… Letters take about 14 days to get here, so you see I am some distance from England's shores…Please remember me to all in the office. In conclusion with kindest regards.

Frank

F. Witt, 5th September 1916, Salonika, Greece.

Dear Jack (Naldrett),

Jolly pleased to have a line from you old man, I thought you might possibly have drifted into different quarters 'ere my letter reached you, but I see you are still 'carrying on', and wish you luck. As regards amusements here, things are rather slow except in particular quarters.

There are two cinemas here and that is about all. Numerous cafés abound, and those places I frequent most, for Salonika is a thirsty place and a pint or two in the evening hours is very acceptable. We have a nice little piano here, but am afraid old Gilbert Bushell could only satisfy his desire at the risk of bruising his hands as it is not full compassed, but we get some noise out of it between us. The news of Bill Ford astounds me. He is a dark horse. I can understand now why he has been so silent...With kindest regards to your good self and all whom are known to me in the Audit.

Yours sincerely, Frank

F. Jarrett, a typed account added by the Audit office, date and place unknown.

Frederick Jarrett late of the Stats. Dept who took part in the East African campaign in the early stages of the war was returning from leave in England, and left London on October 11th. At 7.40am, on October 20th the boat was torpedoed without warning in the Mediterranean and sank in seven minutes, but fortunately all passengers were saved being picked up by French torpedo boat although all baggage and cargo were lost. Fred states that he lost all he possessed with the exception of a pair of pyjamas (in which he had to take a lifeboat) his raincoat and wallet, and that the whole affair seems like a dream now but was real enough at the time. The passengers were landed in Algeria where they were well treated, and subsequently returned to England over land via Marseilles. He will make another attempt to dodge the submarines on November 18th when he sails for Mombassa on the Balmoral Castle via the Cape, there being too much excitement in the Mediterranean at present.

NINE

MARCH 1917

*'Troops were in such bad condition that the doctor sent a report saying
we were not fit for the line.'*

HUGH ANDREW SKILLING

In a letter to the office, H.A. Skilling described in vivid terms why this was
the case. Also this month, the Audit office had news that G. Kemball was
in a military hospital in Covent Garden having been badly wounded by
shrapnel and his wife Hilda, the only female voice in the collection, sent
a letter giving an update on his condition. There was news too that B.L.
Isles and G. Jones did not make it abroad from Longmoor camp as they
needed dental treatment and false teeth and W.J.E. Martin was in hospital
in Cambridge with 'frozen feet'.

Stanley Frost wrote from Dartmouth, fed up whilst on convalescence
but rationalised that it was much better than being in France. On the
other hand, Syd Douce was enjoying his time in hospital, 'it's a ripping
place' and the food is much better than in an ordinary hospital he writes,
certainly excellent in the 'grub stakes'. After his recovery he joined the
3rd Battalion of London Rifle Brigade (Dawlish). Regular writer Arthur
Smith had left his railhead in the Somme district and was recovering from
typhoid in England.

As ever, Gilbert Williams is grateful for supply of cigarettes sent out
by the Audit office. He provided a powerful account of his brigade's role
in the advance of Ancre who captured Beaumont Hamel in November
1916. He said they captured some German trenches and found some
'very young soldiers who burst into tears'. At this time, Williams had

been promoted to Lance Corporal as well as H.A. Skilling. The later, a rare correspondent to the Audit office, described his gruelling time in the trenches and announced that

> *'I expect you will be surprised to hear that I have left the Northamptonshire Regiment and am now attached to the Army Printing and Stationary Services. We are opening a new branch in the photography line and I am here as a photographer.'*

Since the last edition of the newsletter for November 1916, another twenty nine Audit staff had joined up and so this month the office heard about the experience of some those in training at Longmoor and Bordon camps prior to their overseas postings. For example, George Holloway's hut caught fire at Bordon and they had to parade in the mud in rain where it was like *'playing living pictures'* as they had to stand motionless while the band played waltz tunes.

S. Smith at Longmoor Camp said it was a cold and dreary existence. He found life very different after what he was used to, especially having to sleep on the floor. He complained that the men were not given enough food considering the amount of drill they had to practice and wrote

> *'I look like a tramp and my collar, of the colour, something like the office grate.'*

Donald Hambly wrote from Felixstowe, a base where seaplanes were built and tested. He was having a different wartime experience with the Royal Naval Air Service as a stores officer. He vividly described the experience of a raid on his station which involved:

> *'the crack of our gun, the shriek of its shell and the fantasia of a dozen search lights'.*

Quite a few men had called into the office whilst on leave and one of them was Lance Corporal W.C. Davis who was presented with 'a wrist watch and pocket case, and silver pencil case on behalf of his colleagues, as a token from their appreciation of the honour bestowed upon him in receiving the Military Medal' for gallant conduct with the 60th Field Ambulance during an attack near Ginchy on 19th to 20th September 1916.

Finally, the office provided an update on the work of A.E. Evans from the Audit office Passenger department. Evans was the officer in charge of the St John's Ambulance Brigade (no. 37 GWR London Division) and assisted at Charing Cross Hospital in the operating theatre for three days per week. He had been on duty at Paddington during the Zeppelin raids on the city.

D.S.W. Hambly, 21st September 1916, Felixstowe, England.

[This letter has been misfiled by the Audit office and should have appeared with the earlier collection for the November 1916 issue of the newsletter. Possibly it was delayed in the post or Mr. Wood did not hand it over in time].

Dear Mr Wood.

I had meant to write to you when I could tell that I was definitely settled, but as it now seems that some time must lapse before that happy consummation I decided that I would wait no longer.

Felixstowe is the largest and most important of all the home stations. It is an 'experimental and educational' station, i.e. all sorts of machines and inventions are given a chance here and a large number of young officers are taught to fly sea planes. There are between seven hundred and eight hundred men on the station, the greatest proportion being mechanics. So you will readily appreciate that the work of the Stores Officer is no *sinecure*. Another man was sent down with me for training, he served in Gallipoli with a machine gun section and afterwards worried the Senussi *[reference to Western Desert campaign in North Africa]* in an armoured car and as he collected eight machine gun bullets in his anatomy he was sent home and down here for stores work. He is an exceedingly good chap and my great chum. The stores here were being temporarily carried on by the carpenter, a commissioned Warrant Officer and it was quite thought that I or my friend would be appointed, as a matter of fact I was recommended for the post and was halfway through the 'muster' (stock taking) and only awaited confirmation from the Admiralty.

But today orders came to 'stand at ease' and it appears that some other man is being sent here. It is really no disappointment, as I didn't care in the least where I am sent, and I have now learnt enough to take over any old stores. I will let you know when anything is decided.

Of the work of the station I cannot of course tell you much, it is all intensely interesting and one really feels quite near the thing. We have had four raids since I was here, and they are truly fascinating. We have a very lively six inch gun, quite <u>near</u> our billet and when she's busy we begin to enjoy ourselves. The boom of the falling bombs, the crack of our gun, the shriek of its shell and the fantasia of a dozen search lights provide a most excellent entertainment, of course Harwich Harbour and our adjoining Air Station are objectives of the first order.

I shall be very glad to hear from you and to know any changes or events in the Audit office, it all seems very far away and I can't see myself back there again!

I had forty-eight hour's leave for my daughter's wedding on the 23rd of August, she and her husband leave for India on the 23rd instant, a great wrench for me.

I suppose you will have retired before I get back, but I hope we may not altogether lose sight of each other. Regarding this over, it seems all very tame but directly I want to say anything interesting, I am brought up sharp! Kindest regards to you and all my friends in the Agreements.

Yours very sincerely, Donald S.W, Hambly

A' hem! I miss the G.W. magazine. I did not see September number.

D.S.W. Hambly, 6th November 1916, Felixstowe, England.

Dear Mr Wood,

So much has happened since I arrived here on Sunday last that I have not had time or opportunity to write to you even now with the thought of the censor always at the back of my head, it is difficult to tell you much.

I am living in hopes of being sent out much nearer the real thing, but for the present I must possess my soul in patience and carry on with what cheerfulness I can muster. I am very fit, have plenty to eat and drink and smoke and a bed and blankets. Things are rough of course (especially my trip across from Dover last Sunday in a small Torpedo Boat Destroyer! Gale of wind from the southwest) but the warrant officers, who have a Mess of their own here, are a cheery lot, and we really have little to grumble at. One of them hails from St Austell and we sometimes converse in our native language but it generally produces another sort of language from the other members of the Mess.

Remembrances to my friends at Paddington, it seems a long way away, yours sincerely,

Donald S.W. Hambly

A. Smith, 19th November 1916, Addington Park War Hospital, England.

Dear Sir *[Mr Slater]*

I expect you wonder what has become of me as you have not heard from me for such a long time. The reason is that since the 20th September I have been suffering with Enteric. The exact diagnosis of my case being para typhoid B. I have not been up three weeks until next Friday, but since I first got out of bed I have made splendid progress. I was in an isolation hospital in France for six weeks and previous to that in a General Hospital for eight days. I arrived here late last Wednesday night after a very decent journey. This is a beautiful palace surrounded by a park in which we can walk about and we are allowed to go to the post office which is quite near. I am quite happy and comfortable here, it is a splendid hospital. We have a concert or cinema nearly every night in the big hall. Food is good and plentiful. How long it will be before I am considered fit again I have no notion, as a rule it takes months for a person to get right again.

It is a very funny and beastly complaint. During to the whole time I have been in hospital I have received every attention and kindness. During the months of July and August when I was in the Somme district I had a very rough time, was nearly worked to death and had little sleep. At one period we had to commence work at 2am but we were supposed to rest in the day but we could not get any. However, it was all in a good cause and we got through it. Ambulance trains were loaded up at the station where I was and we saw some awful sights. English and German wounded. Perhaps I picked my fever up at this place, but one never knows. While I was in the isolation hospital in France I was kept for three weeks and two days on liquids but I am pleased to say that the doctor has now put me on ordinary diet. With the kindest regards and best wishes to all, I remain yours obediently,

A. Smith

Mrs Hilda Kemball, 23rd November 1916, Upminster, England.

Dear Mr Davies,

Am very glad to tell you that my husband is now at the military Hospital, Endell Street, W.C. I went up to see him yesterday, he looks very ill but says it was only to be expected from what he'd been through. He was three days on the hospital boat, and got to Endell Street at about 1am Tuesday, and was put under an anaesthetic almost immediately and again yesterday morning, so he wasn't feeling particularly grand when I saw him in the afternoon. It is good to have him back again, and the sister told me he would never go out to the front again, as the 'funny bone' is smashed, which will leave his arm stiff, although she says he'll be able to use his fingers. The arm is fractured just above the elbow joint and the wounds on his leg are rather bad especially on the back of the calf, about six inches long, and deep enough to have a tube inserted, which is done to collect all the bad matter, but thank goodness, there are no bones broken in his leg, only flesh wounds.

I should be glad if you will let me have three return from Upminster to Fenchurch Street privilege forms, shall not have to bother you for a pass after all, am thankful to say, the hospital he's at is in a very quiet place so is nice and peaceful, and his ward is 'T Ward'. He is likely to be there for three or four months.

With kind regards, yours sincerely,
Hilda Kemball

R.C.S. Frost, 23rd November 1916, Dartmouth, England.

Dear Mr Hunt,

Many thanks for your most welcome and interesting letter safely received, and I am pleased to hear of the latest news about friends at the office and others in different parts of the world.

I have not had a line from H. Martin for many months, but I hear he has had leave recently, and no doubt he gave you a call. I hoped to have had that pleasure before this time, but I expect to be seeing you one of these fine days.

I am still a patient in hospital, and although at times the life is monotonous in this quiet place, it is preferable to France so I won't grumble. The weather has been so rough and wild of late, that a lot our time is spent by the fireside, and many pleasant hours are passed in comparing notes with men who are patients from minesweepers.

We have had different men from this branch of the Navy for several weeks, and at present five are in my ward. Two of these are survivors from a minesweeper that was blown up by a German mine nearly a fortnight ago, just outside Dartmouth Castle. They are still clearing the sea outside here and the boats return to anchor in the river at night, and the pals of these men visit them this evening. The officers are also very good in calling and leaving gifts and the wounded Tommies share in the fruits thereof!

I have heard from Scotland that the 8th Argylls suffered heavily a short time ago in France, and in the newspapers today I notice the names of nine officers who I knew in France, including the Captain of my company who is killed. I don't know if the 6th Seaforths, who are in the same brigade, were in action at the same time, but I shouldn't be surprised, anyhow I hope *[Gilbert]* Williams came through safely if he was there.

I am enclosing two privilege forms, and will be glad if you will get them signed and returned. I have had some nice afternoons at Torquay and Paignton and was there during the rough weather a short time ago, when the Brixham trawler was wrecked and sea was so rough.

I hope this…will find you very well and undisturbed at the old job…

Sincerely yours, 'Frosty'.

G. Williams, 25th November 1916, France

Dear Bertie *[Hunt]*

Thank you and the other gents very much for the cigarettes which I received yesterday on coming out from the line. We have been having exciting times lately. Our division took a big part in this new advance on the Ancre. In fact, it was our Brigade that captured Beaumont Hamel, and after two days hand fighting the ridge beyond the village. We went over before day break on the 13th November and from there till the evening of 14th we were properly in the midst of it. The greatest handicaps we had were fog and mud. It is really wonderful how the boys kept their direction in the mist which was very thick while the mud began to swallow one up unless one was wary. The Germans thought the village was impregnable, and up to now it has resisted all efforts to capture it. Their artillery and snipers gave us some trouble, but once we were at close quarters with them, they absolutely refused to fight, and were only too eager to be captured. For the most part they were a very measly looking lot and very young and some of them burst into tears when I pointed my bayonet at them. By Jove, Bertie, those Germans look after their creature comforts. Fine deep dugouts and any amount of shirts and socks and cases of soda water etc., I got a souvenir or two, a German helmet and one or two more things. The worst part of the whole business was cleaning up the battlefield afterwards. That's about all the news.

[Lines censored]

Well thanks again for the smokes.

Very sincerely yours, Gilbert Williams

D.S.W. Hambly, 3rd December 1916, Felixstowe, England.

Dear Mr Wood,

I was very glad to get your letter. Hope your hand is under better control now, although I must say your writing shows little evidence of 'intractability'.

From what you tell me, I shall be too bashful to enter the portals of Room No. 13 when, if ever, I return. It will be filled with little things in petticoats, with a grey beard or two to keep them in order. I can almost see mirrors on the wall at the end of every desk and tea cups by the side of every ink pot. Dear, dear! What are we coming to!

So far, over here, we have not felt the results of the submarine menace, but we have been told today that we shall not get any more loaf (beet) sugar, but will have to put up with caster. With the exception of this slight hardship, we can hardly complain of our commissariat*, and I cannot yet describe to the rigors of war!

A man in the corner of the Mess is playing 'Home Sweet Home' on a Japanese fiddle, accompanied by his own grunts. He is a pathetic figure, but I would like to kick him. I have borrowed a fiddle for tonight and then revenge!

Yours sincerely, Donald S. W. Hambly

R.C.S. Frost, 12th December 1916, Dartmouth, England

Please thank Mr Levett for Mag. Safely received.

Dear Mr Hunt,

Many thanks for your welcome letter, with the orders and I shall be much obliged if you will get two more signed for me. I am afraid I am putting you to a lot of trouble, but a visit to Torquay occasionally is very welcome, as there are more amusements there than Dartmouth could dream of providing! I also expected to have left this part long ago, but now it seems very probable that I shall remain here for Xmas.

I am rather surprised *[censored words]* has not been 'bucked up' during his military career, but then you would hardly say he is in the army! I guess he was rather an eyesore to *[censored word]*.

In my ward here we have a Dusky Britisher from Jamaica, who enlisted in the Royal Engineers at Cardiff, and for smartness he is absolutely 'it' and consequently he ranks as a Corporal. He came here from a paddle steamer on its way to Mesopotamia and was landed with sickness. He is now quite well and up to all kinds of jokes.

There is not much to write about as I will close, by wishing you and all old friends in the Audit a very Happy Xmas and a Prosperous New Year.

Yours sincerely, 'Frosty'.

S.C. Douce, 1st January 1917, St. John's Relief Hospital, Harrow, England.

Dear Mr Beak,

Just a few lines to thank you very much for the nice cigs and to wish you a happy new year. This is a ripping place and we get the same treatment as if we were in an ordinary hospital only everything is so much nicer, especially the grub stakes! I manage to get to town occasionally. Was hoping to get as far as Paddington to see you all but we are only allowed to go within a certain radius, and another thing, I don't feel comfortable getting about just at present. My wound is not yet healed and with one boot on one foot and a flat slipper on the other, and a couple of sticks to push myself along you can imagine how awkward it is. They put me on massage treatment the other day. Perhaps that will help matters on a little. Hoping you are quite well. Sincerely yours,

Syd C. Douce

H.A. Skilling, 5th January 1917, France

Dear Mr W.H. Davies,

Just a line to let you know I have not forgotten you. I received a letter on Tuesday 3rd of January 1917 which you sent to me on August 24th 1916. By the marking on the envelope it has been round to various regiments and officers, but it has arrived quite safe at last. I received the letter you wrote in October quite safe. I am sorry I have not written before but we were rather busy when I received your last letter and we could not send more than a field card for about a month. Well I am pleased to tell you that I am still going on first rate. I expect you will be surprised to hear that I have left the Northamptonshire Regiment and am now attached to the Army Printing and Stationary Services. We are opening a new branch in the photography line and I am here as a photographer.

I am unable to tell you more than this up to the present. I expect Harry will be pleased to hear this as he used to give me quite a lot of tuition in this respect.

There are only two of us here up to the present and as the dark rooms are not finished yet we are having an easy time. The Officer is away in England just now getting some more photographic apparatus so we are on our own and I am in charge.

We are billeted with a company of Australian electricians, mechanics, mining and boring engineers and are having a fine time. There are a good lot of fellows and make us very welcome. We had a grand Xmas with them and they know how to enjoy themselves. You can understand what a change this is after being in the line. Just before I came on this job we had over a month in and out of the line waiting to go over the top when the weather was favourable.

We went in for four days then out for a rest for about three days then back again. The water was over our knees in the trenches and it was impossible to use the communication trenches at all. We were holding the front line with two platoons

(I should say our boys' section of the line). Our platoon was twenty two strong including the Officer, and during the bombardment we had eight put out in ten minutes. There were no dugouts of any description there, so you can imagine what it was like to stand there for four nights. We hoped the weather would be alright so that we could go over and get it done with but it was not to be. We were out digging one night when they let us have it for five hours with gas shells, we had two chaps hit with them and put right out.

The sights and smells were awful, as a good many of the chaps lay just as they fell during the advance. It was impossible to bury them. Also there were about a dozen dead horses round about in the mud that were killed by shell fire while bringing up ammunition for the guns. Our guns never cease down there, as soon as one section stop, another lot open out so you can tell there is <u>Somme</u> noise.

The last time we came out, was for forty eight hours' rest then in again and over, but the troops were in such a bad condition that the doctor sent in a report saying we were not fit for the line so two other regiments in our division went over in our place.

We were held in reserve and I am glad to say not required after all. Well I think this is about all, for now, I have been with the A.P. & S.S. since December 1st and I can tell you, I hope I shall stop here. I have no desire to go back to the line. Kindly remember me to all old friends...

Yours sincerely,
H.A. Skilling

R.C.S. Frost, 15th January 1917, Dartmouth, England.

Dear Mr Hunt,

Many thanks for the best wishes from Mr Wood and you all in Agreements department and your last letter, also the note from Jack Symons in violet ink (a reminder of divisions eh!).

I am still haunting Dartmouth as you will observe by the address and cannot say how long I shall remain here. I really expected to go before this, and although one sometimes gets 'fed up' with the present life, it is always wise to remember, I might easily be in a worse shop.

I have been feeling about the same the last month, and although I am not fit yet for a strenuous life in the army, I have improved very much since my arrival in England.

Since last writing to you, we have had the reserve battalion of the 7th London Regiment here in billets for training. Their headquarters are at Hammersmith, so you can guess they are some 'nibs'. Their presence has fairly wakened the place up and the band performances on Wednesday and Saturdays draw large crowds. I say 'large crowds', but if the whole population turned out it would not constitute more than the few people that watch a decent London street fight!

I have a friend who has arrived at Torquay Hospital last week, so I must trouble you again to ask Mr Wood to sign the enclosed orders please, as I should like to see him there…

'Frosty'.

G. Holloway, 17th January 1917, Bordon Camp, England.

Dear Mr Taylor,

As I have now made four changes since arriving at Longmoor I thought perhaps it would now be safe to drop you a line, hoping you are better and back at the office and trusting you remain in the best.

I seem to be alright myself and should find no difficulty in taking to the road when I leave the army. The first day after waiting outside no end of places (by the way I think the motto of this regiment is 'wait outside, dyer 'ere', it might be Kum 'ere git one each a bed (sack of straw) and pillow (ditto) and four blankets. We carried them some distance in the snow, finally found a place to sleep. Struck lucky next day as the R.O.D. were full up, some of us were shifted to the huts at the depot where the Railway Transport Division are, quite like going to Buckingham Palace after the other. Of course that meant carrying your bed about one and half miles through snow. That was too good to last so some were sent to Bordon, that meant playing pack horses, backwards and forwards of course a bit unnecessary but that is all in the game. We arrived at Bordon Monday…

We had partly succeeded in drying things when the hut caught fire, fortunately we were in time to save our things (very expensive to lose anything in the army) scramble them through the windows and find another home. It was comfortable and warm in the depot huts at Longmoor but here sleeping is very cold, the blankets are so poor in fact one of mine I think must have been somebody's muffler before it got in the army. Another, I fancy is a wire netting sample sent to the wrong store. Last night I tried sleeping in my clothes, overcoat, all except boots, was not warm then. I cannot say the 'Railway Troops' is soldiering nor are we working much down here, but I suppose it will suit my age best. Although, I should like something better from a soldier's point of view. I have been inoculated once, shall have second inoculation and vaccination soon and overseas leave in about a month's time. We were inspected by Officer in Charge, Royal Engineers last Thursday i.e. we wallowed in the mud several hours and when he came he succeeded in picking his way up and down the lines (without tripping over) to the time of the music, it rained all the time, so he was satisfied with the appearance of the men. We played living pictures, that is standing motionless, whilst the band played waltz tunes. Not so difficult as it seems, as we were partly frozen and well down in the mud (twenty-seven men fell out). We are not altogether only a few got kits when I did.

We are well clothed and moderately well fed. It is very surprising the number of young fellows in a corps like this, a very heavy percentage being even under twenty five, a lot of Scotch and northerners. Of course they are from all lines.

The first hut I slept in a driver was there from Buenos Aires, he by the way had a blanket stolen so the Sergeant Major informed him it would be a debit of 15/- against him. I will now conclude with very best wishes to all…

George Holloway.

S. Smith, undated, Longmoor Camp, England.

Dear Mr Beak and all,

My address shows you I am well in now. Oh it is a different life and comes hard at first, four blankets on the floor and it is hard. I didn't get used to it until last night which was my first night's proper rest. The food is fair but served very rough and not enough after the drills you have to go through. The weather has of course been very bad and I am still in the same things as I left London last Monday. I look like a tramp and my collar, of the colour, something like the office grate. I was inoculated last Thursday but was not so bad but some of the fellows felt it. I expect I shall have a time with the next lot but hope I don't as they have not got much sympathy and of course there is no comfort. A lot of fellows (about four hundred and fifty) have been shifted (Saturday and today) to Bordon and we shall all probably go when we get fitted out as they are making a new camp there with three new companies. It cannot be worse than here which is very dreary and lonely and the nearest village (Liss) is three miles away where several of us went on Saturday and Sunday and had tea. That place is I may say, truly rural. I have had a military hair cut tonight and feel that I look like *Bill Sykes*. I am afraid none of our young ladies would care to be seen walking up number 1 *[platform at Paddington Station]* with me as I look at the moment. *[Next paragraph censored]*

There is no leave now, only when you get your overseas leave which is generally after six weeks here and when you come back you are the put on the draft so it isn't long is it? George Jones and Isles will probably stay longer as they are to have false teeth but me, although as you know, I have got a very bad lot of teeth was passed and they are not touching mine. Army ways are funny and I have already found out a lot of which I trust I shall one day be able to tell you.

I forget to tell you we all got split up into different huts when we arrived and mine is about a mile away from the camp. It is very comfortable however much better accommodation than at the camp. Three other of our fellows were put in there with me and I found some others, also some very nice L. & N.W. Railway chaps, one of whom knew Mr Bryant and all the Fares office chaps. He was the head of the Season Ticket Office at Euston. I might say that they have been very good to me and assisted me more than some of our chaps, one or two of whom I am sorry to say have not done what they might to assist others and I (together with some of the others) have been surprised but of this more anon when we meet. Well I bid you all *adieu* for the present. I think of you all often and only wish I was back again but it has to be done and one can only hope the end will come soon. I hope poor old Syd Douce is getting on alright as we have not heard how he is. Now good luck to you all and every success and tell them all that could go to keep out of this life as long as they can. Goodnight.

I may say that four of our chaps who were lucky to get their outfit last week were moved to Bordon this afternoon: G. Holloway, Isles, Borrough, G.R.J. Jones.

Yours very sincerely,
S. Smith.

W.G. Croft, 12th February 1917, France.

Dear Jack *[Symons]*

Received the *G.W. magazine*. Thanks very much. There is not much news now in it is there. Sorry to hear about Mr Thear, he went off quick didn't he? This war is certainly making a difference. All the old hands are going. How are you getting on? Still going strong in the Audit? I suppose they have had a clear out there. More girls eh! I don't think the war will last long now. There seems to be a great deal of peace talk. Albert *[his brother]* is still going on safe. He says it is fine out there, very warm. It is not the same here. It is the coldest winter France has had since 1903. Plenty of skating on the ponds here. The worst of it all is there is a shortage of coal. It's becoming a thing of the past. If the war lasts much longer goodness knows what will happen. Never mind we must cheer up. 'All for the Good of the cause',

Cheerio, Best luck
Wal Croft

J.H. Porter, 5th February 1917, Bordon Camp, England.

Dear Stan,

I thank you very much for your letter of 23rd January and am sorry I have not written and thanked you before this for the handkerchiefs which you kindly sent me.

Well Stan the boots are still troubling me. I should be A1 so to speak, if it were not for that. Still I hope to get used to them some time or other. You will be interested to know that Cousins, Anglesey and Starchy went off to France yesterday. I am indeed sorry we did not go out together. They were sent out without overseas leave and I am I am pretty certain that I too shall go without the leave which has been previously granted down here after five Sundays had gone by. We have seventeen hundred or more men in camp here at Bordon and there must be nearly as many at Longmoor. There is too a great number of men who have been transferred from various regiments. They appear to approach to about

50% of the men here and some rare lads some of them are, mostly north-country chaps. I must say, Stan, that since the first week we have had very good weather, but it has been very cold most of the time and today there is a layer of about four to six inches of snow.

We had a march out this morning starting at 10 and back at 12.30. I wasn't sorry when I got back, I must say, solely on account of sore trilbies *[slang for feet]* but otherwise it was a beautiful walk round.

The country looked splendid under the covering of snow and our march took us through avenues of pine trees and across moorlands. It looked a real fairy land Stan.

It is true that Joe *[J.C. Storer]* has been taken to hospital at Aldershot? It is a double rupture which has sent him there. I am very sorry for him. He looked real starved up with the cold the first week he was here.

I have been vaccinated, Stan but just my luck I have had no sick leave on account of it. We were called out one morning for the operation, Starchy, Anglesey, Cousins and all the rest, but just as we were about to go into the doctor the whole of the men who happened to be living in the same hut as myself were told to go back to it at once and forthwith were isolated for four days, a young fellow having died from diphtheria or something in the hut. When the rest of the crowd were inspected a week later, they were discovered that they had not been done, so we had to undergo vaccination there and then, consequently, through the mix up have lost our leave (sick) for it. Cousins had a very queer arm through it when he went off.

Well Stan, I am very glad to hear you are not alarmed over the complaint, whatever it is, that affects your heart. I hope you will go on alright, as undoubtedly you will, so long as you are leading no strenuous life. G.R.J *[Jones]*, Borrough and Isles are now in the hut with me, but I believe we shall be moved again tomorrow.

I must thank you very much indeed for the 'wipes', *[handkerchiefs]* Stan. They have already proved useful for I have the usual cold.

Jim

TEN

OCTOBER 1917

'Get this job over then home sweet home when one can sit by the fire knowing that it will hardly be possible for old stagers like myself to have to don the King's uniform again.'

WILLIAM ERNEST EDWARDS

'Taffy' Edwards writing in a letter dated 11th February 1917. He was to die ten months later in France. He wrote sometimes animatedly and positively about his experiences, but at times seemed to let his guard down, and wrote longingly of the safety and security of home. Here he described his regular attendance at a French church:

'You cannot realise what it means just one short hour to escape the sight of guns and men and preparations for war. It takes one right back to pre-war days when everything was bright and peaceful…'

For Taffy his visits to church fulfilled a similar role as his letters to and from home. Letter writing served as an escape from his current situation, a way of absorbing himself in thoughts of home, and the best way of connecting with it. Several times he expressed a desire to return home and one gets the sense that he found his absence from home overwhelming, but was trying to remain upbeat:

'My present work bears no comparison with office life, quill driving is child's play to it.'

Loss of life amongst the office staff was greatest in the latter part of 1917. The Audit newsletter relayed news of the death of five colleagues, including regular writers Monty Pond and Freddy Woodhams. We have unusually detailed information about the loss of Monty Pond from a letter of condolence sent from his commanding Officer to the Audit office:

'In Honour of the Fallen

We regret to place on record the following who have been killed in action. M.P. Pond, late of the Agreements dept, while serving with the Railway Transport Operating Corps in France, was killed by shell fire on a Sunday afternoon early in May. His father was the recipient of some very comforting letters written by the Officer Commanding, extracts of which are given hereunder.

Captain Macdona writes, 'I have for some time been in charge of the department for which your son was working. I know him sufficiently well to know his worth and also your loss. He was one of my best men and there was nothing I would not have trusted him to do for me.'

Again two days later he writes, 'He has been buried in a cemetery nearby and the grave has been duly registered. Captain Pauling, who is my representative, was there yesterday and is making arrangements for a durable cross to be placed on the grave. I shall satisfy myself that everything possible has been done to honour his last resting place.

I feel it almost vitally, as I was very attached to your son. He died a soldier's death and no man could give more than his life. The loss is to you and all who knew him, of whom I am certainly one, I do not fear for him, he lies in peace.'

Four other deaths were mentioned in much less detail, probably because information about the circumstances of their deaths was scant:

R.W.S. Court (Agreements) was, we are informed, killed in action on 26/3/17. Reggie was always a good sport, especially in connection with the rowing club.

F.G. Woodhams (Goods Audit) was killed in action on 16/8/17. He has done a deal of hard work for his country throughout this terrible war, being wounded twice before meeting with his death by being struck with shrapnel. His father

has been the recipient of many letters from friends and the officer commanding
his son's Company.

E.M.C. Stewart, reported as missing, is now reported to have been killed in action.

Unfortunately none of the letters that were sent *to* the Audit soldiers
survive at The National Archives as they would have been kept by the
soldiers themselves rather than filed at their office. As a result, reading
these letters sometimes feels like listening to one side of a conversation.

However, it is clear that the topic of railways gripped our letter writers
both at Paddington and abroad:

'There are hundreds of engines and wagons here but I have only seen one GW
engine although I have noticed plenty of sleepers marked GW.'

The railway was a subject which bound the group together; a common
ground which was shared by the entire GWR staff. One could say that
it was the only common experience that was held by those at home and
abroad, yet the censor forbade them from talking about it in any great
detail. Taffy Edwards said:

'I am unable to enlarge on railway operating as the subject is barred, so must wait
until the war is over before enlightening you thereof.'

W.E. Edwards, 27th January 1917, Bordon Camp, England.

Dear George (Rivers),

God what a life! What oh ye merry sapper no name only a blessed
number like a bally convict, oh if mother could only see me now? Fit
hale and hearty and as giddy as a kitten. We got down to Longmoor on
Wednesday afternoon and after hanging around the orderly room for a
couple of hours were marched off to dinner which was very acceptable.
At 7.30 we paraded and processed to the station and entrained for
Bordon reaching there about 10.30 paid a visit to the stores, gathered
up four blankets and a bag filled with straw and proceeded to Hut 28

where we all endeavoured to settle down to sleep after having a basin of tea each. I don't think any of us got to sleep as the bally bed was so uncomfortable.

Thursday morning we turned out for 8.45 parade and damned if we were not all marched off to receive our first inoculation, some dropped down before they were done and a few soon afterwards but personally I have felt very little effect only a stiffness in the arm. We were examined for teeth at the same time and this morning were marched off to hospital for treatment, the doctor looked at mine, said have toothache? –no sir– can you eat your food? –yes sir– 'fit' said he so out I went patting myself on the back to think I had escaped one lot of torture. Our food here is rough and ready, of course if no available plate smack the meat and spuds on the bare table and carry on. The cooking is not what you would expect to get at the Troc *[Trocadero]*; but when one is hungry just shut your eyes and slog in hard and it is astonishing how well the food goes down...

(I am) sleeping on the floor, tell Dick Kirrage the wool muffler has been a godsend to me at nights especially. I make a balaclava helmet of it and all draught is excluded. Of course it is no protection against rats which tried hard to find an entrance to our hut last night. We have men of all regiments here, transfers, the Non-Commissioned Officers lose their stripes on arriving and <u>curse</u> but apparently they had no option in coming as railway men are coming in daily. I expect we shall have our pals here from Longmoor on Thursday as E Co. are being transferred to the place. We expect our second inoculation next Saturday... and we should have eight days leave from duty but not to go home. All leave appears to be stopped but I understand there is trouble brewing over it so we may get a few days leave after all. Well George, the country round here is fine and in summer must be simply lovely. At present everything is frost-bound and on the parade ground you want to keep moving as the wind cuts like a knife...

Well old boy I suppose I must draw my horns in and close up. Give my kind regards to... old friends, tell them I am quite happy here and am making the best of a bad job. Cheer oh.
Yours sincerely, Taffy

W.E. Edwards, 11th February 1917, France.

Dear George (Rivers),

Here we are again bright and breezy and fit as a fiddle. We have had both doses of inoculation and am now in the throes of vaccination and the itching stage is now on. I have lost my chum Bushell; he was ordered for draft at 3.30pm Friday and took his departure at 9.45pm amidst the strains of 'pack up your troubles' and voluminous cheers. I certainly feel his loss as we were of one mind and pulled together splendidly. My own departure will not be long delayed as nearly all who came down with me are on orders for next draft, probably leaving here on Wednesday so my next address will be just over the water. Have had rather a good time here but the 'forming fours' on the parade ground gets rather monotonous after a time and if it was not for the occasional route march one would soon get the humph. We had a course of gas drill on Friday, donning a helmet. Proceeded to a six foot trench and walked through whilst poison gas was pumped in. It was rather an uncanny feeling at first but one looked upon the event more or less as a joke. After a very short time, the smell of the gas is still in my clothes and bright buttons presented a sorry spectacle after coming into contact with the gas. Well George I am pleased to say I am fit and well but should be glad to say a farewell visit to Slough before departing overseas. Still I suppose personal desires must be sacrificed in the good of the cause and after all is said and done, it would mean another leave taking if I did get a day off and you know the fewer of them the better.

Get this job over then home sweet home when one can sit by the fire knowing that it will hardly be possible for old stagers like myself to have to don the King's uniform again. I don't know yet what I am going out as, either shunter, brakesman or ground signalman, but have received my overseas equipment today. We are all like a lot of school boys, rather excited at the prospects of crossing the water and hoping to avoid the uncomfortable U-boat campaign. Of course getting to work on the railway will be more in our line than squad drill and we all hope to make a good show in our new sphere. Am glad to say all our boys are fit, I don't think the new conditions of life are hurting anybody, but the boots certainly are a bugbear to be feared, as blisters are plentiful and hobbling cheap… Well I suppose the next letter you get from me will be from 'somewhere in France' and I will not delay writing you from there. I suppose this must now wind up with usual best wishes and kindest regards to all.

Yours sincerely, Taffy

W.E. Edwards, 10th March 1917, France.

Dear George,

At last I can drop you a few lines from this side of the water. What with fatigues and work, principally the former, my spare time has been rather limited. We left Bordon at 11.15pm on Feb 16th and after travelling all night eventually reached Folkestone at 7am and were marched off to a rest camp on Marine Parade for breakfast and then on to the boat, each man being served out with a life belt. There the sea journey ended for the time being as we returned to our rest camp and it was not until the Tuesday morning that we left the homeland accompanied by several destroyers for escort and had a most enjoyable trip across. That night we slept in tents at a rest camp where we dropped across Dick Gilson and I for one was extremely surprised at the warmth in the tent for the time of year. We left there at 10.30am and entrained in carriages of the most ramshackle description; the wheels on one side of our coach revolved about twice every mile and skidded the rest, still after just on 12 hours' travelling we reached our destination for the night, some slept on the floor in the Expeditionary Force canteen, others in barns and a few like myself on the floor of a stable loft. Thursday off again but 'padding the hoof' *[travelling on foot]* this time, with our kit bags on our shoulders we set off singing merrily, but before long the bags got weightier and were cursed loudly before we arrived at our billet, and what a billet to be sure, a large barn rigged up with bunks, tier upon tier, the topmost men being on the fourth storey, and we slept on wire netting, each man receiving two blankets and a waterproof sheet… We commenced work of the navvy order, pick and shovel being the weapons served out to us, and alongside the Canadians we slogged in either cutting out chalk, or packing up the rails on the line, or carrying either timber or rails. We had working near us on several occasions a party of German prisoners who appeared to be quite contented with their lot… Whilst I am writing this our guns are playing hell's delight. I am part of this squad and we are gradually approaching the trenches, which are very few miles from us. Of course I cannot mention and place names but this is a small town, or rather was, as previous bombardments have made havoc of the majority of houses, the church has escaped with very little damage. Our billet is minus windows and doors also one end of the house, still we have made ourselves quite a comfortable residence with the aid of sacking to keep out the draught and for warmth have a very decent stove. The shops here are not like those in Westbourne Grove, still they do not get patronised like the Scottish canteen where prices are far more reasonable, but wine shops are plentiful, and although debarred from selling spirits or liqueurs, do a pretty good trade in French and English beers, the price of the former meeting the Tommy's packet the best.

Our work here is not yet in full swing as the Canadians have not fully evacuated the premises, but light railway working is not like being on the main line as there are no signals and one has to look out whilst travelling to see points are in the proper position as no pointsman is in attendance… I have made several trips in daylight and two at night, arriving home at 11.30pm and 1am respectively, and can assure you it is no joy ride on a dark night as the track is practically a smudge and the mules a blur so you have to keep your eyes well skinned to avoid running down your team. We carry food for man and presents for somebody else who will not appreciate their arrival and personally I quite enjoy these little jaunts as they are apt to be quite exciting at times.

Of course one meets civilians who still stick to their ruined homes, but they are hopelessly outnumbered by the army and even at church still the army, but it is the only place where one can really feel they are in touch with those they have left behind to keep the home fires burning. You cannot realise what it means just one short hour to escape the sight of guns and men and preparations for war. It takes one right back to pre-war days when everything was bright and peaceful, and it also gives one the necessary time to face things as they are and resolve to carry out their duty however disagreeable or dangerous the task allotted to them may be...

After my late arrival (1am) last night or rather this morning I was excused first parade, but as a rule I dish out the food to our party of eleven men and so far have given general satisfaction, each man getting his fair proportion, and must say here we are much better fed than in our former billet– no complaints.

I can see the censor counting these sheets so must have some consideration for him and you must be content with this until I get a communication from you, so here ended the first epistle. Cheer oh, old sport, trust all well at home and all correct in the office. *[Censored]*.

Au revoir, yours sincerely, Taffy

S. Smith, 19th March 1916, France.

My Dear Elton and all,

I expect you are wondering why I have never written since leaving England. Well the fact is I have never had a chance for it has been a cook's tour since I was last with you. Perhaps I had better try and give you some idea of my adventures from the time we last met. It was not many hours after seeing you all that we were dispatched for France... We landed at a town after a nice long trip... At this spot, a rest camp so called, we spent about a week. What with parades in the daytime for various reasons and employed at the docks all night, unloading flour was the job that came my way you can imagine the rest we had. However we then went on to another base and here owing to illness, we were all isolated for ten days and no letters could be sent. Within a day or two of being released from this I alone of all our boys was packed off to another depot so that was the last I have seen for the time being of our crowd, and have been on my own since. After a couple of nights at this depot I was sent to a point to get experience in the work I came here for. This turned out to be the best thing I had touched for the staff were billeted out and I slept in a feather bed which was great for it was under canvas... I soon found out that my luck was in and that happiness and comfort would be my lot whilst there... Alas my dream was soon dispelled, and after a week of civilised existence, I was sent for by the depot. After another 48 hours there I was sent away again to some other spot, but en route, was detained at a rest camp for two days, apparently owing to the absence of trains to the point I was going...

Covered vans are used here to convey soldiers about. Strange to say the actual truck I made this last journey in I saw again the next day loaded with sick horses, so being used for any purpose you can guess they cannot be compared to the carriages in which we made our daily trips to town and back. To continue my travels, the next day I was sent to the point I am now writing from, and which I think will be my residence for some little time as I have now taken up regular duties. It is a terrible, godforsaken and desolate spot. There is naught to be seen except shell holes and rats and these latter are an abomination...There is little to be heard here at night except gun fire and rats and one soon gets used to both. I went to a village, the nearest here, about two miles away, on Sunday last and it was really an awful sight to see how it had been smashed by shell fire. You can now I trust realise the reason for my not writing before, in fact I have only written to my wife and father, and have only received one letter from each of them and that was a few days ago. I can tell you that I hunger for news of home after being here a month without a word... It is also almost impossible to buy anything for there is nowhere to get it...

I trust all is well with everyone... If Miss Welsh's little affair has come off I wish her the very best of luck and trust she will have all happiness... Please write to me soon some of you...

Your old pal, Sid

W.E. Edwards, 4th April 1917, France.

Dear George (Rivers),

Your letter... came safely to hand but I have been too busy to answer until now. As you say my present work bears no comparison with office life, quill driving is child's play to it and if I was not fit and well could not endure for long. In daytime it is fatigues (hewers of wood and drawers of water) and work actually starts about 6pm and continues until 4 or 5am, sometimes as late as 8 or 9am when one returns to the billet fairly knocked up as night work plays the devil with one... We were roused up at 4.30am and marched off to take cover as there was a fear of Fritz sending over messages of hate, so no more sleep...

　　Our first casualties today as some went out this morning and got caught (wounded). Fritz is unkind today. Perhaps somewhat annoyed at the prize packets sent him last night, still one must expect retaliation. I am unable to enlarge on railway operating as the subject is barred, so must wait until the war is over before enlightening you thereof... As regards the commissions you mention, those people who obtained them are welcome to them as far as I am concerned, may they appreciate the work the sappers have to do when they come out here. I was glad to get the magazine, and as we have other GW men here they appreciate a perusal of the former as much as I do. Am glad to hear things are settling down again at the office and hope peace and quietness will reign for some time to come. One never knows when you will drop across a chum in these parts. Read of the stats is near here and I called upon him the other evening as I was walking some stuff to his place, strange meeting eh? Kind regards to all in the office...

Taffy (Edwards)

F.E. Andrews, 4th April 1917, France.

Dear George,

I expect you have wondered what has happened to us all, well old chap, our party of Audit chaps is split up, for there are only four of us left at the camp. Crane and I are in the same tent... We never know from one day to another when we may get marching orders for another depot, as far as the work goes, up to now it has not been of a very interesting character, and our railway work up to now consists of loading and unloading timber and rails, carting ballast, cleaning engines and all sorts of nice little jobs of that kind, so you can imagine what a change it is for us after pen pushing, but I live in hope of a change later on, for I think there will be lots of work on the railway in the near future and we may touch lucky later on, meanwhile I am managing to keep fit and cheery in spite of the rotten weather we are having, snow and hailstorms almost every day and rivers of mud everywhere...

Now old chap, how are things going at the office, 'anything doing', let's have a line when you can find time and tell us all the news... Have you had to go up for re-examination yet? I very often run across GW chaps I know. I must dry up now as <u>duty calls</u>.

With kind regards, yours etc,
Fred Andrews

S.C. Hills, 6th April 1917, place unknown.

Dear Mr Davies,

Many thanks for your interesting letter of 6th July. I only received it the other day, our mails having been held up for some time. Am very glad to hear you are 'pretty fit' in spite of the potato famine etc. We out here have seen a little more of 'Johnny Turk' *[the Turkish army]* just lately and are expecting to have another bout at him any time now. According to the calendar it's Good Friday today, otherwise we shouldn't know. Still there's plenty of fellows far worse off than we are– that's our one great consolation. It also seems as if things are serious in England now, as regards food I mean.

With Best regards. S.C. Hills

W.G. Croft, 8th April 1917, Salonika, Greece.

On Active Service
Dear Jack,

Received mag. again this morning. Many thanks. How are you going on. Still busy. Heard nothing about coming out here again have you?

Well. Cheero. Best Luck, Wal

R.C.S. Frost, 10th April 1917, North Camp, England.

Dear Mr Hunt,

I was very glad to get another letter from you, with all the news respecting old colleagues in the office. Yes, it is sad about young Turner, as he was so keen to join the army. It is strange how things work out, isn't it?

I have not started serious training yet, in fact my life is easier now than when I last wrote to you, and by that you will imagine I am doing nothing at all, and reality you won't be far wrong. I was examined by the doctor a fortnight ago, for classification, and he wouldn't pass me as fit, so I have got to appear before a Travelling Medical Board sometime in the near future, when it calls at Ripon... There are about a dozen of us, and this afternoon we were taken for a walk for an hour. This is a new order, and really a welcome one, as the days drag out so when cooped up in a hut all the time...

There are some great lads in this hut, and the one who particularly shines is a chap who is still feeling the after effects of sun stroke caught in Egypt. One night (pay night!) he came in and started sparring at the stove pipe, and eventually gave it a knockout blow! A rather silly trick he is fond of doing when he cannot get a seat around the stove, is to put live

257

cartridges in the fire, and naturally everyone makes a dash away from it. After the report he invariably secures a seat in the general scramble. On another pay night he strolled in, with one of the battalion name boards, which he had broken off in the ground where the camp road is crossed by another... Of course this board had to be removed before the officer's morning inspection of the hut, so it served a useful purpose in kindling the fire in the morning! No wonder the war is costing us so much, as an officer remarked when a chap told him. He had lost a spoon, at a kit inspection. I hope you are keeping A1 and enjoyed your Easter holiday...

Sincerely yours, S. Frost

J.W. Hyam, 22nd April 1917, Salisbury Plain, England.

Dear Bertie,

Here we are again back in England after an attack of shell shock but now quite recovered. We were only transferred to R.F.A. a fortnight ago and got put on a draft right away. It's all up with the Huns now. I think if you can imagine what machine guns are like, just think what the big guns are like, practically going at the same rate of course, I mean all the guns together. It is awful. This is an awful place here only tin huts and soldiers and the grub is not enough to feed a kid. I hope you will excuse writing but I can't keep still. Sometimes I feel in the pink and then I get a relapse. I am in a good Battery plenty of football we played the Army Service Corps for charity in aid of St Dunstan's home for blind soldiers and won 1-0. About 2,000 watching and excitement was great right up to the finish.

How is everybody at Padd. Please remember me to Freddy Woodhams and... all the girls of course no luck here as regards flappers. How is Tinker? Is Jack Symons still living? The plains are looking a treat now if you ever suffer from bad appetite come here for a five mile gallop over the plain it's the real thing. I have a nice mare as my mount she was a hunter and can jump like a cat and move well *[censored]*...

I met two of the Bruges football team at Rouen who played against the GW team over in Belgium. Strange eh. One had the Croix de Guerre and the other a Commissioner. Called at *Red Lamp* and had a wine. Well must pack up now. Hope you all are in the best of health up in the smoke just drop a line telling me where the boys are.

Yours J.W. Hyam...

F.R. Morris, 26th April 1917, 'in the field', France.

Letter and a programme

Dear Mr Taylor,

No doubt you think that I have forgotten all about you and my friends of the Audit, but never let it be said (this is an army term, if you please.) Truth to tell I have been going to write time after time, but have had to put it off for various reasons. I am taking this opportunity of writing to you, while I am in charge of tonight's guard. I get this job about once a week now, it's not so bad, I have three men and a man in waiting; we mount at 5pm and dismiss at 7am. We make ourselves as comfortable as we can, in the guard tent, which just covers over the top of the sand bags, and these have got grass growing out of them now. The sand bags are about 4ft high and make a good protection. April 1st I got my two stripes up, after being a 1st Air Mechanic for 12 months, the Non-Commissioned Officers have a very decent mess here, and everything is ok. I am corporal in charge of wireless, photographic, electrical and all instruments used on aeroplanes, I have had a very good education on all those subjects, but the one I like best is the wireless, it's far more interesting than photography, which is a very big thing indeed out here, and a lot depends upon a good photograph of the Hun lines...

Yesterday I saw a nice little game between one of ours and one of theirs, after our anti-aircraft fire had taken it up a bit higher, our machine went for it and got well over the top of it, then two more of ours came along and forced it down, she tried all manner of tricks, but down she came alright, and landed a clean machine, not broken in any part, and the two Huns inside it quite well.

We gave a *revue [theatrical show]* to our chaps here on the 13th, it went off alright, we started at 9pm and gave a two hours show, am enclosing programme, and will forward a photo of myself as the 'oldest inhabitant' as soon as I receive them from the Frenchman who took them...Kind regards to all of the section and the remainder of the agreements, and hoping you are fit and well. Good bye.

Yours sincerely, F.R. Morris

P.S. Do you think the programme is worth putting in the GW mag, with one or two photos of the show? If you do, and would get it put in. I will write a description and send it along.

G. Holloway, 13th May 1917, France.

Dear Mr Taylor,

... Have been going to write many times, but been some time getting settled. Have rather an interesting job... Locomotives clerk... The weather now is fine... I am rather high up, so we get the extremes, very cold or very hot. Have nothing to complain about so far but shall not be sorry when it is all over. I cannot tell you anything interesting, as a matter of fact a part of my wanderings I was unable to write at all (forbidden), but of course should like to hear a little news from home... The tents were covered in snow, but I now live in a hut; something like Park Lane. We had a football match yesterday Railway Operating Division and Argyle and Sutherland Highlanders. A fine game and the R.O.D. won. I should like a bit of exercise myself, but there is nothing doing in the aquatic line. In fact the scenery is poor to my mind, owing to the lack of water. Saw some good views round Rouen, but would give a week's pay for a look at the Thames, even at Hammersmith. Have just seen the May mag: too many photos. *[Holloway is referring to the magazine's inclusion of a photograph of each soldier who had lost his life.]*

With best wishes hoping all are well...

G. Holloway

R.C.S. Frost, 9th July 1917, France.

Dear Mr Hunt,

I need hardly say how pleased I was to receive your welcome letter forwarded from Ripon, with all the latest news about old friends at the office. Yes it must seem strange to see the great number of vacant places in the Agreements dept, and possibly to the select few who remain there would be a tinge of sadness at the sight, when you call to mind the busy throng in pre-war days, working far into the night… if it were not for the fact that it is for the duration only. There are a few unfortunately, that will not return, and I was sorry to learn from home is Monty Pond, who will be greatly missed by us on the Agreements section…

Probably you will be surprised to see my address, but I have been on the continent now three weeks. After the medical board at which I was recommended for gradual training in class AIII*, an order came out for all men in that category to proceed to the base in France for such training, so I had to come across here. I have finished my period of training and am now practically 'marking time' so to speak. Specialists only go to units as they are required, so I may have to remain here for some time. Of late we have been filling up our time doing guards, or picquets, or attend funerals, or an occasional route march, or argument! If the latter argument would finish a war, we should have brought peace long ago, as there is always someone in the tent anxious to argue, when there is nothing else to do. Not all these discussions are on war topics, or the various merits of Scotch regiments, but quite a lot of time will be spent on deciding which paddle steamer on the Clyde has the most boilers, or why are army biscuits made so hard! The latter problem is not hard to solve when notice is taken of the large staff of dentists employed at the base, and as I have already broken one of my teeth in the process of mastication.

I am pleased to hear about Fatty Hyam, and will drop him 'a line' in a few days. So you are in the fashion of going in for vegetable growing? I hope you will have the same success that was your reward in the finer art of flower cultivation in peace time. One sees amusing sketches in papers about the talk in city-bound trains, at the present time, and the prominent part the allotment plays. Is that the state of affairs in the local trains to Paddington now? I really must dry up now, and hope these lines will find you well.

Yours sincerely, Frosty

A.P. Barron, July 29th 1917, France.

Dear Mr Hunt,

I have duly received your welcome letter and as you say I now know something about army life… I have not run across any of our chaps excepting two or three of the Railway Clearing House fellows who were the last lot to go, they are stationed where I am so you can guess it is a big depot because I was here about seven weeks before I ran across them, and then it was only luck. I am very pleased to hear Kemball is better, and trust he will soon be well enough to resume his old office work, and when you next see him kindly remember me to him…I am very sorry to hear about young Turner losing his arm and trust he will soon make well… I had heard before I left about poor Reg Court and Stewart. Fancy 'Mug' Morris a Corporal in the R.F.C… I think our chaps are doing well don't you so don't be surprised to hear one of these days that I have been made a Sergeant or something more (I don't think). I heard about poor Pond's death and it must be nice for his father to know he was so much respected. Fancy young Bratchell a 2nd Lieut, I am surprised but at the same time pleased to know our office is doing so well and also that Williams has passed the Officer Training Corps exams…

Yours sincerely, A.P. Barron

There are hundreds of engines and wagons here but I have only seen one GW engine although I have noticed plenty of sleepers marked GW.

J.C. Kibblewhite, 1st September 1917, Malta.

Dear Sir,

I trust you will excuse the liberty I have taken in writing you, after such a long absence from England, but the difficulties of active service is my excuse, although I am sorry to say laziness has a lot to do with it.

No doubt you will wonder what I am doing wasting my time in Malta; well, I came here last January through an attack of dysentery followed by constipation, there I remained, and am likely to do so, unless something very unexpected happens.

I have been taken on the temporary staff, and am acting as parade staff sergeant, quite a nice easy position, except when we are receiving or sending troops away.

How are things in general, looking at Paddington, I suppose the office is full of ladies and men who are over the age limit.

I saw a Great Western Magazine a few days ago, and I noticed that a large number of the 'chiefs' have retired, also that Artlett has not given up trying to bring sports honours to the Audit with the Bowls team.

The weather here is absolutely glorious, and our camp is right against the sea, we get some lovely bathing and boating, in fact it is almost as good as any resort in England. We are about ten miles from Valletta, but we can always get a ride in a motor lorry or a gharry. I have only met one GW man since I have been here and that is Cowles of the Agreements. He has been here since the Dardanelles; and he is acting chief clerk to the commanding officer of the Company camp...

I have not given up hope of getting to England yet, as since I have been here I have contracted malaria, also my heart is not good enough to allow me to carry a pack for a while, so I have been marked unfit for over three months, and I may give you all a surprise by walking into the office one of these fine days.

Well, sir, when is the war going to end, I think it would have been all over now, bar the shouting, if it had not been for Russia.

I think the Great Western Railway according to the magazine have reaped a fair share of the awards for bravery etc, on the field.

Well, sir, I trust it will not be long before I have the pleasure of receiving a reply to my letter, and kindly remember me to all that are left of the old room 19…

I am, Sir, Yours respectfully, J.C. Kibblewhite Sgt.

H. Beaumont, 2nd March 1917, Aratia, Yemen.

Dear Bertie,

Many thanks for your long and interesting letter, which has now reached me; I will reply to it at length at a more opportune moment.

As you will see by above address I have left India. The regiment left the N.W. Indian frontier in January where the winter had been bitterly cold and embarked at Karachi after a three day's train journey, then six day's most pleasant voyage to Aden where we landed and now join part of the Aden Field Force. I have been stationed with a strong detachment on the desert in close proximity to a Turkish force who frequently shelled us, but without any material damage. The heat after the cold winter in India is very trying, scorching hot sun, endless sand and myriads of torturing flies. Life is very different here as compared to India. I never pictured myself riding across the Arabian dessert on a camel. Am pleased to say I am splendidly fit and well, but should be glad when the struggle is over and hope I shall be amongst those who return home safely. Trusting you are well. Best of wishes, kind regards to the remnants of the Audit staff.

Yours most sincerely, Harry Beaumont

ELEVEN

MARCH 1918

'As no doubt many have told you, letters are always a godsend out here.'
STANLEY CLARKE HILLS

This month's edition of the newsletter was not so heavy with correspondence however, as S.C. Hill's comment makes clear, letters from the office were still critical for morale. Arthur Smith wrote from France having recovered from typhoid. He was delighted to network with several other characters from the office out there and exchange news. He also noted that

'We were all very sorry to hear of Pond's death. He was an exceedingly nice fellow and was liked by us all.'

Frost was back in France after his spell in hospital but subsequent letters showed him on leave in the 'Delectable Duchy', that is, Cornwall. Men who were previously wounded such as George Kemball, F.T. Turner, G.R. Jones, and A.E. Rippington had been welcomed back to their desks at home and at the same time, two more Audit staff had joined, including officer messenger F.W.J. Ford to the Royal Flying Corps. Mr Burgoyne, or 'Burgie' as addressed by some, left the Audit to work at the War Office.

E.W. Jackson according to the newsletter notes was back in England. He had recovered from illness when on leave and was then attached to the Artillery at Colchester, then moved to Crowborough but was kicking his heels to be back in France.

The office received interesting word from Kenneth Sharland in India for the first time. He described his long journey to Kirkee, Pashan Camp. He clearly had two very different travel experiences on the White Star liner *Suevic* and the Cunard Company's *Laconia* whilst in transit. In India he also observed that

'strange as it may seem to English people, native women do most of the work here.'

He had also found an Italian restaurant in Poona which was 'very good and quite the equal of most London restaurants.' Football obsessed 'Fatty' Hyam in Winchester on the other hand gave the full breakdown of the 10th Battery Royal Garrison Artillery football team and his impressions of the 'Yankees' based with him. Continuing the football theme, A.P. Barron also noted that he had met several more men from Paddington and

'the latest arrival is Radnage the footballer who was in the Chief Goods Office, I expect you know him he used to play for Queens Park Rangers.'

Frederick Ernest Andrews, of the Rail Operating Division of the Royal Engineers wrote about his time in France. He too, was sorry to hear of Pond's death and added that

'our family has had to pay the penalty of war that so many thousands of families have done, for I am now the only one out here, one brother has just been discharged after nine months in hospital, the second one was killed at Ypres about a month ago and the third is now in a London hospital with a bad shrapnel wound in the thigh'.

This month, William Wiggs managed to convey the sheer immediacy of combat in a short note to the office:

'A matter of about five minutes ago Fritz was bombing us, and I have just got up off the ground where I was laying for about twenty minutes. One fellow has been hit, but not severely by shrapnel. This is his second visit this evening.'

The March newsletter also reported that Corporal F.J. Serjent of the 180th Brigade, Royal Field Artillery had been commended for his gallant conduct and devotion to duty in the field on July 7th 1917 with the Irish Division. Percy Ham of the Agreements department who had been reported killed in action in June 1917, was very much alive according to the notes and had been awarded a military medal: it was actually his brother who had been killed in action.

Lastly, in honour of the fallen, details were given regarding Lieutenant W.H. Cronin who

'held the rank of Acting Captain when on leave from Egypt the latter part of last summer, shortly after his return to active service in Palestine, we heard the sad news of his being mortally wounded, thus passed away yet another of the Audit's old rowing sports.'

H.W. Cronin, newspaper clipping, dated 8th December 1917, included in the newsletter

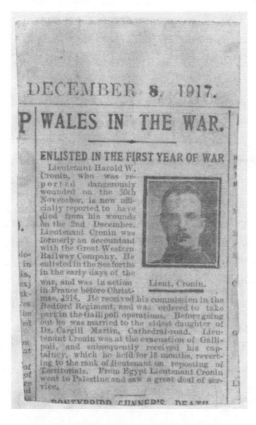

K.B.W. Sharland, 26th July 1917, Pashan Camp, Kirkee, India.

My dear Mr Biggs

The writing mood is on me so I take the opportunity to send you a few lines to let you know how I am getting on, at the same time hoping that at some future date I may have the pleasure of hearing from you. Your letter is bound to be very interesting to me as I have not seen or heard from anybody at Paddington for over six months.

I left Aldershot on March 16th and travelled as far as Durban via Sierra Leone and Cape Town on the White Star Liner *Suevic*. This part of the journey was delightful, the food and accommodation was very good for a troopship. Of course this is accounted for by the fact that it is an Australian troopship. Everything was done that could be to make the journey enjoyable for the one thousand seven hundred men on board. We stayed just outside Sierre Leone for three days but were not allowed to leave. We arrived at Cape Town on Saturday afternoon four weeks after leaving Keyham and had a route march round the town the same evening. The next day we were allowed to roam about at will all day and a right jolly time we had although it was very hot indeed for winter. Cape Town is a beautiful place and the inhabitants made our visit very enjoyable.

The patriotism of the South African is wonderful to us after the coolness of the English (especially Aldershot). On the Monday we sailed for Durban arriving there on the Thursday evening after a rather rough journey round the Cape. We did not land till the Saturday afternoon and then bid goodbye to the *Suevic*. She went on to Australia. We had two weeks at Durban and had a glorious time in a rest camp on Ocean Beach. Every day we went bathing and only had parades up to 12 noon each day. The trams were free to us all over the city and invitations were showered upon us by the English residents. You can rest assured that we were very sorry to leave such a delightful spot, still all good things come to end and we finally had to go on board the *Laconia* belonging to the Cunard company for four weeks' misery, we lay in the harbour for one week longing to go ashore before we started on the last stage of our journey to India. This ship was actually lousy *[infested with lice]* and we had to put up with a shirt inspection every day. The food was bad and very little of it and to back it all up the canteen was rotten as well. I was glad to get to Bombay and get off such a rotten ship. I lost a stone in weight during that four weeks.

We arrived in India during the monsoon period and have had plenty of rain more than we like I can assure you.

Kirkee is only about hundred miles from Bombay and is about six thousand feet above the sea. We will while here never have the extremes of weather as the climatic conditions are considered to be ideal here.

Strange as it may seem to English people native women do most of the work here, and actually act as bricklayers' labourers carrying pans of 'mortar' on their heads, the men do very little indeed. Sunday is the same as any other day to them. As they have their own religious days when they have what they call *Ram Jamees*. All cartage is done by oxen and is rather slow and cumbersome. Kirkee Bazar is about three quarters of an hour's walk from Pashan Camp and is rather interesting but is very dirty, children run about naked and the drainage and dwellings are very bad indeed. Cigarettes made by the Turkish tobacco company *Bandra* can obtained for eleven annas *[former unit of Indian currency]* per 100 (eleven pence) and are very good indeed, being better than the Nebka. Poona is the nearest city and is about five miles away. I walked there last Thursday to have a look round, this place boasts of one or two hotels and an Italian restaurant but is otherwise an exact counterpart of Kirkee and quite as dirty. The Italian restaurant is very good and is quite the equal of most London restaurants.

We do not receive a very many letters out here, as the mail is so uncertain, we never know when the next one will arrive.

When you are writing you must let me know all the news, I wonder whether your section will ever be established again as it was before.

Since I came out here I have taken up signalling and find it very useful, there is just a possibility I might be able to learn wireless, if so I don't doubt that it might be useful to me, when we get back to *Blighty* if there is half a chance to do so I will cease it.

Our Battalion is at Aden and unless the signalling alters my destination I will eventually find myself there. It is not exactly the place I should choose if I had my own way but of course there is no choice about it.

Well I think I have given you all the news now and am sure you are tired of reading this letter by now, so will close with best wishes to you all from, yours sincerely,

Kenneth W. Sharland

A. Smith, 18th September 1917, France.

Dear Sir *[Mr Slater]*

A few more lines to let you know that am still alive and kicking. I was very pleased to get your letter of 9th May and to know all the office news, but from various sources since then, I have heard of great changes. In fact about five weeks ago I had quite a field day with G.W. men. I went up to G.H.Q. in the car with my officer and when I got there I found several old British Expeditionary Forces chums and a number of G.W. men so I had quite an enjoyable time. The G.W. men I saw were Russell (Audit) who is a corporal, Burgoyne (General Manager's Office) who is a Company Sergeant Major, Horton (G.M.'s Office) who is a second corporal and to my great astonishment I saw Mr Dent of Parcels department (Audit) fame up there. He had only been out a fortnight then. He seemed to be jogging along steadily and taking things as they came. Russell and I sealed our friendship with them by having a mug of tea each in the Y.M.C.A. at his expense. At G.H.Q. I also met a Sergeant Pocock who was one of the L. & N.W. Railway auditors who used to come to Paddington and check coal accounts etc. Through going to G.H.Q, I was able to learn news of other Audit men and have since got into communication with Tom Crathern who is quite well

We were all very sorry to hear of Pond's death. He was an exceedingly nice fellow and was liked by us all. Crathern told me in a letter that he had been to see his grave and that someone had put up a very nice cross. In fact the Military Forwarding Officer has a photo of it in his office

In June I went on another fine trip in the car with my officer, down to our principal base. The weather was grand which made the trip perfectly enjoyable

On the first of this month a promotion order was issued, and it may interest you to know that I am now a Sergeant. Speller of the G.M.'s Office, who is here, was promoted to Company Sergeant Major and Webb of the Passenger Department, Audit was made a Lance Corporal. We had ten promotions in the headquarters all together so we did well

A few of us have been fishing in our spare time. We have caught a few but we are not very enthusiastic about it. The proper fisherman has a stone jar by his side doesn't he? Perhaps that is the attraction

I think this all for the present, so with my kindest regards and best wishes to all, I remain, yours obediently,

A. Smith

S.C. Hills, 7th October 1917, Egypt.

Dear Mr Davies

Thanks very much indeed for your letter of September 19th, it was most interesting. I will certainly keep a look out for the 10th Middlesex Regiment and for Paddy Norwood.

At present we are about six miles behind the line doing a little training, sometimes amounting to nine hours a day which we think is a bit too much. However we always smile when a mail arrives no matter how pushed we have been. I don't mean we only smile when we get a letter, it's far from that, but as no doubt many have told you, letters are always a godsend out here. I saw a *GWR. Magazine* the other day, there were any number of changes among some of the big pots.

I see Mr Potter's son has had another lift up. I am very pleased to hear that so many of you older ones are keeping well and sticking it especially Mr Couch and yourself. I hope your good luck will continue in the way of good health. Best regards to yourself and all.

Yours very sincerely,

S.C. Hills

When you knock against Mr Goodall will you give him my best regards. Thanks.

F.E. Andrews, 16th October 1917, France.

Dear Mr Slater

Just a few lines to let you know how things are going with me, I have been going to write to before this, but on each occasion I have had to postpone it for some reason or other. I have been at this place since April. It is a fairly large city and has at one time been a very nice place, but it is now a heap of ruins, not a habitable house anywhere and no civilians, it is the nearest railhead to this part of the line and when we first came here things were pretty lively, but Fritz is gradually being pushed back here and has not troubled us for some time now I don't mind if he has forgotten we're here. Naldrett, Dawson and Anglesey and several other Audit chaps were up here a short time ago, but their detachment has now been moved to another part of the line, they are on the Light Railway and shift about more.

It was nice to meet some of the old office pals again and I spent several pleasant hours with them while they were here, for I am the only G.W. man in this detachment. McMeeken is in the Railway Transport Officer's office about three miles from here and I see him occasionally. I was very sorry to hear of the deaths of Pond and Woodhams and no doubt there are other casualties amongst our office chaps but I seldom hear any office news. Our family has had to pay the penalty of war that so many thousands of families have done, for I am now the only one out here, one brother has just been discharged after nine months in hospital, the second one was killed at Ypres about a month ago and the third is now in a London hospital with a bad shrapnel wound in the thigh. I have had a variety of jobs, including navvy's work, carrying rails and

sleepers, guard, point oiler and various other jobs. I am now a checker
and number taker which job suits me much better, for it combines a lot
of indoor clerical work with outdoor checking and now that we have to
face another winter out here, it will be something to spend a little of my
time indoors for I still have memories of last winter under canvas, but
I shall not be so badly off this winter for we are living in railway vans
which will be much warmer. I have now been in France nearly nine
months and there does not appear to be any prospect of leave, for there
are more here who have been eighteen months without leave and at the
rate the R.O.D. men are going at present it will be well into next year
before my turn comes.

I understand that north London has suffered rather badly in the
recent air raids but I hope you came through all right. My wife and
family have had to get away from home, for it was upsetting their nerves
and I am pleased to think that they are out of the danger zone.

I am keeping fairly fit in health and always manage to keep cheery,
which wants a bit of doing sometimes especially now the muddy season
has started, but let's hope this will be our last out here and by this time
next year we may be all settling down to civilian life again. Please
remember me to Mr Wood, Bert Hunt and all other Audit friends. Yours
sincerely

F.E. Andrews...

J.W. Hyam, 31st October 1917, Winchester, England.

Dear Bertie

No doubt you have been wondering what has become of me. Well, I have
got another shift as you see and it is a trifle better than Bulford, more
life. We can go to theatre or cinema occasionally; that is what we could
never do at Bulford. By the way I have written to Frosty about a month
ago and up to the present have had no reply. I hope he is well, have you
heard from him lately? How are all the boys? Are all the girls married

yet? And has Bill Butler got married yet? We have one good thing in this
Battery that is a rattling good football team.

The forward's right wing two officers are both amateur
Internationals, centre forward Fatty, left wing a Preston N.E. and Everton
regular player and Wickham of Sittingbourne a Kent County player. Left
half: Lancashire Accrington Stanley, C.H. [centre half] a Scottish Junior
International and he has also played regularly for Patrick Thistle Scottish
League, R.H. [right half] a Motherwell man, R.B [right back] Walsall
& Exeter City, L.B. [left back] Bristol Rovers and G.K. [goal keeper] a
Welsh amateur International. We have played five, won them all and got
twenty-five goals and one against a penalty in the 1st match. How is the
GW team going on, is Ginger still there? I suppose a few of the old ones
discharged.

This is a heavy Battery of sixty pounders [guns] and today they
warned all A1 men for a draft for Italy and also Non-Commissioned
Officers, that is, in the gunner section. We the drivers have fifty-eight
out of a hundred odd warned for Salonika, so we shall be pretty well
cleared out by Xmas eh! I hope the wife is well and if any remember
me to Freddie Woodhams, Jack Symons and Dickie. We have a lot of
W.A.A.C.* here, flappers and old 'uns. Some of them have been working
in munitions but are now cooks and know absolutely nothing about it
yet, but I suppose they will soon pick it up. We have some good talent
here in the concert line and get some very pleasant evenings. We have
altogether quite a number of clever men here, artists, B.Sc., B.A., M.D.
Well, must pack up now remember me to all the boys etc...

Yours sincerely, Fatty

R.C.S. Frost, 20th November 1917, France.

Mr Levett,

Just a few lines to thank you for the monthly supply of *G.W. Magazines*,
and to let you have my proper address. The magazines have been sent
on from the base alright, but you know a good soldier doesn't like his

friends to think he is always stuck at the base!!! Of course this is not my only reason for writing but I thought it about time to let you know I am still kicking about France. Since leaving the base last August, I have not had such a bad time. I have renewed my acquaintance with the trenches and was in the big push on September 20th last. I am glad to have enjoyed good health, and escaped being damaged up to the present. A few of us are away from the Battalion billeted in a French village. Life in a place like this is pretty quiet, and mud abounds everywhere as usual. I have spent some decent evenings with fellows from my old Battalion who are also here, which help to pass these dark nights. We miss such places for recreation as Y.M.C.A. huts etc. which are always found in the forward areas, and bases. However what we lose in this respect, we gain in safety from shell fire and bombs.

Last Tuesday we celebrated the anniversary of the 'Scotchman's day' at Beaumont Hamel, by enjoying a holiday from the usual routine. The army rations were increased and sports held in the morning. After dinner there was a free beer parade for such as like to 'gaze upon the vintage when it is crimson', but I was found on the T.T. [teetotal] parade of course.

How are all good people getting on at the office? I shall be glad of a few lines from any of you, when 'divisions' will allow! Please remember me to Messrs Hunt, J.B. Taylor, Symons and Woodhams. With kind regards to you all,

Sincerely yours, 'Frosty'...

A.P. Barron, 27th November 1917, France.

Dear Mr Hunt,

Just a few lines to let you know that I am still alive and in the best of health. I have not heard from anyone at the office for some time past and naturally I wonder if you are still there and how things are going. Our messenger Ford promised to send me the magazine each month so as I could keep in touch with things, but I only had *October* and have since written him regarding *November* and have had no reply. I was wondering if he has left, if so, would you kindly ask one of our other chaps to send it to me and I will pay when I get home on leave

I am pleased to say I have a job at present in the Low Stores and I like it very much and can manage it for the duration. What do you think of the news lately, fine isn't it and I think it will continue so as long as the weather keeps fine, it has been bitter cold out here this past few days but I suppose we cannot grumble as the weather has been lovely for the time of year. Is Hibberd still there? If so you might ask him if he received my letter as I have written to several at the office and not one has answered only you and Mr Rivers. I suppose you are all beginning to think about Xmas now and I expect the shops are beginning to look pretty. Has Mr Kemball come back to the office yet? If so, you might remember me kindly to him also his wife

I am afraid I must now close we cannot say too much, my address now is… and should be pleased to hear from anyone. In case I don't get the opportunity of writing you again I now wish you and all friends a Merry Xmas and Happy New Year, trusting we shall be with you this time next year.

A.P. Barron.

R.C.S. Frost, 20th December 1917, Cornwall, England.

Dear Mr Levett,

Just a few lines to thanks you for your splendid long letter which I received from France last Saturday. I need hardly say how much I appreciate your kindness in telling me about old friends at the office, although I have had the pleasure of seeing you since your letter was written

I am now spending a few quiet days in the Delectable Duchy, and having very good weather, although cold, so please excuse this short note.

With best wishes for a Happy Xmas to Messrs Taylor, Hunt, Symons and Meyers, and accept the same yourself. Sincerely yours,

S. Frost.

A.P. Barron, 28th December 1917, France.

(We had a fine time at Xmas and I think every man was more than pleased)

Dear Mr Hunt,

I received your very welcome letter on Xmas Eve and am pleased to hear you liked the card I sent, I have had a letter from Ford since writing you and was very much surprised to hear that he had joined the Royal Flying Corps

I am more than obliged to you for kindly offering to send me a magazine each month, fancy Hyam training troops. Is he a non-commissioned officer? I am very sorry to hear that your father has been ill and sincerely hope by now that he has quite recovered

Remember me kindly to Hibberd and Jack [Symons] also all friends at the office. Fancy poor Cronin gone under, I suppose we have lost quite a few men by now, I must now draw to a close, wishing you a happy and Prosperous New year

Yours sincerely, A.P. Barron

W. Wiggs, field card, 8th January 1918, location not given.

This was sent to Mr J.R. Smith at the Audit office and Wiggs indicated
that he was well and had received a letter

A.P. Barron, 12th February 1918, France.

(Give my kindest regards to all in the office)

Dear Mr Hunt,

Just a few lines to let you know that I received magazine alright today
and thank you very much for the same

I was sorry to see that poor old Bertie Edwards has passed away, although I expect it was a happy release for all concerned. I have met several Paddington men here lately and the latest arrival is Radnage the footballer who was in the Chief Goods Office, I expect you know him he used to play for Queens Park Rangers

Pryor, who was in the General Manager's Office has I see been made Sergeant, he went home on leave about two weeks ago, did he call in the Audit?

I must close now as things are just the same here from day to day, hence the small letter, so hoping you are quite well as I am pleased to say I am at present. I remain yours sincerely,

A.P. Barron.

Could you do with a couple of chickens this week?

W. Wiggs, 23rd December 1917, France.

Dear Mr Smith,

I hope you will accept my apology for not writing before. It has not been want of will it has been lack of opportunity. I wonder how you all are. I am fairly well now but was very queer for several weeks recently. I also often wonder how you are all getting on and should like to hear

A matter of about five minutes ago Fritz was bombing us, and I have just got up off the ground where I was laying for about twenty minutes. One fellow has been hit, but not severely by shrapnel. This is his second visit this evening

It will soon be twelve months since I left you. It seems a very long time ago. I am afraid I have very little I may tell you, so will conclude by asking you to accept my best wishes for the New year and desiring that you will remember me kindly to any enquiring friends. Believe me, dear Mr Smith, sincerely yours,

W. Wiggs

R.C.S. Frost, 26th February 1918, Wimbledon Camp, England.

Dear Mr Hunt,

I am afraid I must ask you again for some more privilege orders between Wimbledon and Ealing, when you have a few moments to spare. Many thanks for the last three, safely received

    I was hoping to give you a call today as I am going to Leicester Square Dental Hospital but... I doubt if there will be time. The custom was (until today) to report at the hospital at 9am, but probably owing to the rationing business, we must have as much food from the military people as possible. I hope it won't make any difference to our weekend passes as one never knows when a brain wave may strike a War Office official, and he will think of the simplest method of feeding soldiers on weekend pass viz. by stopping such leave!

With kindest regards, sincerely yours, 'Frosty'

J.W. Hyam, undated, Winchester, England.

My Dear Bertie,

So sorry I have not written before but we've been so busy here as all the day long we are training recruits from A.S.C, R.E and Royal Field Artillery and Royal Garrison Artillery coast defence unit whose places they are filling with category men. I am now assisting in riding school and take a class. It's very interesting and at times laughable as you can imagine. I wrote to Frosty about six weeks ago but have had no answer. Have you heard anything of him? We have a lot of Yankees here and they are some knuts *[slang for an aristocrat or dandy]* here, played merry hell, broke into quarters of the W.A.A.C

    They all carry revolvers and picquets carry loaded sticks. They march in quite a ragtime manner just like the French and they all wear gloves... Our football team still going strong; still unbeaten. Shall have to come and play G.W. team, eh!

Yours sincerely, Fatty

TWELVE

AUGUST 1918

'When will it all be over... when?'
JOHN EDWARD RANDLE WHITE

This was the final collection of war letters issued by the office. The number of men writing to Paddington had dwindled: far fewer letters were included in this issue. We can't know exactly why this was, but several factors probably played a part. Prolific letter writer Jack Symons had returned to the office after being discharged due to damage from an episode of 'trench feet'. Others who had written often, such as Monty Pond, Taffy Williams and Harold Cronin had been killed in action.

This would have affected the morale of the colleagues still fighting, who could probably have been described as 'war weary' by now. It must have been hard to sustain the momentum of letter writing over a period of years, and to endeavour to remain upbeat and cheerful when writing, which was the convention for this group.

For the people left behind in the office, perhaps it was difficult to find motivation for the task of collating and distributing the letters. By now, letters had been collected for four years. Two men who were involved in their collation, Gerald Burgoyne ('Burgy') and P.F. Dalton, had by March 1918 left the office to work in other government departments. In addition to this, we believe that some of the older staff who started collecting the letters may have retired.

For the families of men, who had been urged to lend letters to the office for inclusion in the newsletter, the novelty of the letter collections would probably have faded along with their ties to the office.

News of major events in the soldier's lives still reached the office. Of W.J.E. Martin, a Messenger of the 3rd Grenadier Guards, the newsletter said:

> '[Martin], *we are proud to report, won distinction, being awarded the Military Medal, has had some very narrow escapes since going back in November last, arriving just in time for a big street fight, having to pull down doors and make stretchers for the wounded, at the same time using the German prisoners as stretcher bearers.*'

News had also reached the office that a frequent writer, W.E. 'Taffy' Edwards, had been killed:

> '*The News reached the Audit about 3/4/18 of his being seriously wounded in heavy shell fire and with regret we place another name on record with the fallen, for on the following day we had the news that poor Taffy had succumbed to his terrible injuries, passing away on Good Friday.*'

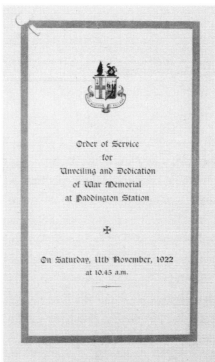

Order of Service
for
Unveiling and Dedication
of War Memorial
at Paddington Station

✠

On Saturday, 11th November, 1922
at 10.45 a.m.

There was, it seems, a feeling that things were winding down, at least for those who were still writing to the office at this late stage. This extract from the Audit newsletter says:

'We hear news of the following…

Jackson E.W. again in France, having quite recovered from his chill…

Peacock, G. Was in hospital for 2 months at Stockport having a poisoned finger, eventually losing the top joint…

Watts T.H. Very much alive, as usual.'

Frost was training in the UK, 'dodging the column'* by his own admission. He said *'there is ample provision for sport here, including football, rugby, cricket, tennis and boxing, and it is very much encouraged.'* Fatty Hyam wrote during his journey to Mesopotamia, then again from India: *'there is an abundance of sport and grub here'*. None of our authors wrote that they experienced fighting in this period, but no one here seemed to sense that the war would be over by the end of the year either. J.E.R. White wrote our opening quote from a gruelling training course in England; *'When will it all be over… when?'* One can almost hear Walter Croft's anguish when he wrote *'I shall be more than happy to see it all finished. Am absolutely fed up now.'*

C.E. Faulkner, Castledown Bere, Ireland, undated.

'All's well but properly isolated on top of a mountain, 700 feet above sea level, and very cold, even for July: what will it be in winter? We are 18 in a hut, not half enough room, and sleep in hammocks, and on the floor, one lot of hammocks up to the roof. The water we get about 200 yards down the hill, where we also wash, which is a treat about 4.30 in the morning, with the wind blowing off the Atlantic. We never see a soul and are 9 miles from Castledown, the chaps say it's like being in the Blockhouses in South Africa.'

J.W. Hyam, 10th March 1918, France.

Dear Dickie,

Here we go again merry and bright. Had a fine crossing no incident of note. Off to Mesopotamia tomorrow at least start our journey. May well meet some of the boys and Beaumont on way at Rawalpindi in India. Of course I shall try and have a game of footer and a flutter on the Ace.

Yours J.W. Hyam

W.G. Croft, 5th April 1918, place unknown.

Dear Jack,

How are you? Have not heard from you for some time now. Guess you are rather busy at present. Are you still in the Audit? Better than being in the army, what say you. This last affair was some do, wasn't it? Guess they are biting off more than they can chew… I suppose everything is getting dearer and dearer. Some war this. Heard from Dicky Davis the other day. Told me of one or two changes in the office, also of one or two visitors they had… Well, Jack, I shall be more than happy to see it all finished. Am absolutely fed up now.

Heard from Albert today. He is still on the move out there. Poor old chap, he does stick it. Apparently the only thing to do. Well, cheero. Best luck and good wishes.

Yours ever, Wal

R.C.S. Frost, 21st April 1918, Wimbledon Common Camp, England.

Dear Mr Hunt,

Many thanks for your last welcome letter, with the enclosures. I am very sorry to hear of the latest Audit casualties. What a space there will be in the old office after the war.

As you are probably aware today's weather was the limit, especially when confined to camp on duty, as is my lot, however I am trying to pass the time in writing letters. My days are numbered here, as I am expecting to go on the next draft to an Officer Commanding Battalion and I shall be rather glad to get away, as the 'vertical breeze' has been right up of late, on account of the events in France, and the need for men overseas. We get all sorts of rumours, medical tests, and educational tests, with the constant threat of being returned to France for misconduct etc., so when I get to a school, I shall feel more settled.

Quite a fair percentage of budding officers have been turned down on medical grounds here, although returned fit from France. The doctors spent two busy days last week putting us through it, but I managed to get through alright.

As there are so few other people here, except the cadet details, we get the constant attention of nearly everyone from the Commanding Officer down, much to our regret of course. However one has only to remember France and you soon decide to forgive everyone here for making you remain in camp, when you would prefer to be elsewhere. I should be much obliged for another dose of privilege orders please, when you are not too busy. I hope you are keeping fit…Sincerely yours

Frosty

A.P. Barron, 7th May 1918, France.

Mr Hunt,

Have received your letter of the 3rd inst. Glad to hear that you have forwarded mag. and will let you know when I receive it. I expect you will be surprised to hear that I am once more back at my old address… The first one I met on arriving was G. Jones of Season tickets, looking as fat as ever and he told me he had only just come out (some people are lucky) but he has now left here. I am very pleased to hear of Martin winning the Military Medal, and if you write to him at any time give him my best regards and say how pleased I was to hear the news and that

I wish him the best of luck, I don't know how long I shall be here, but hope it will be a few weeks as I have had it rather warm lately. I must now close with kindest regards to you and all friends.

Yours sincerely, A.P. Barron

R.C.S. Frost, 16th May 1918, Bushey, England.

Dear Mr Hunt,

You will observe by my address that I have left Wimbledon at last! About forty of us arrived here last Friday, and have taken on the role of cadets with the Guards. The hall is beautifully situated quite close to Watford, so you will see I have not gone far away, but of course there are not very many opportunities for getting home. The company I am in is sleeping under canvas in the grounds, on account of the lack of accommodation inside. However, this is a pleasure more than a hardship at this time of year, as only three sleep in each tent, and we have bedsteads, and other things to make us comfortable.

As one would expect, the discipline maintained is of a high standard and the parades still pretty stiff. From 8.15 to 1pm our time is fully occupied, with usually a couple of hours' drill, an hour of physical and a lecture. Then we carry on from 2.15 to 5pm. By a new arrangement just made we do evening study from 4-5pm instead of from 9-10pm, so now our evenings are free for sport.

Wednesday and Saturday are half days, for which we are thankful. Altogether we are very well off here, and very comfortable, as naturally the training is the best in the country. There is ample provision for sport here including football, rugby, cricket, tennis and boxing, and it is very much encouraged.

How are things getting on at the office? I suppose you will soon be thinking of holidays. At present we are allowed weekend leave to 15% of our number, which involves a railway journey, while a further 10% are given leave to within ten miles of here, but not to travel by train. As you may know the motor buses run from Watford to London!

It is almost time for dinner so I must make myself presentable and will bring these few lines to a close.

With kindest regards to all. Sincerely yours, Frosty.
P.S. The badge we wear is found on the envelope. You will notice it has the initials of the Guards on it.

J.E.R. White, 5th July 1918, Narborough, England.

Dear Mr Williams,

I believe I have owed you a letter for some considerable time, and now that there is some time at my disposal, I will endeavour to remove my arrears.

It was during the first half of the course at Bath that I last wrote. At half term we had eight days' leave. Upon our return from that we learnt that for our company the course had been reduced from six to five months. No one was sorry for that; long are the five months. When completed we were only too keen to get away. That may appear strange, more particularly when one considered that 80% had returned from France for the course, but I can assure you I never had a harder time. During the course we had about 20% of the men returned to their units for one reason or another, but I am glad to say that all who went in for the examination on the 28th June successfully passed. The following day we had our farewell dinner and concert, leaving bath on Thursday for leave pending gazette. I do not know to what regiment I shall be gazetted, but hope it will be either the Indian Army or the Machine Gun Corps, both of which I have applied for.

For the past week I have been making the best of my leave, visiting friends and having a nice lazy time. Have you had news recently of the old Audit men in France and elsewhere? Occasionally in the GWR magazine I see interesting items, but beyond that, nothing. When will it all be over… when? Please remember me to those of my old comrades who still remain. Kind regards…

J.E.R. White, Cadet

A.P. Barron, 12th July 1918, France.

Dear Mr Hunt,

I received magazine alright last evening and am much obliged to you for same, I hope you will forgive me not running up again to wish you goodbye, only I had such a lot to see that it was impossible to get to all that I wanted to, but I know you will understand and not mind.

I am glad to say that we had a good passage this time. It was not bad in the least. Give my kindest regards to George and tell him I hope to be with you all once again, and I hope the next time will be final. I must now close,

A.P. Barron

R.C.S. Frost, 20th July 1918, Bushey, England.

Dear Mr Hunt,

I hope these few lines will find you still busy at the office. So many changes are taking place amongst people in civilian life, even some of the staid veterans have received the call, that I have begun to fear your position at the office may be insecure, but I hope you are still among the indispensables.

I am glad to be able to report all OK from here. I have got quite used to doing things, as the guards will have them done, even to putting out shoes on the left of boots every morning, at the bottom of the bed. This company is still under canvas, with two cadets in each tent, which gives us plenty of room, also plenty of work on Friday mornings, when tent boards must be taken out and scrubbed before the first parade of 1½ hours P.J. or 'physical jerks'. You can guess we are fully awake for that parade!

However life is very pleasant here, and after parades we have a real good time, with plenty of sport. I believe the course has been extended to seven months now, so I have great hopes of seeing another Xmas in England. I am afraid my plans for dodging the column will be exhausted then!

The time will soon pass though, and we have our half term exam in a fortnight's time, as there is eight days' leave to follow. I hope to get a chance of seeing you at the office then and hear all the news. I manage to get home for a few hours on Saturdays, without a pass, so I have no reason for getting fed up yet. I thought I might trouble you to send a few privilege orders if you don't mind, between Bushey and Willesden... We only get passes to travel on steam trains once a month, so my 'buckshee' journeys are limited to Saturdays as the electric line is closed from Willesden on Sundays. I hope these few lines will find you keeping well... Very sincerely yours

Frosty

J.W. Hyam, 15th April 1918, Roorkee, India.

My Dear Bertie,

Have arrived in India for the purpose of relieving some A1 men here who have been here for a long period. It's not a bad show here just above Delhi but so d____d hot: risen to 106 degrees in the shade and we have more hot weather just coming. Our parades are as follows 6.30-7.45 and 9 to 10 and finish for day. There is an abundance of sport and grub here. Fancy getting eggs laid too. A supper of say ½ new mutton chop, potatoes, peas, broccoli and tea 4d. The things that are expensive are goods from England especially English soap, sauces, writing paper and of course we are unable to get English made fags. We had a grand journey from England; route was Southampton to Cherbourg then to Italy. In Italy we went to Alexandria, stayed there three days had a grand time streets of red lamps etc. and lovely shops. No two houses in main stretch are alike. Then from Alexandria we come to Port Suez by train then on P. and O. Liner *Kaiser I. Hind* to Bombay had two days there and that's a grand place too, lovely wide streets and grand buildings. They have a sea front very much like Hastings and all the big boys have their after dinner drive there and form a queue by shore. Some stuff there too. Lots of Europeans knocking about too. Had a game of footer for the Railway Operatives depot last night, 6pm, with King's Own and won... But it was so ruddy warm and I felt like a wash out at finish. Kind regards to all. Give Bill Butler my address and ask him to drop a line.

J.W. Hyam. Fatty.

How are the tours going is Frosty still serving?

CONCLUSION

❖

The final letter in this collection was written on 20th July 1918, by Stanley Frost, who wrote from a training camp in Bushey, England. This camp was only about 12 miles from his familial home in Ealing, West London. Indeed, he stated that he usually got a chance to visit home for a few hours every Saturday. At the time he wrote this letter, he was part way through a seven month training course. When war ended on 11th November 1918, we believe that he was still based close to home. Presumably his homecoming would have been far removed from the dramatic and visually arresting images of soldiers landing on British soil which one is familiar with: he probably got the train or bus home.

In reading Frosty's letter, one would never guess that it was to be his last. In fact, the same could be said for all of our final letters. After the Armistice was declared on 11th November, not one single soldier wrote to the Audit office. The abrupt end of this letter collection is quite unsatisfactory for the reader; we do not know how the soldiers heard about the end of war, how they felt, how they celebrated and the circumstances under which they returned home and to work.

To try to deduce a little of the experience of these men after the war ended, we can turn to other accounts of the war. We do know that demobilisation was a slow process. GWR men, like other soldiers, would not have returned immediately. Some battalions had so much work still to do that they remained abroad for many more months. Those staff who had been working on the railway infrastructure in France were still trickling home well into 1919.

In terms of finding out about the lives of individual soldiers outside of the war, several record series prove useful. The 1911 census entry for

Stanley Frost, our most prolific writer, states that he lived at 39 Broughton Street, Ealing, with his parents, sister, two brothers and their wives. He was 26 when war broke out in 1914. The GWR Register of Clerks us that he joined the company aged 14 as a railway clerk. Frost returned to the office on 15th January 1919, two months after war ended. By 1922, he had moved to 21 Campbell Road in Hanwell, London, though we don't know who with. Frost retired from the GWR on 30th January 1948, and we think he died in 1962.

Jack Symons' position amongst our letter writers is unusual. He went to war, but was injured and subsequently discharged on Saturday 5th August 1916. He was back at his old desk the following Monday, a mere three days later. Symons' point of view had changed, from a soldier writing to the Audit office, to a recipient of letters from those who were still fighting. Symons worked at the GWR until his retirement in 1935, and records indicate that he probably died in 1941.

Gilbert Williams was 20 when he went off to war in 1914. He did not return to work in the office until six years later, on 19th January 1920. Williams also fought in the Second World War, leaving in August 1939 and returning from war in November 1948. He retired from the GWR in 1959 after 49 years working for the railway, but for 15 of those he'd been away in the Army.

The register of railway clerks reveals that 'Fatty' Hyam resigned from the Audit office on 7th July 1914, after working there for eight years. We don't know his precise date of enlistment, but by August 1915 Fatty is well established in a remount depot in England. It is unclear why Fatty resigned from the Audit office so soon before joining the army, since the GWR aimed to keep soldiers' jobs open, and to pay them whilst they were away. There must have been something in his personal circumstances which the records don't tell us. Despite his resignation, Fatty still wrote back to friends in the Audit office throughout the war. In April 1917 he wrote from hospital in Salisbury, where he was recovering from a case of shellshock. He had been transferred to the Royal Field Artillery and sent to fight in France. As noted previously, his letter shows the effects of this shellshock. The last time we hear from Fatty he is in Bombay, India, enjoying a peaceful period and enjoying the 'footer'.

The Great Western Railway was quite rightly proud of the contribution its staff had made to the war, and of the provisos they had put in place in a bid to look after the wellbeing of staff who had served. For example, the GWR endeavoured to keep the jobs of men who went to war open for their return and tried to accommodate staff who had been injured at war. A document held at The National Archives contains notes made in preparation for the Chairman's speech at the unveiling of the war memorial at Paddington station in 1922. At the unveiling, the Chairman was keen to emphasise that:

> *'The Company have given particular attention to the question of employing disabled ex-service men… the name of the Company is inserted on the King's Roll in connection with the National Scheme, and upwards of 5,000 disabled ex-service men are now employed.' (Document reference RAIL 258/447)*

After the war had ended and troops had returned, the GWR was able to quantify the contribution that it had made to the cause. The contribution made by the Audit office was high: 55.5 per cent of male staff enlisted, whereas the average rate of enlistment across the GWR was 32.6 per cent. This amounted to 184 men, 17 of whom lost their lives.

It took some time for the GWR to decide how to memorialise those staff who had died in battle. Over the years numerous gestures were made to mark loss of life or medals gained. The first GWR roll of honour appeared at platform 1, Paddington station at the end of 1915. In 1920, the Audit office had unveiled a roll of honour within its boardroom, 'in memory of 17 members of the staff of the office, who lost their lives in war.' The photo of the unveiling ceremony (overleaf) was featured in the June 1920 GWR magazine. Similar memorials were made for individual railway departments and displayed at stations across the west of England.

A view of the Memorial.

Reproduced with kind permission of Steam,
The Museum of the Great Western Railway.

Documents held at The National Archives hint at the deliberations which the GWR underwent as they tried to decide upon one fitting memorial to all members of their staff who had lost their lives (document reference RAIL 258/447). On 11th November 1922, a memorial dedicated to all 2,524 staff who had died in battle was unveiled on platform 1, Paddington station. The unveiling formed part of a formal memorial service.

The GWR invited close relatives of those who had lost their lives to come to the service, saying that 'the opportunity should be afforded to relatives of the Great Western men who fell in the war to be present at the ceremony.'

The statue was designed by C.S. Jagger, a sculptor who had himself seen active service in the First World War. A casket containing a list of the names of all GWR war dead sits underneath the figure of a soldier. The soldier is reading a letter from home, with a faint smile on his tired face. This collection of letters shows us how important letter writing was for these men, who wrote not only to their families but to their workplace too. It seems very fitting that the men in this book have been memorialised in this way.

Copyright, reproduced with kind permission of Steam,
The Museum of the Great Western Railway.

SOLDIER
BIOGRAPHIES

Where known, we have outlined some basic information about the lives of our letter writers.

F.E. Andrews (Frederick Ernest)
Born: 15 November 1879, Joined GWR: 16 November 1896, Joined up for service: 8 January 1917, Regiment: Railway Operatives Division, Royal Engineers, Regiment number: 218857, Rank: Sapper, Returned to office: 26 May 1919, Retired: 15 November 1939.

A.P. Barron (Arthur Pearson)
Born: March 1882, Joined GWR: 18 May 1899, as a messenger, Regiment: Railway Operatives Division, Royal Engineers, Regiment number: 270807, Rank: Sapper.

H. Beaumont (Harry)
Born: 17 October 1873, Joined GWR: 25 July 1988, Regiment: 1/6 East Surrey Regiment, Regiment number: 2297, Rank: Quarter Master Sergeant, Returned to office: 14 May 1919, Retired: 17 October 1933 after 45 years' service, Died: Oct-Dec 1952. Note: Beaumont was engaged in coal and merchandise private settlement accounts section. He was a member of volunteer army as a young man. He was a life governor of Richmond Hospital, London and was a Freemason. He also held an M.B.E. (Military Division).

N. Boyce (Nicholas, Nick, Nic)
Born: 21 October 1879, Joined GWR: 10 February 1896, Joined up for service: 12 November 1915, Regiment: Railway Troop, Royal Engineers, Regiment number: 138015, Rank: Sapper, Returned to office: 16 June 1919, Retired: 21 October 1939.

E.H. Brackenbury (Edgar Harry)
Born: 21 September 1894, Joined GWR: 3 April 1911, Regiment: Railway Troop, Royal Engineers, Regiment number: 8711, Rank: Sapper, Returned to office: 7 July 1919, Died: Jan- Mar 1965.

E.W. Bratchell (Ernest William)
Born: 28 July 1893, Joined GWR: 3 February 1908, Regiment: 1/3 (City of London) Battalion (Royal Fusiliers), Regiment number: 2176, Rank: Private, Returned to office: 29 March 1920, Died: Jul- Sep 1969.

H. Bullen (Henry)
Born: 25 April 1893, Joined GWR: 6 June 1910, Joined up for service: 27 October 1914, Regiment: 2/10 Middlesex regiment, Regiment number: 2858 Rank: Private, Returned to office: 31 March 1919, Died: 11 February 1942. Note: Bullen spent his whole career in Chief Accountant's Office. He was a bandman and a cricketer in West Drayton where he lived.

T. Cautley (Thomas Henry)
Born: 21st November 1882, Joined GWR: 18 January 1909, Joined up for service: 31st March 1915, Regiment: Railway Troop, Royal Engineers, Regiment number: 87714, Rank: Sapper, Returned to office: 14 July 1919, Retired: 21st November 1842, Died: Oct- Dec 1972.

S.W.C. Court (Stanley William Claude)
Born: 21st February 1897, Joined GWR: 30 June 1911, Joined up for service: 9 August

1914, Regiment: 2/16 (County of London) Battalion (Queen's Westminster Rifles), Regiment number: 1816, Rank: Corporal, Died: Died of wounds on 30 July 1916 at Neuville-Saint-Vaast, France.

R.W.S. Court (Reginald Walter Southwood, Reggie)

Born: 20 December 1881, Joined GWR: 16 February 1897, Joined up for service: 3rd November 1914, Regiment: 3/1 Hereford regiment, Regiment number: 2818 Rank: 2nd Lieutenant, Died: Killed in action on 26 March 1917. Buried in Jerusalem, Israel.

E.J. Cowles (Ernest John)

Born: 8 August 1893, Joined GWR: 29 June 1903, Joined up for service: 5 August 1914, Regiment: Royal Buckinghamshire Hussars; Royal Army Medical Corps, Regiment number: 713; 434085, Rank: Corporal, Returned to office: 10 February 1919, Retired: 8 August 1954, Died: Jul- Sep 1967.

S.W.C. Court (Stanley William Claude)

Born: 21 February 1897, Joined GWR: 30 June 1911, Joined up for service: 9 August 1914, Regiment: 2/16 (County of London) Battalion (Queen's Westminster Rifles), Regiment number: 1816, Rank: Corporal, Died: Died of wounds on 30 July 1916 at Neuville-Saint-Vaast.

R.W.S. Court (Reginald Walter Southwood)

Born: 20 December 1881, Joined GWR: 16 February 1897, Joined up for service: 3 November 1914, Regiment: 3/1 Hereford Regiment, Regiment number: 2818 Rank: 2nd Lieutenant, Died: Killed in action on 26 March 1917. Buried in Jerusalem, Israel.

W.G. Croft (Walter George, Wal)

Born: 11 May 1896, Joined GWR: 8 May 1911. Croft resigned on 7 September 1921, re-joining GWR in 1923. Joined up for service: 5 August 1914, Regiment: 13 County of London Battalion of London Regiment, Regiment number: 1589; 490193, Rank: Private; Corporal, Returned to office: 26 May 1919, Retired: Retired due to illness on 21st September 1932.

H.W. Cronin (Harold William)

Born: 9 May 1880, Joined GWR: 3 February 1886, Joined up for service: 8 September 1914, Regiment: 4 Seaforth Highlanders. Promoted to Lieutenant in 5 Bedfordshire Regiment on 20 May 1915, Rank: See above, Died: 2nd December 1917 at 35 Casualty Clearing Station in Palestine, leaving £268 19s to his widow Muriel, Note: Immediately prior to war he was a travelling auditor for South Wales District.

J. Davies (James)

Regiment: 6 City of London Rifles, Regiment number: 3343, Rank: Lance Corporal.

W.C. Davis (William Charles, Will, Dicky)

Born: 12 November 1884, Joined GWR: 12 January 1900, Joined up for service: 2 September 1914, Regiment: Royal Army Medical Corps, Regiment number: 31223, Rank: Lance Corporal; Sergeant, Returned to office: 10 February 1919 Retired: 12 November 1944, Note: His surname was often misspelled as Davies by his colleagues.

S.C. Douce (Sydney Charles, Syd)

Born: 17 November 1882, Joined GWR: 28 November 1898, Joined up for service: 1 December 1915, Regiment: 1/5 London Regiment; 3rd Battalion London Rifle Brigade; Royal Army Medical Corps, Regiment number: 3701; 202204; 536657, Rank: Private, Returned to office: 17 February 1919, Died: 29 May 1933.

S.H. Dunton (Samuel Harry, Sal)

Born: 7 January 1888, Joined GWR: 7 May 1902, Joined up for service: 8 September 1914, Regiment: 5 London Rifle Brigade; 17 Middlesex; Royal Engineers, Rank: 2 Lieutenant; Captain, Returned to office: 20 July 1920, Retired: 21 November 1942, Died: 21 July 1961.

R.A.W. Dyer (Ronald Arthur William, Ron)

Born: 11 April 1895, Joined GWR: 29 August 1910, Joined up for service: 6 September 1914, Regiment: 2 Bedfordshire Regiment, attached to Signal Company, Royal Engineers, 47 Division, Regiment number: 14833, Rank: Private, Returned to office: 17 February 1919, Died: Jul- Sep 1969.

W.E. Edwards (William Ernest, Taffy)

Born: 21 March 1879, Joined GWR: 26 August 1895, Joined up for service: 24 January 1917, Regiment: Royal Engineers, Railway Operating Division; Royal Engineers 19 Light Railway Operative Company, Regiment number: 229675 Rank: Sapper, Died: 29 March 1918 in France.

C.E. Faulkner (Charles Edmund)

Born: 6 September 1868, Joined GWR: 4 December 1882, Joined up for service: 8 January 1915, Regiment: 32 Company, London Guard National Reserve, Returned to office: 24 February 1919, Retired: 6 September 1928, Died: Oct- Dec 1941

F.H. Ferdinand (Frederick Horace, Fred, Ferdi)

Born: 6 December 1893, Joined GWR: 29 June 1908, Joined up for service: 31st March 1915, Regiment: Attached to Military Forwarding Officer, Royal Engineers, Regiment number: 87725, Rank: Sapper, Returned to office: 23 June 1919, Retired: 30 September 1959, Died: Oct- Dec 1977.

R.C.S. Frost (Richard Charles Stanley, Stanley, Frosty)

Born: 30 January 1888, Joined GWR: 26 May 1902, Joined up for service: 18 September 1914, Regiment: 8 Argyll and Sutherland Highlanders; Duke of Cornwall's Light Infantry, Regiment number: 1998; 300470, Rank: Private; Second Lieutenant, Returned to office: 15 January 1919, Retired: 30 January 1948, Died: Records indicate at Frost died on Apr- Jun 1962.

H. Giles (Harold George)

Born: 18 May 1898, Joined GWR: 7 August 1912, Joined up for service: 19 March 1915, Regiment: Royal Bucks Hussars, Regiment number: 2125; 205745 Rank: Private, Returned to office: 28 April 1919, Retired: Resigned from Audit office on 9 May 1920.

R. Gilson (Richard, Dick, Dicky)

Born: 20 September 1887, Joined GWR: 4 March 1902, Joined up for service: 8 September 1914, Regiment: 4 Seaforth Highlanders, Regiment number: 2076; 200415, Rank: Acting Colour Sergeant, Returned to office: 24 February 1919 Retired: 20 September 1947, Died: Jan- Mar 1961.

G.F.W. Halls (Gerald Frederick Williams)

Born: 18 June 1897, Joined GWR: 24 January 1912, Joined up for service: 29 December 1915, Regiment: Royal Flying Corps, Regiment number: 16927, Returned to office: 20 January 1919, Died: 2 December 1958

D.S.W. Hambly (Donald Stewart Wharton)

Born: 9 March 1865 in Plymouth, Joined GWR: 3 March 1884, Joined up for service: 14 August 1916, Regiment: Royal Naval Air Service, Rank: Lieutenant; Captain, Returned to office: 11 June 1919, Retired: 8 March 1925, Died: April 1 1930, Note: Hambly served as an equipment officer of Air Force, first as a Lieutenant R.N.V.R. with the R.N.A.S. and afterwards as a Captain in the R.A.F. He served three years in France and Belgium, was Mentioned in Despatches and received Croix de Guerre from the King of Belgium.

W.A. Hastings (William Albert, Billy)

Born: 17 March 1888, Joined GWR: 5 June 1903, Joined up for service: 7 September 1914, Regiment: 4 Seaforth Highlanders, Regiment number: 2092, Rank: Sergeant, Returned to office: 5 February 1919, Died: Jan- Mar 1937.

E.F. Henderson (Edwin Frank)
Born: 1 March 1892, Joined GWR: 11 March 1907, Joined up for service: 29 March 1915, Regiment: Army Service Corps, Regiment number: S4/072629, Rank: Private; Sergeant, Returned to office: 28 July 1919, Retired: 1 March 1952, Died: Apr- Jun 1982.

J.R.H. Higgs (John Reginald Herrman)
Born: 24 September 1892, Joined GWR: 22 May 1897, Joined up for service: 2 February 1916, Regiment: Railway Troop, Royal Engineers, Regiment number: 149896, Rank: Sapper, Returned to office: 27 January 1919, Retired: 24 September 1942.

S.C. Hills (Stanley Clarke)
Born: 21 November 1897, Joined GWR: 29 April 1912, Joined up for service: 22 April 1915, Regiment: 3rd Berkshire Regiment; Hampshire Regiment, Regiment number: 3099; 331290, Returned to office: 24 February 1919, Died: Jul- Sep 1970.

S.B. Hodges (Sidney Broad)
Born: 7 January 1884, Joined GWR: 26 February 1900, Joined up for service: 12 November 1915, Regiment: Royal Engineers, Railway Troop, Regiment number: 138032, Rank: Sapper, Returned to office: 7 September 1919, Retired: 7 January 1944, Died: Jan- Mar 1956.

G. Holloway (George)
Born: 31 January 1879, Joined GWR: 4 June 1894, Joined up for service: 8 January 1917, Regiment: Royal Engineers, Railway Troop, Regiment number: 218856, Rank: Sapper, Returned to office: 30 January 1919, Retired: 31 January 1939, Died: Apr- Jun 1967.

R.F. Hull (Richard Frederick, Fred)
Born: 4 June 1892, Joined GWR: 25 July 1908, Joined up for service: 17 September 1914, Regiment: 1/6 Seaforth Highlanders, 1st Highland Infantry Brigade, Regiment number: 2161, Rank: Lance Corporal, Returned to office: 17 March 1919, Retired: 5 December 1953, Died: Oct- Dec 1974.

J.W. Hyam (James Walter, Fatty)
Born: 24 July 1891, Joined GWR: 26 April 1906, Regiment: 11 Hussars, C. Squadron; Royal Field Artillery; Royal Garrison Artillery, Regiment number: 223725; 184963, Rank: Gunner, Retired: Resigned from Audit office on 7 July 1914, Died: Jan- Mar 1951.

E.W. Jackson (Ernest Wilfred, Jacko)
Born: 12 April 1868, Joined GWR: 9 November 1883, Joined up for service: 5 August 1914, Regiment: Railway Troop, Royal Engineers; 1st Queen's Westminster Rifles, Regiment number: 6, Rank: Quarter Master; Hon. Lieut, Returned to office: 1 January 1920, Retired: 12 April 1928, Note: In July 1916 Jackson is promoted to Quarter Master, which his reported in London Gazette.

R. James (Richard James, Dick)
Born: 8 January 1894, Joined GWR: 10 May 1910, Joined up for service: 5 August 1914, Regiment: Royal Field Artillery, Rank: Corporal, Returned to office: 17 March 1919, Retired: 8 January 1959, Died: Oct- Dec 1969

F. Jarrett (Frederick, Fred)
Born: 10 June 1891, Joined GWR: 26 November 1906, Resigned from Audit Office: 5 March 1913, Note: In March 1919 Jarrett was promoted to Acting Assistant Chief Accountant of Uganda Railway. He left GWR service for East Africa in March 1913 and served in East African Campaign. In 1935 he became Colonial Treasurer for St Helena.

G.F.M. Kemball (George Frank Moir)
Born: 6 August 1882, Joined GWR: 18 January 1897, Joined up for service: 18 September 1914, Regiment: 1/6 Seaforth Highlanders, Regiment number: 2181; 265671, Rank: Private; Lance Corporal, Returned to office: 4 March 1918, Retired: Resigned from Audit office on 20 October 1918, Died: Jan- Mar 1956.

J.C. Kibblewhite (James Claude)
Born: 14 June 1895, Joined GWR: 26 January 1911, Joined up for service: 2nd September

1914, Regiment: 2/13 Battalion London Regiment, Regiment number: 490602, Rank: Sergeant, Returned to office: 5 May 1919, Died: 20 December 1951.

A.E. Kirk (Archibald Ernest, Arch)
Born: 16 July 1883, Joined GWR: 27 November 1899, Joined up for service: 12 November 1915, Regiment: Railway Troop, Royal Engineers, Regiment number: 138039, Rank: Sapper, Returned to office: 30 June 1919, Retired: 2 September 1942, Died: It is thought at Kirk died in Oct- Dec 1949.

A.H. Lambert (Arthur Howard)
Born: 15 March 1889, Joined GWR: 20 October 1903, Joined up for service: 29 December 1915, Regiment: Royal Flying Corps, Regiment number: 16928, Rank: Sergeant Major, Returned to office: 27 November 1919, Retired: 31 March 1951, Died: Oct- Dec 1974.

H.G. Langford (Henry George)
Born: 20 July 1891, Joined GWR: 23 October 1905.

F.E. Lewis (Frederick Ernest, Effie)
Born: 31 July 1875, Joined GWR: 18 November 1889, Joined up for service: 18 October 1915, Regiment: 2nd Middlesex Hussars, Returned to office: 10 February 1919, Retired: 31 July 1935.

W.P. Mansbridge (William Perrin)
Born: 11 February 1889, Joined GWR: 12 October 1904, Joined up for service: 29 December 1915, Regiment: Royal Flying Corps, Regiment number: 16929, Returned to office: 3 March 1919, Retired: 31 July 1951, Died: Oct- Dec 1973.

H.W. Martin (Henry William)
Born: 21 August 1888, Joined GWR: 18 September 1902, Joined up for service: 14 April 1915, Regiment: 54 Railway Supply Detachment, Army Service Corps, Regiment number: S4/086987, Rank: Private, Returned to office: 20 January 1919, Retired: 21 August 1948.

W.J.E. Martin (William)
Regiment: 3rd Battalion Grenadier Guards, Regiment number: 20348, Rank: Private, Note: Martin was awarded military medal. His medal card list qualifying date as 12 June 1918.

C.D. Mayo (Charles Douglas, Charlie)
Born: 30 June 1893, Joined GWR: 8 November 1909, Joined up for service: 5 August 1914, Regiment: Artists' Rifles; 2nd Royal Scots Regiment, Rank: Lieutenant; 2nd Lieutenant, Retired: Resigned 17 February 1919 but seems to have re-joined GWR on 17 November 1924 and subsequently retired on 16 April 1955.

W.A. McConnell (William Alexander)
Born: 30 July 1881, Joined GWR: 8 November 1897, Joined up for service: 3 June 1915, Regiment: Royal Army Medical Corps, Returned to office: 27 October 1919, Note: McConnell was undertaking clerical work in Royal Free hospital, England, a hospital turned over to military.

A.J. Morris (Arthur James)
Born: 24 September 1891, Joined GWR: 15 August 1906, Joined up for service: 8 September 1914, Regiment: 19 Hussars, Rank: Lance Corporal, Returned to office: 3 March 1919, Retired: 24 September 1951.

F.R. Morris (Frederick Ronald, Muggins, Mug)
Born: 1 April 1893, Joined GWR: 9 January 1908, Joined up for service: 29 December 1915, Regiment: Royal Flying Corps, Regiment number: 16922, Rank: 1st class Air Mechanic, Returned to office: 10 March 1919, Retired: Resigned on 25 March 1925.

M.P. Pond (Montague Percy, Monty)
Born: 13 September 1888, Joined GWR: 19 May 1904, Joined up for service: 31 March 1915, Regiment: Railway Troop, Royal Engineers, Regiment number: 87749, Rank: Sapper, Died: Killed in action on 6 May 1917 while serving with Railway Transport Operating Corps.

J.H. Porter (James Henry)
Born: 29 April 1888, Joined GWR: 22nd July 1902, Joined up for service: 5 January 1917, Regiment: Railway Operating Division, Royal Engineers, Regiment number: 218771, Rank: Sapper, Returned to office: 15 September 1919, Retired: 29 April 1948.

A.E. Rippington (Albert Edwin, Rip)
Born: 21 November 1893, Joined GWR: 29 June 1911, Regiment: 5 London Rifle Brigade, Returned to office: 5 November 1917, discharged due to injury, Retired: 21 November 1958, Died: Oct- Dec 1982.

D.J. Robertson (David Joseph, Joe)
Born: 5 January 1877, Joined GWR: 24 June 1892, Joined up for service: 12 November 1915, Regiment: Railway Troop, Royal Engineers, Regiment number: 138054, Rank: Sapper, Returned to office: 5 May 1919.

M.A. Russell (Mark Anthony)
Born: 30 March 1883, Joined GWR: 26 June 1889, Joined up for service: 12 November 1915, Regiment: Railway Troop, Royal Engineers, Regiment number: 138053, Rank: Sapper, Returned to office: 23 June 1919, Retired: 30 March 1943, Died: Apr- Jun 1965.

F.J. Serjent (Frederick James)
Born: 4 April 1891, Joined GWR: 19 July 1907, Joined up for service: 5 November 1914, Regiment: 182 Brigade, Royal Field Artillery; 180 Brigade, Royal Field Artillery, Regiment number: 3321; 39427, Rank: Corporal, Returned to office: 16 May 1919, Died: 12 August 1942.

K.B.W. Sharland (Kenneth William)
Born: 25 September 1888, Joined GWR: 7 April 1903, Joined up for service: 29 October 1914, Regiment: 1/6 East Surrey Regiment; Bedfordshire Regiment; Bedfordshire and Hertfordshire Regiment, Regiment number: 34173; 32376, Rank: Private, Returned to office: 26 November 1919, Retired: 25 September 1948, Died: Jan- Mar 1967.

L.W. Sharpe (Leonard William)
Born: 23 September 1893, Joined GWR: 2 September 1908, Joined up for service: 6 September 1914, Regiment: Bedfordshire regiment, Regiment number: 14834, Rank: Private, Returned to office: 31 March 1919, Retired: 25 August 1956, Died: Jan- Mar 1983.

G. Shipley (George William)
Born: 18 August 1878, Joined GWR: 17 July 1893, Joined up for service: 19 September 1914, Regiment: 10 Middlesex Regiment, Regiment number: 2594, Rank: Company Sergeant Major, Died: 2 December 1915.

H.A. Skilling (Hugh Andrew)
Born: 17 April 1891, Joined GWR: 16 November 1905, Joined up for service: 10 February 1916, Regiment: 3 Battalion Bedfordshire Regiment; 7 London Brigade Field Artillery, Regiment number: 43228, Rank: Lance Corporal, Returned to office: 13 October 1919, Retired: 17 April 1951, Died: Jan- Mar 1970.

A. Smith (Arthur)
Born: 8 March 1895, Joined GWR: 7 March 1911, Joined up for service: 31 March 1915, Regiment: Railway Troop, Royal Engineers, Regiment number: 87760, Rank: Lance Corporal, Returned to office: 16 June 1919, Retired: 30 September 1955.

S. Smith (Sidney, Sid)
Born: 20 October 1881, Joined GWR: 30 January 1896, Joined up for service: 8 January 1917, Regiment: Railway Operatives Division, Royal Engineers, Regiment number: 218849, Rank: Sapper, Returned to office: 19 May 1919, Retired: 20 October 1941.

E.H.C. Stewart (Edward Henry Cecil)
Born: 13 November 1891, Joined GWR: 18 March 1907, Joined up for service: 28 October 1914, Regiment: 1/5 Grenadier Company, London Rifle Brigade, Regiment number: 1167; 300717, Rank: Private, Died: 1 July 1916.

J. Symons (Jonathan George, Jack)

Born: 22 August 1875, Joined GWR: 28 October 1889, Joined up for service: 3 September 1914, Regiment: 13 County of London Regiment (King's Royal Rifles Corps), Regiment number: 6389, Returned to office: 7 August 1916, Retired: 22 August 1935, Died: Records indicate at Symons died in Oct- Dec 1941. Note: Symons had joined City of London Imperial Volunteers to serve in Boer War on 5 January 1900, returning to office on 1 December 1900.

F.T. Turner (Frank Thayer)

Born: 22 October 1897, Joined GWR: 13 April 1912, Joined up for service: 28 November 1915, Regiment: Company 3/18 London Irish Regiment, Returned to office: 5 November 1917, Died: 28 May 1937.

T.H. Watts (Thomas Harold, Watty)

Born: 28 August 1884, Joined GWR: 19 January 1900, Joined up for service: 4 August 1914, Regiment: Drakes Battalion, Royal Naval Volunteer Reserve, Retired: 24 July 1919, Died: 11 September 1953.

W. Wiggs (William Charles Frederick)

Born: 2 February 1881, Joined GWR: 11 November 1896, Joined up for service: 8 January 1917, Regiment: Royal Engineers, Railway Troop, Regiment number: 218855, Rank: 2nd Corporal, Returned to office: 1 August 1919, Died: Oct- Dec 1971.

J.E.R. White (John Edward Randle)

Born: 20 March 1896, Joined GWR: 28 June 1911, Joined up for service: 30 October 1914, Regiment: Army Pay Corps; Machine Gun Corps, Regiment number: 2644, Rank: Private, Returned to office: 29 May 1919.

G. Williams (Gilbert)

Born: 18 April 1894, Joined GWR: 30 August 1910, Joined up for service: 17 September 1914, Regiment: 1/6 Seaforth Highlanders, Regiment number: 2175, Rank: Private, Returned to office: 19 January 1920, Retired: 18 April 1959, Died: Records indicate at Williams died between Oct- Dec 1967. Note: Williams also fought in Second World War, leaving on 25 August 1939 and returning from war on 15 November 1948.

F. Witt (Francis, Frank)

Born: 8 February 1893, Joined GWR: 9 March 1908, Regiment: Royal Engineers, Mediterranean Expeditionary Force. Transferred to Office of Superintendent of Line on 15 June 1914. Regiment number: 138069; WR296343, Rank: Sapper, Died: Jan- Mar 1970.

F.G. Woodhams (Frederick, Freddy)

Regiment: 13 London Rifles, Regiment number: 1383, Rank: Private; Lance Corporal; Sergeant, Died: Woodhams was killed in action on 16 August 1917, having been struck by shrapnel. Prior to this, he had been wounded twice., Note: Freddy's father, Frederick William Woodhams, also worked in Audit office.

Office workers

Details of some of the men who remained in the Audit office are given below.

G. Burgoyne (Gerald, Burgie)

Born: 3 November 1887, Joined GWR: 1 December 1902, Retired: 14 September 1942, Note: Records indicate at Burgoyne died between Apr- June 1963.

H. Hunt (Herbert, Bertie)

Born: 1 April 1869, Joined GWR: 23 September 1884, Retired: 1 April 1929

G.H. Rivers (George Henry, Mr Rivers)

Born: 2 April 1879, Joined GWR: 14 July 1894, Retired: 2 April 1939
H. Taylor (Mr Taylor, Henry, Tinker), Born: 11 February 1857, Joined GWR: 5 May 1875

R.P. Wood (Robert Pocock)

Born: 14 February 1874, Joined GWR: 7 November 1888, Retired: 14 February 1934.

Mr Frederick William Woodhams

Born: 27 September 1870, Joined GWR: 11 May 1885, Retired: 27 September 1930, Died: Jan- Mar 1943, Note: father of F.G. Woodhams, who went to war.

People mentioned in the letters

E.C. Chamberlain (Ernest Charles, Joe)

Born: 19 March 1892, Joined GWR: 10 January 1907, Joined up for service: 1 September 1914 Regiment: 13 London Regiment, Regiment Number: 2473, Rank: Sergeant, Died: Killed in action on 9 May 1915.

J.J. Radnage (Joseph John)

Born: 21 February 1884, Joined GWR: 5 June 1899, Joined up for service: 18 November 1915, Regiment: Royal Engineers, Railway Troop, Regiment Number: 289276; WR/274734, Rank: Sapper; Corporal, Died: Jul-Sep 1947, Note: Radnage was signed to play for Queen's Park Rangers football team in 1909, having previously played for Reading football team. In 1918 Barron writes: 'the latest arrival is Radnage footballer who was in Chief Goods Office, I expect you know him he used to play for Queens Park Rangers.' On his service record (document reference WO 363/R 41, extract below), he states that the only harm that befell him during active service was a shin injury whilst playing football in France in 1919.

Army Form B 178B.

STATEMENT BY A SOLDIER CONCERNING HIS OWN CASE.

NOTE.—This Form is to be filled in by every soldier prior to the compilation of Army Form B 179A, whether a patient in hospital or not, and attached thereto. The questions are to be answered in the soldier's own words, and the Form is to be signed by him and the signature witnessed. In the event of the soldier being unable to write he should affix his mark, such act being witnessed.

Regimental No. *WR. 274734*   Rank *Corporal*

Name *Radnage*   *Joseph John*   Unit and Corps *ROD RE.*

(Surname)   (Christian Names)

Note.—Before answering the questions below, the soldier is to note that

    (a) The statements made by him will be checked by official records.

    (b) In answering Question 2 any special matters which in his opinion caused any unfitness from which he may be suffering or which aggravated it should be clearly stated.

If the soldier is unable to read, the above notes are to be read to him by an officer.

1. (a) In what countries have you served during this war, and for what periods?	England & France. Enlisted Nov. 1915. Overseas Jany 1918. & Evacuated to England April 1919.	
(b) In what capacity?	Orderly Room Work. - Clerk. &c.	
2. If you are suffering from any disease, wound, or injury, state what it is, the date upon which it started, and what, in your opinion, was the cause of it. (If more space is required a sheet of foolscap should be used, and firmly attached to this form.)	Wound on Right Shin caused on March 9th/1919 through a kick whilst playing football at Beaurainville, France. (Accident duly reported to R.E. Records)	

SELECT
BIBLIOGRAPHY

❖

Trench Talk: Words of the First World War; P. Doyle & J. Walker, Published 2012, Spellmount, imprint of The History Press, Stroud, Gloucestershire, ISBN 9780752471549.

The Great Western Railway in the First World War: Sandra Gittins; The History Press, Published 2010, ISBN 9780752456324.

DOCUMENTS

RAIL 253/516: The newsletters.

RAIL 253/789: Organisational chart of the Audit office, 1914.

RAIL 258/447: Papers including memorial service programme on the War Memorial Paddington

RAIL 264: Staff records for the GWR, which have been digitised and are searchable on www.ancestry.co.uk.

ZPER 19/27-31: Copies of the GWR magazine for the war years.

1911 Census: Available on http://www.1911census.co.uk/

RESOURCES

The National Archives educational resource **Telling Tommies' tales** includes copies of a selection of letters, a film short in which a soldier looks at the letters, links to a Flickr gallery of the collection and four podcasts based on the letters. http://www.nationalarchives.gov.uk/education/resources/telling-tommies-tales/